HENRY VIII's IMPRISONED WOMEN

This book is for you, Dadda. I wish you were here to read it.

HENRY VIII's IMPRISONED WOMEN

The Women of the Tower

NEHA ROY

PEN & SWORD HISTORY

AN IMPRINT OF PEN & SWORD BOOKS LTD.
YORKSHIRE – PHILADELPHIA

First published in Great Britain in 2023 by
PEN AND SWORD HISTORY
An imprint of
Pen & Sword Books Ltd
Yorkshire – Philadelphia

ISBN 978 1 39909 576 1

A CIP catalogue record for this book is available from the British Library.

Typeset in Times New Roman 11.5/14 by
SJmagic DESIGN SERVICES, India.
Printed and bound in the UK by CPI Group (UK) Ltd.

Pen & Sword Books Limited incorporates the imprints of Atlas, Archaeology, Aviation, Discovery, Family History, Fiction, History, Maritime, Military, Military Classics, Politics, Select, Transport, True Crime, Air World, Frontline Publishing, Leo Cooper, Remember When, Seaforth Publishing, The Praetorian Press, Wharncliffe Local History, Wharncliffe Transport, Wharncliffe True Crime and White Owl.

For a complete list of Pen & Sword titles please contact
PEN & SWORD BOOKS LIMITED
47 Church Street, Barnsley, South Yorkshire, S70 2AS, England
E-mail: enquiries@pen-and-sword.co.uk
Website: www.pen-and-sword.co.uk

Or

PEN AND SWORD BOOKS
1950 Lawrence Rd, Havertown, PA 19083, USA
E-mail: Uspen-and-sword@casematepublishers.com
Website: www.penandswordbooks.com

MIX
Paper | Supporting responsible forestry
FSC® C013604

Contents

SECTION 1

1

The History of the Tower of London

The Tower of London is easily the most notable and noticeable tourist landmark of the city today. The impregnable fortress, built by William the Conqueror in 1066 during the Norman Conquests, has, over the years, served the monarchy of England in many different ways: as a palace, castle, prison, torture chamber, mint, treasury, armoury, records office, observatory and even a zoo.

The Tower of London has played a pivotal role in many events that have shaped the history of the country. From coronations to imprisonments and executions, the Tower has been a silent witness to all. It has been besieged many times as conquering the castle was always of prime importance to control the monarchy and, subsequently, the country.

The Tower earned a bloody reputation during the medieval ages when it witnessed many a great lord and lady fall in disgrace. Many notable people such as Sir Thomas More, Queen Anne Boleyn and Lady Margaret Pole met their grisly ends in its precincts. Mysteries such as the famous disappearance of the two princes and the lesser-known disappearance of Lady Margaret Pole's grandson, Henry Pole, remain unsolved and haunt the Tower to this day.

Post the Tudor reign, the Tower was used as a prison during the First and the Second World Wars and was damaged in the Blitz. Today, it stands tall as a World Heritage site and is cared for by the Historic Royal Palaces.

William the Conqueror

The story of the Tower starts with the Battle of Hastings, fought in the year 1066 between the English, under the leadership of the Anglo-Saxon King Harold Godwinson, against the Norman-French King William the Conqueror.[1] This heralded the start of the Norman conquest in England.

The battle, in which the Normans emerged victorious, was fought approximately 11km north-west of Hastings, close to the present-day East Sussex.

William the Conqueror was crowned King of England on Christmas Day 1066.[2] Despite petty skirmishes and minor altercations, the Battle of Hastings was the decisive end of the Norman Conquest of England.

The new King of England immediately began fortifying his new kingdom by building castles at key locations. Eventually, he turned his sights on to London when he reached Canterbury.

Much to his dismay, he was unable to enter the country's largest city as the fortified bridge to London was held by the Saxon troops. He instead rampaged towards Southwark and lay waste to the town. Following a series of victories, the city of London finally opened its doors to the Norman conqueror and the new King of England in December 1066.

The fortification of the city of London and the castle building began in earnest. William the Conqueror built nearly thirty-six castles between the years 1066 and 1087. However, there are some references in the Domesday Book which suggests that the number of castles established, mainly by his subordinates, may be more.[3]

Quoting William the Conqueror's biographer, William of Poitiers: 'certain fortifications were completed in the city against the restlessness of the huge and brutal populace. For he [William] realised that it was of the utmost importance to overawe the Londoners.'[4]

To achieve this, William the Conqueror prepared to enter the city in state and sent an advance party to London to prepare for the same. He understood the importance of the city, the Westminster Palace was the centre of government and the city was known for its numerous ports. This was essential for the Normans to establish a stronghold over the newly conquered city.

Two more castles – Baynard's Castle and Montfichet's Castle – were built at around the same time as the Tower. The area at the south-east corner of the Roman town walls was chosen as the site for the Tower; the walls served as a readymade defence mechanism. The earliest structure of the Tower, probably built by timber and later replaced by stone, would have been enclosed by a ditch. William the Conqueror may have also considered the River Thames as a potential protective element while drawing up the layout. A timber bulwark may have served as yet another protective measure and an accommodation for William would have most certainly been a part of the plan.

The White Tower, after which the Tower is named, was said to have been constructed around 1076. Gundulf,[5] Bishop of Rochester was in charge of the construction and it is said that building wasn't completed until after William's death in 1087. William the Conqueror's castle was the strongest point, and included a grand accommodation facility for the monarch. We can easily assume that this part of the Tower was completed by 1100 as records suggest that Bishop Ranulf Flambard[6], a corrupt clergyman who exacted harsh taxes, was imprisoned there. Interestingly, Bishop Flambard also holds the distinction of the first person to escape from the Tower.

In 1097, as mentioned in the Anglo-Saxon chronicles, King William II[7] ordered a stone wall, which very likely replaced the timber bulwark, built around the castle. The Norman Conquest also saw the entry of Jews into London.[8] The Jewish community used the Tower as a retreat and also as a safe haven when their security was threatened.

Henry I, Queen Matilda and Stephen of Blois

By 1135, the Tower, an impregnable fortress which was located very strategically, was hardly ever used as a royal residence. It was under the charge of a Constable, Geoffrey de Mandeville,[9] at this time.

The year 1135 saw King Henry I on his death bed and the succession in dire straits. The dying king had urged his barons to swear fealty for Queen Matilda, but it was all in vain as merely a few days after Henry's death Stephen of Blois[10] arrived from France to take charge and stake his claim on the throne of England. The sly Mandeville went to the Queen's side in exchange for money after Stephen of Blois was captured in the Battle of Lincoln in 1141.[11] However, as the queen's support decreased Mandeville sold his loyalty to Stephen, thereby amassing immense wealth, partly due to his position as the Constable of the Tower and also through his underhand dealings. He held secret meetings with Queen Matilda, but when caught Stephen had him arrested and stripped him of his position.[12] The position of the Constable of the Tower was no longer a hereditary one as Stephen had Mandeville replaced with his loyal supporters.

Changes to the original form of the Tower were undertaken during the reign of King Richard I by his Lord Chancellor, William Longchamp.[13] Longchamp was in charge of managing the monarchy in England while the king was away on crusade, and he is said to have spent great sums of money in renovating the castle. Longchamp, according to Roger of Howden, a chronicler, built a moat around the Tower and tried in vain to fill it up with water from the nearby river.

Longchamp, who served as the Constable of the Tower, was preparing for war against Prince John, King Richard's younger brother, who was trying to take advantage of the king's absence to seize power. The Tower was under siege for the very first time in its history and the fortifications and additional defence mechanisms were severely tested as Longchamp held out for three days before surrendering to Prince John, resulting in him being crowned king in 1199.

However, his rule proved an unpopular one and his barons rebelled. In 1214 Robert Fitzwalter[14] laid siege to the Tower with his army, but despite being short-staffed it was successfully defended and the siege was lifted after King John signed the Magna Carta. The king, however, in a perfidious move, broke his promises. This resulted in a rebellious outbreak which we know as the First Barons' War. Robert Fitzwalter maintained his hold on the castle till its regiment of soldiers joined forces with the rebelling barons. King John eventually conceded defeat and the barons offered the throne to Prince Louis, the heir of the French king.

However, there was another faction that backed the deposed King John's son, Henry, to inherit the throne of England. The two factions – one supporting Prince Louis and another supporting Prince Henry – went to war. Despite Fitzwalter maintaining his hold over the city of London and the Tower, Prince Henry's arm prevailed over the army supporting the French heir.

Major renovations took place during the reigns of Kings Henry III (1216-1272) and Edward I (1272-1307) wherein the castle was extended, amidst occasional civil unrest, and took the form that we see today.

King Henry III often held court at the Tower of London and is said to have held Parliament there twice as the barons continued to cause unrest. Henry III[15] did not care much about his barons, which led to a feeling of resentment amongst the latter. To quell the rebelling barons, the king needed to ensure that the Tower was amply fortified. He also ensured that the Tower was a comfortable place in which to live, and for this he began work on the innermost ward. The tradition of whitewashing the White Tower – hence its name – began in 1240, during Henry III's reign. The Royal Mint and the Royal Menagerie were also established in 1248 during the reign of King Henry III.

By way of fortifications, a defense perimeter, which included numerous towers, was built and a ditch was dug on the sides – mainly east, north and west – not protected by the river. Londoners weren't happy with these expansions due to the disruption that it caused and openly celebrated when the gatehouse collapsed in 1240.

The disgruntled barons united under the leadership of Simon de Montfort[16] and compelled the king to accept a list of reforms, one of which was holding regular parliaments. Cornered, the king and his soldiers took refuge at the Tower in 1261. The warring parties came to a truce and, according to the terms, Henry was required to relinquish the control of the Tower.

In 1265 Simon de Montfort was soundly defeated at the Battle of Evesham and regained control over the city and the Tower. In a highly despised move, Cardinal Ottobuono[17] arrived in England and was given the custody of the Tower. He also excommunicated the rebels, which did not sit well with the public.

Disgruntled by the monarch's decision, in 1267, the 6th Earl of Hertford, Gilbert de Clare,[18] besieged the Tower with the view that no foreigner or clergyman should gain control of it. He was, however, defeated and King Henry III regained control of the Tower.

The reigns of King Edward I and King Edward II

A seasoned castle builder, King Edward I carried out various expensive renovations at the Tower. Being an experienced warrior himself he also applied his knowledge of siege warfare to fortify the castle accordingly. Heavily inspired by the empires of the East, Edward was instrumental in introducing the building of arrowslits in the castle. He filled up the trench dug by King Henry III and created a new enclosure by constructing curtain walls. A new entrance was created and the Beauchamp Tower replaced the old gatehouse built by King Henry III. In order to make the castle self-subsistent, King Edward I built watermills.

By 1279 the several mints in the country were brought together under a centralised mint located within the Tower. Outside London only a few mints, including a few ecclesiastical ones, continued to operate. This decision may have been taken after 600 Jews were charged in 1278 with coin clipping and imprisoned in the Tower.

The Privy Wardrobe was founded during the reign of King Edward II who ruled England from 1307 to 1327. The Tower saw very little activity during this period save for the time when Margaret de Clare, Baroness Badlesmere, became the first woman to be imprisoned at the Tower for refusing to admit Queen Isabella[19] at Leeds Castle and ordering her archers to fire at them, resulting in the deaths of six members of the queen's entourage.

The Tower did not make for a very secure prison. In 1323 Roger Mortimer[20], Baron Mortimer, was aided in his escape by the sub-lieutenant who cut out a hole in his cell wall and helped Mortimer flee to a waiting boat which took him to France. Baron Mortimer eventually gained infamy for having an affair with the queen, whom he met in France, and for plotting to overthrow the king.

Mortimer returned to England in 1326, captured the Tower and released its prisoners. Mortimer virtually ruled England as King Edward III was too young, but by 1330 Edward III[21] captured Mortimer and incarcerated him in the Tower. The king's battlefield exploits were legendary: he captured King John II of France during the Battles of Crecy and Poitiers and also King David II of Scotland at Neville's Cross. His royal prisoners complained about the lack of hunting facilities at the Tower, where they were imprisoned, and King Edward III subsequently had it renovated accordingly.

Richard II

King Richard II started the tradition of a procession from the Tower to Westminster Abbey when he was coronated in 1377. He wasn't a very popular ruler and during the Peasant's Revolt[22] in 1381 he was trapped in the Tower as the crowds laid siege to it. As he left to meet Wat Tyler[23] the crowds stormed in and looted the Jewel House. Afraid of the rampaging mobs, Simon Sudbury[24], the Archbishop of Canterbury, sought refuge in St John's Chapel hoping that the rebels would respect the sanctity of the place and spare him.

However, matters for the archbishop took a grim turn as his sanctuary was broken into and he was unceremoniously dragged over to Tower Hill and beheaded. King Richard II was imprisoned in the White Tower as Henry Bolingbroke, the future King Henry IV and the grandson of King Edward III, returned from exile to claim the throne of England for himself. King Henry IV faced a minor revolt and shut himself in the Tower when the supporters of the erstwhile King Richard II staged a coup which ultimately failed[25].

Over the next few years the Tower was home to many distinguished prisoners. King James I of Scotland, when he was still heir to the throne, was kidnapped and held there. The prisoners from the Battle of Agincourt, in which England saw one of its greatest battlefield triumphs under the leadership of King Henry V, were also imprisoned in the Tower until they were ransomed.

Wars of the Roses

In 1460, when the Wars of the Roses were in full swing, the Yorkists forces laid siege to the Tower. The artillery fire, used for the first time during the Battle of Northampton, damaged the Tower and it was during this battle that King Henry VI was captured. After being briefly reinstated as the king in 1470 with the help of Richard Neville, Earl of Warwick, the deposed King Edward IV recaptured Henry VI and imprisoned him in the Tower where he was mysteriously found dead.[26]

The Tower was further fortified during this time to withstand gunfire, and loopholes and a bulwark were constructed for cannons and handguns. During the Siege of London in 1471 the armies of York, who were stationed at the Tower, opened fire at the Lancastrian forces.

King Edward IV committed fratricide when he had his younger brother, George, Duke of Clarence, executed at the Tower. The ever impulsive George made a grave mistake of accusing the Queen of England, Elizabeth Woodville, of witchcraft after the death of his wife, Isabel Neville. The duke was attainted for treason and sentenced to death. He was rumoured to have been drowned in a butt of Malmsey wine, his chosen way to die, in his room in the Tower.

The Tower's greatest mystery, however, was the disappearance of the princes,[27] the two sons of King Edward IV. On King Edward's death in 1483, his son Prince Edward, Prince of Wales, was proclaimed King Edward V. As he was too young to rule, the deceased king's brother, Richard, Duke of Gloucester, was appointed Lord Protector, on the suggestion of his royal brother, to rule the realm on behalf of his twelve-year-old nephew.

Richard took custody of the young king at Stony Stratford while he was returning to London from Wales and lodged him in the Tower whilst imprisoning, and later executing the boy king's uncle, Anthony, Earl Rivers, and his half-brother, Richard Grey. He planned a grand coronation for his nephew which never took place. He, along with his brother, Richard of Shrewsbury, Duke of York, were last seen in public in June 1483 after which they disappeared. Richard, Duke of Gloucester, was then crowned King Richard III. It is believed that they were smothered to death in their sleep but the identity of the murderer, despite the countless conspiracy theories, remains unknown (in 1674, bones believed to be those of the princes were discovered in a box under the stairs of the White Tower). King Richard III was defeated by Henry Tudor, who ascended the throne of England as King Henry VII, at the Battle of Bosworth in 1485.

The Tower under the Tudors

King Henry VII[28] did not use the Tower much as a royal residence; rather, he used it more as an armoury and a prison. He hardly spent a week staying there, visiting on fourteen occasions between 1485 and 1500. The Yeoman Warders of the Tower have been serving as the Royal bodyguards since 1509.

In 1532 Thomas Cromwell spent a huge sum of money in renovating the castle, importing tons of Caen stone for the work. The accommodation facilities, though, remained deplorable and the castle was in no state for any sort of royal accommodation.

The reign of King Henry VIII[29] saw the Tower gain a grim reputation as a place of torture, incarceration and execution. The Tower held a number of notable prisoners, among them Queen Anne Boleyn, Lady Margaret Pole, Countess of Salisbury, and Queen Katheryn Howard, all of whom faced the executioner's axe (or sword in Anne Boleyn's case). It also held the maverick Alice Tankerville, who became infamous as the first woman to escape from the Tower (albeit briefly), Elizabeth Barton, the nun from Kent (who was later hanged to death at Tyburn) and the Protestant martyr Anne Askew (who was later burnt to death at Smithfield).

This book tells us the story of their lives.

2

The Life of Common Women in the Tudor Era

The Tudor era boasted of a number of notable women, aside from the queens of the two monarchs, King Henry VII and his son, King Henry VIII. Apart from the ones whose lives are described in this book, there are many others who were instrumental in leaving an indelible mark on English history: Lady Margaret Beaufort, the matriarch of the Tudor royal family, was a formidable woman who helped shape the fledgling dynasty into a force to reckon with; Elizabeth 'Bessie' Blount gave King Henry VIII his illegitimate son, Henry Fitzroy, whom the king made the Duke of Richmond and seriously considered naming him his heir when he was disillusioned by the birth of his daughters; Mary Boleyn, his mistress whom he discarded for his second queen, Anne Boleyn; Nan Seymour, his favourite queen's sister-in-law; Lady Margaret Douglas, the king's niece, and many more.

However, there is very little written about the common women of that era. One of the few exceptions is Anne Askew who recorded her trials and subsequent torture in *The Examinations of Anne Askew*. So what was life like for a woman in Tudor England?

Inheritance

Although a male dominated society, daughters were allowed to inherit land in the absence of legitimate sons. This was not the case in Wales where the man's inheritance was divided equally amongst his sons, even illegitimate ones. Barony by Writ, too, could be inherited by daughters. In the case of multiple daughters, the barony would not be vested until the family reached an agreement as to which daughter and spouse would inherit it.

Baronies by patent were granted by a written order of the king, especially to the heir of the body which made the said title inheritable by women, the prime example in this case being Margaret Pole being elevated as the Countess of Salisbury in her own right.

Common women, on the other hand – the peasants, farmers and the likes – were usually trained in domestic work with the intention of finding employment in rich households, as was the case with Elizabeth Barton. They were expected to work there till they married, some even continuing after marriage.

Marriage

Marriage for many women was usually an economic agreement between the respective parents. A common woman would find it hard to survive without a partner to support her economically. This can be the reason for multiple marriages in the case of both men and women. Widows remarrying across all strata of English society was not uncommon either. Nor did class hierarchy matter much as it was very common for widows of tradesmen to marry their subordinates in order to carry on with the business.

Marriages in that era were more of a contractual agreement than an act of love. However, one thing common in every class of society with regards to matrimony was consent between the man and the woman. Therefore, marriages fixed in childhood required consent when the children reached majority (twelve in the case of girls and fourteen in the case of boys). However, as children obeyed their parents unquestioningly, consent was not a difficult thing to obtain.

A Dutch resident in London observed that although women were entirely in the control of their husbands, they enjoyed a good amount of freedom. They were not kept behind closed doors like other Europeans but often sat outside their houses and met up with their neighbours. They dressed in good clothes and often left the mundane household work to servants.

Sex and Divorce

With regards to sexual intercourse and displays of affection, the English were notoriously less prudish than their European counterparts. Abstinence was considered unhealthy by doctors, though excessive sex was considered a sin and men were accused of treating their wives as prostitutes.

Women were considered inferior to men and often described by the clergy as driven by their physical desires. The concept of divorce did not exist before the Reformation. If a spouse wished to obtain a divorce, the said person had to prove that the marriage was invalid on one of the following grounds: lack of consent; lack of dispensation in case of a close affinity; an existing precontract with another; insanity of the partner; or non-consummation of marriage. For commoners divorce was an expensive affair, but it was not uncommon amongst the royals and nobility.

Childbirth

The main purpose of marriage during the Tudor era was to provide heirs – whether royal, noble or common. Pregnancy and birth were a complicated affair at that time especially as the former was difficult to diagnose. Phantom pregnancies were commonplace and a woman could only be sure of being pregnant when her child began moving. While the upper classes went into confinement in comfort, lesser privileged ones usually had birthing sheets passed down through generations. It was not unusual for common women to give birth without any preparations. The process of birthing was a perilous affair and it wasn't uncommon for the mother and/or child to lose their life during or after birth.

Crimes

While we can find records about crimes committed by upper-class or noble women, those committed by common women largely went unrecorded. Of those crimes recorded, the most common were adultery and thieving.

With new avenues of learning and religious views becoming a lot more liberal than that in the Plantagenet era, the number of victims – usually women – slowly dwindled. It was during the Plantagenet reign when the dowager queen, Elizabeth Woodville, and her mother, Jacquetta, were accused of being witches and using witchcraft to ensnare King Edward IV into marriage. The allegation raised its head once again during the reign of King Henry VIII when he accused his second

Anne Boleyn – though no charges were pressed – of seducing him through sorcery.

The most common methods of execution for women who committed heinous crimes such as adultery, thieving or murder were being burnt at the stake (those accused of heresy and blasphemy) and execution by the axe. An uncommon method of execution came to the fore during the Alice Tankerville episode when Alice and her husband, John Wolfe, were chained and lowered into the River Thames till they drowned. Hanging was a punishment used on women especially during the Pilgrimage of Grace rebellion. Punishments usually included whipping for minor offences. A 'scold's bride' was a device which went over the head and gagged the mouth; it was used to curtail and punish gossiping women.

A woman's life during the Tudor era wasn't an easy one. Women who tried defying the authorities and breaking with tradition were quickly subdued and put down. No woman, common or aristocrat, was spared if they broke the law or were even accused of doing so, more often than not on false charges as we will find out in this book through the lives of six unfortunate women from different social classes who dared to go against convention and paid the ultimate price.

SECTION 2

3

Henry VIII

'Whoever leads an auspicious life here and governs the commonwealth rightly, as my most noble father did, who promoted all piety and banished all ignorance, has a most certain way to heaven.'[1]

King Henry VIII of England

In the fourteenth century an unostentatious Welsh family with dubious ancestry – they claimed that they descended from Cadwallader – began their rise to dizzying heights when one of theirs wooed and secretly married the Queen of England. Owen Tudor, who landed in England to seek his fortune, found a place and employment at the court of King Henry V as the Master of Wardrobe to Henry's queen, Catherine of Valois. Through means unknown, he entrenched himself in her household and so charmed his mistress that a few years after the demise of her husband, the king, she secretly, and quite possibly without a royal sanction, married Owen Tudor.

The upheaval that the marriage caused was immense. Catherine was banished to Bermondsey Abbey, an eleventh-century Benedictine monastery located in the south-east of London, and Owen Tudor to Newgate Prison. Their two sons, Edmund Tudor, born in 1430 at Much Hadham Palace in Hertfordshire, and Jasper Tudor, born in 1431 at Hatfield in Hertfordshire, were sent to the care of Katherine de la Pole, the sister of William de la Pole, 1st Duke of Suffolk, at Barking Abbey in Essex. Tragically, Queen Catherine died the following year, probably nursing a broken heart, but Owen led quite an intrepid life. He broke free from his prison twice and was recaptured. He even sought sanctuary in the purlieus of Westminster Abbey and had to be coaxed out by being invited to feasts in the nearby taverns, thereby exemplifying his weakness for the lighter pleasures and frivolities in life. He finally met a grisly end when he championed the Lancastrian cause during the Wars of the Roses and was beheaded by the Yorkist King Edward IV after the Battle of Mortimer's Cross.

Edmund and Jasper Tudor, however, enjoyed the royal favour of their half-brother, the Lancastrian King Henry VI. Their legitimacy was formally confirmed and declared by Parliament in 1453. Edmund was first knighted and then created Earl of Richmond and both brothers improved their monetary and social status through the various grants of estates that the king bestowed upon them and through being admitted to King Henry VI's council. The high point of their lives was when Edmund Tudor married the heiress Margaret Beaufort.

The ancestry of the Beauforts was less obscure than the Tudors. They descended through John of Gaunt who had three sons by his mistress, Katherine Swynford, before marrying her. Although in normal circumstances the sons would be legitimized through the Canon Law, the barons were having none of it. They refused to conform the English laws with the Canon laws in this case and hence the offspring of the scandalous union continued to be illegitimate. However, the Beauforts were finally legitimised by King Richard II. King Henry IV, however, added a clause wherein the Beauforts were barred from inheriting the English throne. This explains King Henry VII's hesitation to base his claim to the throne on hereditary right. However, it would be wrong to say that the Beaufort family had no influence in the royal court. One was a cardinal and Bishop of Winchester, another Duke of Exeter and a third was the Earl of Somerset. Margaret remained the sole heir of the family after the male line collapsed in the third generation.

Margaret Beaufort: The Tudor Matriarch

Margaret Beaufort was born in 1443 at Bletsoe Castle in Bedfordshire, a quaint three-storey house surrounded by a moat. Her birth was recorded by her mother, Margaret Beauchamp, in her Book of Hours and she remained the only child of Margaret and her husband, John Beaufort, Duke of Somerset, who inherited the earldom in 1418 following the death of his elder brother, Henry. John travelled to France at the age of fifteen along with his stepfather, Thomas, Duke of Clarence, and his brothers, Thomas and Edmund, as part of the king's army during the Hundred Years' War against France. Fate, however, wasn't too kind on them and their stepfather was killed during the Battle of Bauge. He and his brother Thomas were taken into captivity. He spent seventeen years as a captive of the French during which he lost his brother, Thomas, who died soon after being released. In 1442 he married a widow with six children, Margaret Beauchamp, who gave birth to their daughter, Margaret, the following year.

However, a dark cloud descended upon Somerset's career. He was not very lucky in the war against France and took the disastrous decision of plundering some French towns and embezzled the funds sent to him for his own use. Somerset's behaviour enraged the usually mild-mannered Henry VI and he refused to meet him. Shamed and humiliated, it is speculated that he committed suicide. It was said that Margaret's mother was pregnant at the time of Somerset's death and his suicide and subsequent shock caused her to lose the baby, either due to a miscarriage or a later death. This left Margaret, Somerset's only legitimate child, a rich heiress. Despite his financial impediments, he owned vast estates in the counties of Kent, Lincolnshire, Norfolk, Somerset, Essex, Worcestershire and Sussex.

Left to her own devices and without a male protector, Margaret was thrust into the treacherous world of politics wherein her status as a wealthy beneficiary to her late father's estates made her a befitting yet vulnerable catch in the marriage market.

Noticing this, King Henry VI handed over the wardship of Margaret, who was also his kinswoman, to William de la Pole, Earl of Suffolk, a great favourite of his and later, of his queen, Margaret of Anjou. Suffolk, married to Alice Chaucer, the granddaughter of the celebrated poet Geoffrey Chaucer, had his son's marital prospects in mind when he took over the guardianship of little Margaret Beaufort.

Although it is unlikely that Margaret ever left her mother's care, William de la Pole, following the death of his son's former fiancée, Anne Beauchamp, promptly betrothed his son, John de la Pole, to Margaret.

Keeping her status and her future in mind, Margaret's mother imparted quality education on managing estates and lands amongst other life skills, something that was unheard of in the case of women in that era. Fluent in English and French, though not so much in Latin, Margaret's thirst for knowledge was insatiable.

She was also incredibly religious, a quality that defined her throughout her life. According to historian Nicola Tallis in her book *Uncrowned Queen: The Life of Margaret Beaufort*, Margaret may have been inspired by her half-sister Margaret St John who was later to become the Abbess of Shaftesbury.[2] She tried to make religion as accessible as possible to the public by translating religious texts from Latin and French to English, a knack inherited many years later by her great-granddaughter, Elizabeth.

After the death of Margaret's father, John Beaufort, her mother fell in love and sought to marry John Neville for which she applied for a dispensation from the Pope as they were distantly related. However, for unknown reasons the marriage did not take place. Instead, Margaret (her mother) married Lionel, Lord Welles, who was one of King Henry VI's privy councillors. Margaret was close to all her half-siblings but shared a special bond with Lord Welles' son, John, who was seven years younger than her. Nothing much is known about Margaret's relationship with her stepfather, Lord Welles, who may have been too busy at court to have paid any attention to his stepdaughter's upbringing. Moreover, she was already under the guardianship of William de la Pole, Duke of Suffolk, so we can assume that Lord Welles may have had little or no influence on Margaret's rearing.

His eyes firmly set on Margaret's inheritance, William de la Pole married his son, John de la Pole, to Margaret in some sort of a marriage ceremony. Since both of them were very young, the marriage was never consummated and it is not known about their feelings towards each other later in their lives. Margaret probably did not get along with John de la Pole as he colluded with the Yorkists in order to bring down the Tudor dynasty, despite swearing allegiance to King Henry VII. Margaret never considered John her husband and always referred to Edmund Tudor as her first husband.

Meanwhile, King Henry VI's ineptitude as a ruler and lack of military prowess ensured that England was left with only a couple of French territories for themselves: Calais and Aquitaine. William de la Pole's unpopularity grew and despite protesting his innocence and loyalty, was impeached by Parliament on 28 January 1450. Not knowing his fate prompted the hasty marriage between his son and Margaret. The public clamoured for his arrest and the king was forced to pass the order to pacify his subjects. King Henry VI had no intention of mortally punishing him and hence, after a trial, banished him from England and France. Enraged, the public took matters into their own hands and William de la Pole was found murdered while on his way out of the country. Margaret was only seven at that time.

In February 1453 an almost ten-year-old Margaret was brought to the court in the presence of the king who announced her betrothal to his half-brother, Edmund Tudor. Edmund was extremely loyal to his half-brother and Henry VI wished to repay this loyalty. Edmund stood to gain immense wealth through marriage to Margaret as her vast inheritance would be divided between him and his brother, Jasper. Margaret formally assented to her marriage with Edmund Tudor, later claiming that she had received an indication from the divine to do so. On 1 November 1455 the twelve-year-old Margaret married Edmund Tudor who was twelve years her senior.

By November 1456 a very young Margaret Beaufort was already widowed. Edmund had died of the plague in captivity at Carmarthen on 3 November 1456. Moreover, the young Countess of Richmond, who was yet to turn fourteen, was also pregnant. Two months later she gave birth to a baby boy, Henry Tudor, at Pembroke Castle on 28 January 1457, a process so excruciatingly painful and damaging for her that she did not bear any more children.

Spending most of the time in exile with his uncle, Jasper Tudor, Earl of Pembroke, during the reign of the Yorkist king Edward IV, Henry Tudor briefly returned to England during the brief reinstallation of the Lancastrian king Henry VI. The death of Edward of Westminster, Prince of Wales, in the Battle of Tewkesbury, and the supposed murder of Henry VI thrust Henry Tudor into prominence as the next heir to the Lancastrian throne and his mother, Margaret Beaufort, was determined to make it happen.

Initially reluctant, Henry soon warmed to the idea of acceding the throne of England one day and bided his time in exile till it was safe to return. He finally did so in 1485 (notwithstanding a failed attempt in 1483), meeting King Richard III at Bosworth Field and defeating him on 22 August 1485. He then honoured his promise and united the two warring houses of Lancaster and York by marrying Edward IV's eldest daughter, Elizabeth of York.

Elizabeth bore Henry a total of six children out of which four survived: Arthur, Prince of Wales, Margaret, Henry and Mary. Henry VII's rule was not a very stable one due to numerous rebellions aimed at ousting him from the throne, the most notable ones being that of Francis Lovell, Lambert Simnel and Perkin Warbeck. Although lenient with Simnel, Henry VII did not extend the same mercy towards Warbeck and had him executed along with Edward, Earl of Warwick, whose life and death was a tragic chapter in Henry's reign.

Later in her life a frail Margaret Beaufort adopted a nun-like appearance, wearing a widow's barbe right up to her chin and a wimple.

Ever religious, she immersed herself in charitable deeds and also held immense influence in her son, King Henry VII's court. She was the founder of Christ College and St John's College, Cambridge, and was a sponsor of William Caxton.

Elizabeth of York: A Plantagenet Princess and a Tudor Queen

To understand Henry VIII's psyche, especially when he was crowned King of England, we need to examine his relationship with his parents. Extremely close to his mother, Elizabeth of York, little Henry was devasted by her death. This is evident in the Vaux Passional painting which lay forgotten, until recently, at the National Library of Wales. The painting shows the king being presented a book while two girls, their heads draped in black, sit behind his throne. What is interesting to note here is the little boy in green just beyond the girls. The painting, once in the possession of Joan Vaux, Lady Guildford, who was a close friend of Elizabeth of York, is said to depict the death of the queen, the two girls being Margaret and Mary Tudor, and the boy in green being Henry. The painting shows Henry in an emotionally vulnerable state and in great distress. We may assume that the portrait was commissioned by Lady Guildford on the passing of her friend as a remembrance. The depiction of Henry's vulnerability speaks volumes about the bond between him and his mother.

Elizabeth of York was born to the swashbuckling King Edward IV of England and his highly controversial wife, Elizabeth Wydeville or Woodville (a modern corruption), in 1466 at the Palace of Westminster, the first princess born to an English monarch in over a century. The palace was being renovated at the time of Elizabeth Woodville's confinement and she was lodged in the newly constructed chamber specially done up for her. Pregnancies in those days were a risky affair and Elizabeth most likely had her mother, the enigmatic Jacquetta Woodville, Duchess of Bedford, to assist and comfort her along with her other ladies. The little 'Lady Princess' was baptised in the same month in a new font built by her kinsman, George Neville, the brother of Richard 'Kingmaker' Neville, Earl of Warwick.

The eldest daughter of the king, Elizabeth grew up in opulence in a vast household. The court was a dynamic one and Elizabeth moved from one palace to another with her royal family and the courtiers, ladies and servants. Her mother, the queen, despite her detractors, carried on in her role with dignity. However, the resentment of Richard Neville, Earl of Warwick, grew by day and he finally rebelled. Elizabeth was said to have been briefly betrothed to George Neville but it was called off after Richard Neville's revolt. Her parents then were in talks with Louis XI of France for his son, Charles, the Dauphin of France's hand for marriage in 1475, to which Louis agreed. The princess' delighted parents even started calling her 'La Dauphine'. However, in 1482 Louis went back on his promise and broke the betrothal.

She was said to be docile by nature and got along well with her little brood of siblings: Cecily, Mary, Edward (briefly the King of England and then one of the Princes in the Tower), Margaret, Richard (The other Prince in the Tower), Anne, Catherine and Bridget. The Earl of Warwick's rebellion forced Edward IV to go into exile and Elizabeth Woodville, along with her brood, sought sanctuary at Westminster Abbey. It was quite a tumultuous time for Elizabeth who was then restored to prominence when Edward IV won back the throne of England.

Following the death of her father, her brother Edward V was declared the King of England, along with her uncle, Richard, Duke of Gloucester, acting as the regent and Lord Protector of the minor king as demanded by her father on his death bed. However, Richard captured her brother and sent her uncle, Anthony, Earl Rivers, to his death. He lodged Edward, and later Richard, in the Tower of London, presumably for their safety. But that was not meant to be. Having been seen in public just once after their capture and imprisonment when they were spotted shooting arrows in the Tower gardens, Edward and Richard mysteriously disappeared, giving rise to many questions that remain unanswered to this day.

Despite the uprisings of Lambert Simnel and, later, Perkin Warbeck threatening to cast a dark shadow on her reign as Queen of England, Elizabeth made a mark by being an amenable and quite a fertile wife to her husband, Henry VII. Elizabeth's first child, Prince Arthur, was born in September 1486, just about eight months after her marriage to Henry VII. This did raise a few eyebrows but the thought of an heir coming along so quickly into the new regime may have quashed any feelings of doubt in the citizens of England. Amidst a few miscarriages she bore three more children – a daughter 'Margaret'; a son 'Henry', the future Henry VIII; and another daughter 'Mary' – before eventually dying on her thirty-seventh birthday while giving birth to her final child, Katherine, who tragically died a few days after her mother.

Her death was mourned deeply as people remembered her kind and gentle nature. Despite not involving herself in any of the political decisions, Elizabeth took the education of her children extremely seriously.

The Early Life of King Henry VIII

On 28 June 1491 at Greenwich Palace, a second son was born to King Henry VII and Queen Elizabeth of York. Named Henry, most probably after his father, little Henry, or Harry as he was affectionately called, was a robust infant compared to his rather weak older brother, Arthur, who was, quite grandly, named after the king's supposed ancestor, the legendary King Arthur.

When he reached his third birthday Henry was created the Duke of York, most likely in retaliation to the imposter 'Perkin Warbeck's' claim to the said dukedom. Lord Herbert Cherbury, Henry's earliest biographer, claimed that the prince was destined for the church as wished by his father, but destiny had other plans. Being a spare, no one imagined that Henry would one day inherit the throne and the kingdom of England.

One year prior to the death of his mother, Henry's life took a complete about turn when his elder brother, Arthur, Prince of Wales, died suddenly on 2 April 1502 at Ludlow Castle in Wales, probably of the deadly sweating sickness. Newly married to Katharine of Aragon, Arthur was the glittering result of the unity and reconciliation between the two warring Houses of the Wars of the Roses: Lancaster and York. It is believed that Arthur was always a delicate and a calm child, as opposed to his virile and gregarious younger brother, Henry. We can only assume that Henry may have been sad at the death of his brother, but the fact that he was now Prince of Wales and stood to inherit the throne must have pleased him immensely.

Upbringing and Education

Prince Henry was said to be a passionate and eager learner. The celebrated poet, John Skelton, along with a William Hone, was one of his first tutors. It is likely that it was Margaret Beaufort's influence that helped

Skelton – blessed with a sarcastic wit which won him many enemies rather than friends – secure his appointment as the prince's tutor.

Duly impressed by the skills of his illustrious pupil, Skelton may be the one who taught the prince to read and write in an elegant hand. He was, however, relieved of his post as the prince's tutor following a minor misdemeanor which led to him being imprisoned. It is also believed that the late Prince Arthur's tutor, Bernard Andre, the poet, was one of his teachers. Andre probably taught him Latin while Giles D'Ewes may have taught him French. He even managed to learn Spanish thanks to Katharine of Aragon, thus displaying his linguistic skills.

He also had a musical ear and, although we are not sure whether he is the composer of 'Greensleeves', he is credited for composing the lively 'Pastime in Good Company'.

Post the demise of his brother, the newly created Prince of Wales and heir to the throne of England received instructions in horse riding, jousting, archery, tennis and hunting; all the activities that the future king of England should excel at. And excel he did! Born with a natural tenacity and eagerness to succeed in whatever he did, Prince Henry's confidence and competitive spirit were the two qualities that defined him as a king and also his reign.

Prince Henry was extremely well-read for someone his age. Erasmus, on a visit to England, visited the royal children at Eltham Palace on the request of his friend, Sir Thomas More.

In Sir Thomas' own words: 'I prithee, bear me company to a certain great house nigh to here. There thou shalt find friends, who have a great desire to see thee.'

The 'friends' here refer to the children of King Henry VII. We don't know about the others, but Erasmus' visit brought great joy to the academically inclined Prince Henry who later kept up a lively correspondence with the Dutch humanist, often emulating the latter's style of writing in his letters. Initially suspecting the prince's tutors of helping him, Erasmus was surprised to find out that the letters were written by the prince himself with no assistance from his tutors. In addition to this, Prince Henry was also a remarkable orator.

Blessed with an almost eidetic memory and a discerning eye for detail, Prince Henry was, in the words of a Venetian, 'in every respect the most accomplished prince'.

Among his many academic passions was his love for the stars in the sky. Prince Henry loved astronomy and his astrolabe can still be seen at the British Museum today. He was also interested in cartography and owned many maps and mapmaking tools.

However, despite his talents, King Henry VII, after the death of Prince Arthur, kept Prince Henry, his new heir, on a tight leash. He restricted his son's movements, occasionally relenting but only under strict supervision by the king's chosen men and only in close vicinity. He wasn't given any royal duties and responsibilities except for lessons in history by the king himself. He spent his time alone in his room, which was almost connected to the king's bedchambers. No one was allowed to speak to him and the prince himself spoke up only when asked to. What King Henry VII hoped to achieve by this autocratic behaviour we don't know, but his once gregarious and fun-loving son must have surely chafed under such harsh restrictions.

Prince Henry's miserable existence finally came to an end as he ascended the throne of England following his father's death in 1509.

King Henry VIII's reign: The Early Years

One of Henry VIII's first acts as king was to marry Katharine of Aragon, his brother's widow. Katharine had quite a tough life post widowhood with her father-in-law forcing her to live an almost hand-to-mouth existence by being tight with money. However, her miseries came to an end after her marriage to Henry, an act that required a papal dispensation.

On 11 June 1509 the young King Henry VIII and Katharine of Aragon wed in an intimate ceremony in the Queen's Closet at Greenwich Palace with the Archbishop of Canterbury, William Warham, officiating. The palace, formerly known as Bella Court, was built five miles down the river from London by Humphrey, Duke of Gloucester, for his wife, the scandalous Eleanor Cobham. After the ignominious fall of the duke and the duchess, the ownership of the palace passed on to the wife of King Henry VI, Margaret of Anjou, who promptly renamed it Palace of Placentia, or Plesaunce, or the Palace of Pleasure.

Keeping the wedding ceremony as low-key as possible, no public celebrations were planned, nor did they observe the ceremonial bedding ceremony as was the case in Katharine's marriage to Arthur.

Her primary role as a Queen Consort of England was to provide heirs to the throne and participate in philanthropic acts. Nevertheless, Katharine was known to be an active participant in the political management of the realm, displaying her acumen from time to time.

Amassing a great fortune as an inheritance, Henry soon started planning for a grand coronation wherein many glittering public displays and jousts were planned as a show of his wealth. Money flowed like water as fabrics of various colours from as far afield as Flanders were procured for the celebrations.

On 21 June Henry VIII kept the coronation tradition alive as he moved to the Tower of London to prepare for his crowning as the King of England. The next day he appointed many of his closest companions who served him in the privy council as the Knights of the Bath.

The next day, on 23 June, King Henry VIII and Katharine of Aragon participated in a procession that took them through the various parts of London as the public strained to catch a glimpse of their new sovereigns. They wound their way through the narrow streets where the buildings were covered in draperies, and wine flowed freely.

Wearing a gold embroidered doublet which was studded with many precious gems, Henry looked every inch the king as he rode beneath a canopy while clad in white satin and ermine, while Katharine rode behind her royal husband in a litter.

They finally arrived at Westminster Palace where they kept a night-long vigil at the Chapel of St Stephen. The next day, on 24 June, Henry and Katharine walked on a herb- and flower-strewn carpet into Westminster Abbey wearing the royal robes, ready to be proclaimed the sovereigns of England. Henry then swore his coronation oath, was anointed with the Holy Oil and was finally crowned King of England by William Warham, the Archbishop of Canterbury. He was then led to his throne by thirty-eight bishops as the crowds sang the 'Te Deum'. Katharine was then crowned in another ceremony, after which the royal couple proceeded , amidst the deafening cheers of the public, to Westminster Hall for the banquet.

After a grand feast which saw some innovatively crafted dishes, the celebrations continued with glittering public displays and jousts. However, the death of Margaret Beaufort, on 29 June, a day after Henry's eighteenth birthday, brought the celebrations to a halt.

King Henry VIII put together a grand funeral for his grandmother wherein he ordered the church bells to toll for six days and her confessor, John Fisher, the Bishop of Rochester, paid her a beautiful tribute. She was then buried at Westminster Abbey.

Barring this minor hiccup, King Henry VIII's reign had now begun.

The Reign of King Henry VIII

Adonis of fresh colour,
Of youth, the goodly flower,
Our Prince of high honour,
Our paves, our succour,
Our King, Our Emperor,
Our Priamus of Troy,
Our wealth, our worldly joy!
Upon us he doth reign,
That maketh our hearts glad,
As king most sovereign,
That ever England had,
Demure, sober and sad,
And Mars' lusty knight,
God save him in his right.[3]

John Skelton on King Henry VIII

Prince Henry Tudor, the second son of King Henry VII and his queen, Elizabeth of York, ascended the throne of England as King Henry VIII. As evident in the poem above by the irascible English poet, John Skelton, the young prince was anointed the King of England amidst much joy and celebration, especially after the rather staid rule of his father, the miserly King Henry VII.

The king in the Tudor era was considered to be an almost divine being. Being anointed with the Holy Water and Holy Oil accorded the king of the status of being a representative of the Almighty. In accordance with this belief, the king and his position in society was distinct from others. His people believed that their king had a special place in Heaven. Therefore, they expected their monarch to be just and noble and rule them honourably. The institute of monarchy was a hallowed one and treason against it was considered the most serious crime in the kingdom, attracting the ultimate penalty, one that was usually carried out by the gruesome method of hanging, drawing and quartering. For higher status prisoners on death row, the preferred method of execution was beheading.

During the reign of the Tudors the power entrusted with the king united all branches of his government, among them the Parliament, the Privy Council, the courtiers, the noblemen, judges and mayors.

In a society that placed a great deal of importance on the rank and status of an individual, it was imperative for the monarch to display his power and authority. It also worked as a propaganda tool for visiting dignitaries and ambassadors.

King Henry VIII's court was touted as one of the most magnificent of that era. He wore extravagant clothes and spent a fortune building palaces and castles. He also did not hold back when it came to organising lavish feasts and masques, especially during a visit of foreign dignitaries and ambassadors.

King Henry VIII began his rule by executing two corrupt and hated ministers of his late father, King Henry VII, Empson and Dudley. This act endeared him to his subjects who were finally hopeful of a golden future with the young king.

4

People and Events in the life of King Henry VIII

Cardinal Thomas Wolsey

Cardinal Thomas Wolsey, a statesman and a bishop, was born in around 1473 to Robert Wolsey of Ipswich and Joan Daundy. It is a popular belief that his father was a butcher, which became a main topic of criticism later in the cardinal's life. Wolsey attended Ipswich School and Magdalen College School before going on to study theology at Magdalen College, Oxford.

Thomas Wolsey entered the royal court in the service of King Henry VII in 1507. However, his star rose during the reign of King Henry VIII as the king sought to limit the powers that the nobles held. The king appointed him as the royal chaplain and Wolsey served as a secretary to Richard Foxe who recognised his capabilities. As Wolsey grew in stature and position, so did his wealth, which soon became a bone of contention to many. He had the king's ear and advised him on many state affairs which often ignited a feeling of jealousy in other courtiers and nobles.

Wolsey ultimately rose to be Lord Chancellor wherein he was referred to as *alter rex* (the other king). Wolsey fell out of royal favour when he failed to secure a divorce for the king from his queen of twenty-five years, Katharine of Aragon. A broken man, Wolsey died at Leicester while he was on his way to London to answer to charges of treason.

Katharine of Aragon

Katharine of Aragon was the youngest surviving daughter of King Ferdinand of Aragon and Queen Isabella of Castile, born at the Archbishop's Palace of Alcala de Henares near Madrid. Blessed with long, red hair, a round face and wide, blue eyes, Katharine descended from the House of Lancaster on her maternal side. Tutored by Alessandro Geraldini, Katharine studied arithmetic, canon and civil law, religion, history, theology, and genealogy. She was also taught Castilian Spanish, Latin, and later French.

From a very young age Katharine was aware that she was promised in marriage to Arthur, Prince of Wales. The marriage would validate the claim of the Tudors on the throne of England. Katharine and Arthur were married by proxy on 19 May 1499. They kept up a correspondence in Latin till Arthur turned fifteen, after which they were deemed old enough to officially marry.

Katharine left Spain for England on 17 August 1501, and after a gruelling sea voyage met Prince Arthur at Dogmersfield in Hampshire. They were married on 14 November 1501 at Old St Paul's Cathedral.

The couple were then sent to Ludlow Castle in Wales to preside over the Council of Wales and the Marshes. Merely a few months into their marriage, they were both afflicted by the sweating sickness which claimed the life of Prince Arthur. Devastated by her husband's death and pushed into penury due to her father and father-in-law haggling over her dowry, despite her being betrothed to Prince Harry, Katharine spent several years shuttling between various derelict residences in England before the death of King Henry VII. The political scenario changed as King Henry VIII ascended the throne of England and married Katharine on 11 June 1509.

Although their marriage was harmonious, it was a known fact that King Henry VIII took mistresses. It was rumoured that he had his eyes set on one of the sisters, most likely Anne Hastings, Countess of Huntingdon, of Edward Stafford, Duke of Buckingham (much to his chagrin). One of the most well-known of Henry's mistresses was Elizabeth 'Bessie' Blount, who gave birth to his illegitimate son, Henry FitzRoy.

After three miscarriages and losing a son after seven weeks of birth, Katharine finally gave birth to their daughter, Princess Mary, on 18 February 1516 at Greenwich.

Field of Cloth of Gold

The Field of Cloth of Gold was a meeting between King Henry VIII and Francis I of France that took place at Balinghem from 7 to 24 June

1520. The objective of this meeting was to enhance the bond of friendship between England and France following the treaty between the two countries that was signed in 1514. Each king attempted to outshine the other through ostentatious shows of wealth and gold, feasts, jousts and games. Banquets were held in honour of the two queens: Queen Katharine of Aragon of England and Queen Claude of France. Sports such as archery and wrestling kept the participants entertained and the summit broke up on 24 June after a Mass by Cardinal Thomas Wolsey.

The English Reformation

It was King Henry VIII who brought about the English Reformation: the transformation of England from a Catholic country to a Protestant one. In 1527, Henry, a devout Catholic, appealed to the Pope for an annulment from his wife of twenty-five years, Katharine of Aragon, on the grounds that his marriage was invalid as she was his older brother's widow and must have consummated her marriage with him. Katharine vehemently denied this charge, defending herself with elan in the ecclesiastical court. The annulment was difficult to obtain as the papacy was now under the control of Charles V, Holy Roman Emperor and Katharine's nephew.

This was the trigger for Henry to accept the papal supremacy in England. Between 1532 and 1537 he introduced various statutes which concerned the relationship between himself and the Pope and, consequently, the structure of the English Church. These included the Statute in Restraint of Appeals, which ensured the death penalty for those who brought in papal bulls in the country. Amidst many other such acts that restricted papal authority in England, the Peter's Pence Act stated that England had 'no superior under God, but only Your Grace'. The king received unconditional support in this from Archbishop Thomas Cranmer.

Henry insisted on using Parliament's time in discussing matters of faith much to the chagrin of Thomas Cromwell. This move gave rise to the Six Articles Act wherein six major questions were answered by advocating religious orthodoxy, thus hindering the reform movement. This was followed by the commencement of reformed liturgy and the Book of Common Prayers. Throughout the reign of King Henry VIII England witnessed an abstruse shift from religious orthodoxy, which was compounded with the executions of prominent personalities such as Sir Thomas More and Bishop John Fisher as they refused to give up the papal authority. Henry established a political theology of compliance with the Crown which reflected Martin Luther's new interpretation of the fourth commandment that was brought into England by William Tyndale. Protestant Reformers faced discrimination over Henry's decision to annul his marriage to Katharine of Aragon and a great many, including William Tyndale, were put to death.

Sir Thomas More

Born in Milk Street in London on 7 February 1478 to Sir John More and Agnes More, Sir Thomas More, or Saint Thomas More, was an English lawyer, statesman, philosopher, author and humanist. He served King Henry VIII as Lord Chancellor from 1529 to 1532. More, the author of *Utopia*, a book that describes the political system of an imaginary island, opposed the Protestant Reformation and spoke out against the likes of Martin Luther and William Tyndale. He opposed Henry's separation from the Church and refused to accept the king as the Supreme Head of the English Church. He also refused to accept the annulment of his marriage to Katharine of Aragon, leading to him being arrested for treason and executed on Tower Hill.

Eustace Chapuys

Eustace Chapuys was a diplomat from the Duchy of Savoy, born to Louis Chapuys and Guigonne Dupuys at Annecy, in the Holy Roman Empire. He served Charles V, Holy Roman Emperor, in the capacity of an ambassador to England from 1529 to 1545. Renowned for his writings and extensive records of official correspondences, Chapuys began his education at Annecy and in 1507 attended the University of Turin for five years. He also studied law at the University of

Valence and boasted Heinrich Cornelius Agrippa, Sir Thomas More, and Bishop John Fisher amongst many others as his friends. He had a deep respect for Erasmus and also corresponded with him, though the two never met. Chapuys first visited England in September 1526 and was then appointed Imperial ambassador to England on 25 June 1529. He stayed at Austin Friars and was a neighbour of Thomas Cromwell. His legal background helped him defend Katharine of Aragon during the King's Great Matter and he remained a lifelong friend of Katharine and her daughter, Mary. He lost and could never see Anne Boleyn eye to eye, always referring to her as 'the whore' or 'concubine'. Chapuys opposed the French despite being fluent in their language.

Despite suffering from gout, Chapuys remained in England till 1545. After a few more ambassadorial positions in Antwerp and Bourborg, Chapuys finally retired. After his retirement as an ambassador he acted as an adviser to Charles V from 1547 to 1549. He died on 21 January 1556 and is buried at the Chapel of the College of Savoy

Thomas Cranmer

Thomas Cranmer, Archbishop of Canterbury and the leader of the English Reformation, was born on 2 July 1489 to Thomas Cranmer and Agnes Hatfield at Aslockton, Nottinghamshire. He was instrumental in helping King Henry VIII annul his marriage to Queen Katharine of Aragon and marry Anne Boleyn. He, along with Thomas Cromwell, supported the royal supremacy over the Church in England. Cranmer did not make any major changes in the Church during King Henry VIII's rule due to the tussle between Conservatives and Reformers. He, however, established the first doctrinal and liturgical structures of the reformed Church of England.

His career flourished during the reign of the fiercely Protestant King Edward VI, but was arrested and imprisoned during the reign of his half-sister, Queen Mary I. Under pressure from the Catholic Church, Cranmer recanted many times but to no avail, finally reconciling himself with the Roman Church. He was sentenced to death, and on the day of his execution he withdrew his recantation and was burnt at the stake as a heretic.

Dissolution of the Monasteries

The Dissolution of the Monasteries was a legal and administrative process between 1536 and 1541 wherein King Henry VIII dissolved several monasteries, convents, priories and friaries in England, Ireland and Wales through the authority granted to him by the Act of Supremacy in which the king was the Supreme Head of the English Church. He seized their income, disposed of their assets and supported their former personnel in a financial capacity. Although originally planned to increase the regular income of the Crown, the funds seized from the monasteries were used to fund King Henry VIII's military expeditions. This project was created by Lord Chancellor Thomas Audeley and Richard Rich, Court Augmentations Head. Thomas Cromwell is often named as the person instrumental for bringing this dissolution about, but he only oversaw the project to bring in reforms and not to close or seize them.

Queen Jane Seymour

Jane Seymour was the third wife and Queen Consort of King Henry VIII. Born to Sir John Seymour and Margery Wentworth at Wulfhall in Wiltshire, Jane married the king at Whitehall on 30 May 1536 after the execution of his second wife, Anne Boleyn. Not as highly educated as Queen Katharine of Aragon or Anne Boleyn, Jane was well-known and well-liked for her amiable nature and for her efforts in reconciling King Henry VIII with his daughters. She barely involved herself in state matters save for one recorded moment when she had asked for pardon for the rebels of the Pilgrimage of Grace. Jane Seymour gave birth to Henry's long-awaited son and heir, Edward, on 12 October 1537 at Hampton Court Palace. She lost her life twelve days after her son's birth, most likely due to puerperal or childbed fever.

Edward Seymour, Earl of Hertford

Edward Seymour was the oldest surviving brother of Queen Jane Seymour, and the son of John Seymour and his wife, Margery Wentworth. He joined the household of Mary Tudor, Queen of France, at the age of fourteen. He served Charles Brandon, Duke of Suffolk, during his campaign in France and also accompanied Cardinal Thomas Wolsey on his embassy to France. He was created Viscount Beauchamp after his sister Jane's marriage to King Henry VIII. He also became the Warden of the Scottish Marches, and his royal favour did not wane even after the death of his sister in 1537. He also served the king as Lord High Admiral, a post that he gave up for John Dudley, the future Earl of Northumberland. He was also made the lieutenant-general of the north and was instructed to punish the Scots for the repudiation of the treaty of marriage between Prince Edward and Mary, Queen of Scots. He landed at Leith in May 1544 and pillaged Edinburgh before returning to England, burning villages and castles on the way. He was also appointed the lieutenant of the realm under the regency of Queen Catherine Parr while King Henry VIII was away in France.

Pilgrimage of Grace

The Pilgrimage of Grace was a popular rebellion that began in Yorkshire in October 1536. It then spread to other parts of England, namely Cumberland, Northumberland, and north Lancashire, under the leadership of Robert Aske. The rebellion was in protest at King Henry VIII's break from the Roman Catholic Church, the Dissolution of the Monasteries, and the policies of Thomas Cromwell, apart from other social, political and financial complaints. Following the failure of the Lincolnshire Uprising, the Pilgrimage of Grace broke out on 13 October 1536. A barrister from London, Robert Aske, was chosen to lead the rebels.

Thomas Cromwell

An English lawyer and a statesmen, Thomas Cromwell was the son of a blacksmith from Putney, Walter Cromwell, and his wife, Katherine Meverell. He served as the chief minister to King Henry VIII from 1534 till his death in 1540. Little is known about Cromwell's humble beginnings, but he shone at the royal court where he was the strongest and most powerful supporter of the English Reformation. He was instrumental in the downfall of Anne Boleyn, an erstwhile friend and champion of his. Amassing many enemies during his tenure as chief minister, Thomas Cromwell fell spectacularly from grace after he arranged a disastrous marriage for the king to Anne of Cleves hoping to bring a fresh direction to the Reformation. He was instead attainted for treason and heresy and beheaded on 28 July 1540 at Tower Hill. King Henry VII later regretted his decision.

Queen Anne of Cleves

Anne of Cleves, born in Dusseldorf to John III, Duke of Cleves, and Maria, was the fourth wife and queen of King Henry VIII. Marriage negotiations began in March 1539 as Henry wished to forge an alliance with her brother, Wilhelm, Duke of Cleves, who was a leader of the Protestants in Western Germany. Anne married Henry on 6 December 1540 at Greenwich. Henry gave her a generous allowance and premium estates following the annulment and termed her as the King's Beloved Sister. She remained in England for the rest of her life, outliving Henry, and finally dying at Chelsea Old Manor on 16 July 1557. She is the only one of King Henry VIII's queens to be buried at the hallowed Westminster Abbey.

Bishop Stephen Gardiner

An English bishop and a politician, Stephen Gardiner was born in Bury St Edmunds. Although the identity of his father is disputed, his mother is said to have been an illegitimate daughter of Jasper Tudor, King Henry VII's uncle. He was educated at Trinity Hall in Cambridge and excelled in class, his forte being Greek classics. He went on to study canon and civil law and became immensely proficient in them. He then found employment as Cardinal Thomas Wolsey's secretary and was with him at The More when the Treaty of More was signed. In 1527, along with Sir Thomas More, he was commissioned to bring about a treaty with the French for the support of an army against Charles V, Holy Roman Emperor. Despite being unsuccessful in the King's Great Matter, he was appointed King Henry VIII's secretary in 1529. He took part in various foreign embassies and was instrumental in the enactment of the Six Articles Act which led to the resignation of eminent priests such as Nicholas Shaxton and the persecution of Protestants. After the execution of Thomas Cromwell he was elected the Chancellor of the University of Cambridge. Being a religious conservative, he tried to charge Archbishop Thomas Cranmer with heresy and also attempted to implicate Queen Catherine Parr for secretly sympathising with the Protestants, especially Anne Askew.

Queen Catherine Parr

Queen Catherine Parr, the sixth and final queen of King Henry VIII, was the eldest child of Sir Thomas Parr and Maud Parr who was a close friend of Queen Katharine of Aragon. Twice widowed, she married Henry on 12 July 1543 at Hampton Court Palace. Catherine enjoyed a close friendship with all three of Henry's children, sharing a special bond with Princess Elizabeth whose education and upbringing she personally oversaw. She was instrumental in restoring Mary and Elizabeth to the line of succession through the passing of the Third Succession Act in 1543. Her book, *Prayers or Meditations*, became the first to be published by an English queen under her own name. Catherine sympathised with the Protestants, which provoked the religious conservatives who tried in vain to get her arrested.

After Henry's death she was allowed to keep her jewels and dresses. Six months after Henry's death Catherine married Thomas Seymour, her final marriage, which was short-lived. She passed away on 5 September 1548 due to complications during childbirth, a common cause of death in those days. Her daughter, Mary, soon disappeared from the pages of history.

Death of King Henry VIII

Later in life King Henry VIII grew morbidly obese and had to be moved with the help of mechanical devices. Covered with painful, pus-filled boils, he also possibly suffered from gout, most likely due to a jousting accident he met with years earlier. The wound that he sustained proved difficult to heal and would bother him for the rest of his life. The accident also damaged his mental state and he was prone to sudden bouts of anger.

King Henry VIII passed away on 28 January 1547 at the Palace of Whitehall, possibly due to his obesity. He was buried in a vault at St George's Chapel at Windsor Castle, next to the queen who bore him his heir, Jane Seymour.

5

Alice Tankerville

Little Ease

The grim reputation of the Tower of London – as we have read previously – reached its peak during the reign of the Tudors. Known for its plethora of torture paraphernalia, the Tower was infamous for having a special prison cell which was, quite aptly, termed as Little Ease.

Little Ease[1] earned its moniker due to its tiny size which measured only 1.2m^2. This ensured that the prisoner in the cell could not adjust himself/herself into a comfortable position and was compelled to crouch in an awkward position, neither sitting nor standing, for days, or even sometimes weeks on end.

Today, Little Ease is lost to us. The location of the original cell is unknown and all we have today is a replica in the assumed location. The legend that surrounds this particular cell lives on as it may have played host to some notable prisoners such as Guy Fawkes.

One such prisoner who was incarcerated in the tiny cell, although not so well-known as Fawkes, was John Bawd. A former prison guard, his fate is closely linked to another prisoner who earned the infamy of being the only woman to have escaped from the Tower of London: Alice Tankerville.

1534

In the dead of a moonless, chilly January night, two cloaked figures could be seen tiptoeing away from Tower Hill, huddled close together. To anyone oblivious to Alice Tankerville,[2] the two people may have looked like a lovestruck couple – sneaking out for a night-time embrace, or perhaps just cuddling up to each other to protect themselves from the January chill.

However, it was anything but that. They were lovers, but one of the two, Alice Wolfe, née Tankerville or Tankerfelde, was, as mentioned above, on her way to imprint her name into the pages of history as the first woman to escape the infamous Tower of London.

Short-lived was her triumph, though, as moments later, along with her companion, John Bawd, her jailer and lover, she was discovered by the prison guards and was thrown back into the dreary bowels of the Tower.

How did Alice and John manage to pull off this feat, albeit for a brief time? To know this, we need to go back three years.

1531

Not much is known about Alice's early life apart from the fact that she certainly was good-looking. We can safely assume that her parents did not belong to the nobility given Alice's checkered past.

Alice knew how to use her looks and charm to her advantage and in no time ended up as a common law wife to John Wolfe. Indeed, Edward Hall, a member of Parliament and lawyer of Gray's Inn, believed her to be a 'harlot'.[3]

John Wolfe was a Merchant of the Steelyard. This was an area in London, near Blackfriars, and was the place where the Hanseatic merchants operated under their own laws. The Hanseatic League[4] was a medieval commercial and defensive guild of merchant groups and towns in central and northern Europe. It was formed to protect the members against piracy and also promote mutual commercial interests.

By 1531 King Henry VIII's coffers were almost empty and the king was expecting a shipment of 366 gold crowns to arrive any day. That day arrived and the king's men hurried to the London docks to collect the money. However, they were in for a shock: the ship had returned empty.

Despite the money being transported in an iron chest that was locked and chained to the floor of the ship, the theft had taken place and no one knew who did it or how the thief managed to steal the money.

A major investigation was launched but initially met with little success. Fate finally smiled upon the investigators when, nearly two years later, the scanty evidence pointed towards John Wolfe as the perpetrator of the crime. However, the evidence in question was just the fact that Wolfe was a part of the crew that was aboard when the ship in question was docked in London. Given the situation, this was enough for the Crown to issue an arrest warrant for Wolfe, who was immediately apprehended and taken to the Tower of London, where he awaited his trial on charges of theft and treason.

Prisoners held captive in the Tower were expected to pay for their own food and bedding. Alice Tankerville, his common-law wife, fulfilled her wifely duties to the tee as she brought him fresh clothes and bedding, and home-cooked food.

However, the notoriously seductive Alice lost no time in entrancing two of her husband's jailers, William Denys and John Bawd, who were so taken in with her charms that they allowed her to bring in fine treats and wine for Wolfe. It is clear that they did not extend these favours to her and her husband for nothing in return. And Alice was only to happy to oblige them.

Luck favoured the couple as the case against Wolfe crumbled due to lack of evidence and he was released. Instead of celebrating his success, Wolfe wisely decided to lay low in Ireland till the case against him was forgotten. But before he left for Ireland, he had one job to do.

He met John Bawd, his erstwhile jailer, privately and asked him to keep his wife, Alice, safe while he was away. Needless to say, Bawd readily agreed.

If John Wolfe and Alice Tankerville assumed that his absence would bury the case against him, they were sadly mistaken. Barely a few weeks had passed since Wolfe's departure that new evidence turned up in the case of the missing gold. And this time it incriminated Alice as an accomplice.

Fearing another Houdini-like act by Alice, the couple were tried in *absentia* so that Alice was kept in the dark about the allegations against her. Only when they were found guilty of theft and treason against the Crown were the arrest warrants issued.

February 1534

Merely a month before the First Act of Succession – which proclaimed the validity of King Henry VIII's marriage to Anne Boleyn and recognised the right of their future offspring to succeed their father to the throne of England – was passed, Alice was finally captured. She was then thrown into a drab, windowless cell in Coldharbour Gate tower where the only light trickled through a small, barred window on the heavy oak door.

She was shackled to the walls of her cell with her hands and feet bound securely by iron manacles. This was an unusually cruel treatment, so much so that the daughter of Edmund Walshingham, the Lieutenant of the Tower, pleaded for leniency for Alice. Giving in to his daughter's demands, Walshingham ordered for Alice's shackles to be taken off.

In a relatively more comfortable environment now, Alice was further pleased to know that one of her jailers included her one-time friend William Denys. Denys visited Alice often, even when he was off-duty, and brought her small treats. However, Denys wasn't particularly discreet about his regular visits and very soon his superior, Sir John Walshingham, got wind of it. Denys was promptly fired from his job.

Alice did not miss Denys for long as John Bawd soon managed to change his schedule so that he was Alice's guard almost every day. Aware of his predecessor's fate, Bawd was seemingly more prudent in handling matters. Gradually, a romance between the guard and his prisoner blossomed behind the closed oak door.

Desperate to get out of her squalid condition, Alice and her lover hatched an escape plan. Alice told Bawd that Denys had happened to mention a possible escape route in Coldharbour Gate tower and asked Bawd to check the veracity of his claims. Once discovering this to be true, Bawd, blinded by his love towards Alice, agreed to help her escape, risking his job and his own life.

Bawd started executing the escape plan by first taking his close friend, Jeffrey Harrison, into his confidence. He also spoke to a hosteller who owned a stable of horses close to the Tower. He then purchased two lengths of rope from a merchant named Sampson and found a smooth, round stick.

Bawd now needed a key to the outer door of Coldharbour Gate tower which was always kept locked. The guards were ordered to return the keys to the main office once the last guard went off-duty at 10pm every night. Bawd began making a duplicate of the key that he needed, filing it little by little. He hid his duplicate key in his uniform and worked on it diligently till the key worked perfectly.

His handiwork complete, Bawd passed the key, the stick and the rope through the bars of Alice's cell for her to hide them under the straw in her room. Then their wait began.

On a moonless winter night, two weeks later, the two of them decided to put their plan into action. Once Bawd's shift ended that night, he asked

Alice to pass the rope to him through her cell door and then hurried out of the tower.

Alice tucked the duplicate key in her bodice and got to work. She reached out through the gap under her cell door with the help of the stick that Bawd had smuggled to her and began poking around blindly for the pin that held the clasp on the door.

After a few nerve-wracking moments, Alice finally located the pin and started tapping it upwards to unfasten it from the clasp. The pin soon fell on the ground and Alice swung the door open triumphantly. She then felt her way through the dark passages and reached the outer door. Alice unlocked the outer door and walked out into the yard.

Alice was smart enough to cover herself from head to toe in a black cloak so as to make herself practically invisible as she made her way out from captivity. Enveloped in the darkness of the night, she felt her way through the narrow alleyways and made her way up the stone stairs, reaching the roof of St Thomas' Tower where John Bawd was waiting for her. Keeping an eye on the patrolling night guard, Alice and Bawd made their way out of the Tower by climbing down the rope that Bawd had fastened on to a hook on the stone parapet. They landed on a tiny pier next to Traitors' Gate and silently rowed away towards the Iron Gate steps where prisoners were brought through the Traitors' Gate.

The couple then stepped out of the boat and made their way through the dark roads and alleyways in the Tower complex, passing by the guards' houses. Bawd had rented a couple of horses which were tethered close by and would take them to his friend, Jeffrey Harrison's place. Harrison had agreed to keep his friend and paramour in hiding till the guards gave up searching for them. They then planned to escape London. It is quite possible that they had planned to meet John Wolfe after their escape.

Alice and Bawd walked towards the horses and untied them with nervous excitement, trying to avoid any undue attention. Just as they went around the last corner towards Tower Hill and were about to approach the waiting horses, they were confronted by a small band of people. Bawd recognised them as the patrolling night guards; with them was one of Bawd's oldest friends, Charles Gore.

Gore called out a greeting to his friend who mumbled back incoherently and continued walking with Alice, trying to avoid getting too close. Just then, Gore happened to catch a closer look at Bawd's companion. Being an occasional guard at the Coldharbour Gate, he recognized his prisoner in an instant and sounded the alarm.

In no time the couple were surrounded by the night guards of the Tower of London. The escaping couple offered little resistance as the guards dragged Alice back to her cell which was now secured with a heavy padlock. John Bawd was taken to the Counter Gaol to be questioned.

Afraid of being tortured, Bawd confessed everything and blamed the 'love and affection that he bore' for Alice for leading him to take such a drastic risk and put everything he held dear on the line. He was then moved to the notorious Little Ease cell and was only taken out to be questioned further or to be racked.

Sir Edmund Walshingham would have lost his job and probably even his head for this fiasco had he not received the news that John Wolfe was apprehended in an attempt to return to England.

Already tried in *absentia* and sentenced to death, Alice Tankerville and John Wolfe met their end in an unusual and macabre manner. On 31 March 1534 the couple were taken from their cells to the stone walls on the embankment on the River Thames where they were chained and lowered into the water during low tide. Slowly and steadily, the filthy water of the Thames crept higher and higher as Alice and Wolfe tried frantically to raise their heads above the rising tide. Onlookers watched as the couple were slowly drowned. So ended the life of the only woman to have escaped the Tower of London, albeit for a fleeting moment.

As for John Bawd, he paid a heavy price for aiding Alice's escape. Despite his confession, he was racked until his limbs hung loose from their joints. In immense pain and completely immobile, Bawd was finally wrapped in chains and suspended over the walls of the Tower where he died of exhaustion, starvation and hunger. His body was left there for months on end while the ravens and other scavenging birds feasted on his flesh.

Amidst all this brouhaha, the mystery of the king's stolen gold remains unsolved. We truly do not know whether or not Alice Tankerville and John Wolfe were really behind the heist or if they were just a couple of petty criminals who met a gruesome end.

6

Anne Boleyn

19 May 1536: 9am

This was the day England wrote a new, sordid chapter in the annals of its long history. Sure, there were many scandalous queens who sat upon the throne: the Tudor matriarch, Catherine of Valois, for example, married her squire, Owen Tudor, after the death of her husband, King Henry V, thereby causing a lot of bad blood and straining of ties within the nobles in the court of her son, Henry VI. Or Elizabeth Woodville, the commoner wife of the Yorkist King Edward IV who defeated and may have caused the death of Catherine's son, King Henry VI. Edward caused quite a flutter when he surreptitiously married Elizabeth, a Lancastrian widow with two sons, rather than the Princess of Bona, a match that was arranged by 'The Kingmaker', Richard Neville, thereby incurring his wrath and sparking a rebellion the result of which finally terminated the rule of the Lancastrians.

But never before had a Queen of England been executed. This was a first for the citizens of London. Although the execution – beheading by a sword – was meant to be a private one, crowds thronged into Tower Green through a gate which was left open, unintentionally or by design, we don't know. The daily humdrum of life took a break as men, women and children gathered in front of the scaffold to witness the tragic event with a macabre interest.

The queen in question: Anne Boleyn. Also known as the Concubine, a name given to her by the imperial ambassador, Eustace Chapuys. She incurred the wrath of the citizens of her country when she decided to woo the king with a passionate fervour, her eyes set firmly on the crown. Not once, the Londoners said, did she think about the poor Queen Katharine of Aragon – who later called her 'the scandal of Christendom' – who, after almost twenty-five years of marriage to King Henry VIII, was unceremoniously cast away and died, all but forgotten at Kimbolton Castle.

Was Anne really as iniquitous as she was made out to be? Or was she just a pawn in the hands of her powerful family members who correctly gauged her vivacious personality and played their cards well?

Boleyns: A History

The Boleyns, like most of the noble families in the Tudor era, had obscure but not necessarily dubious origins. It is suggested that the family had its roots in France given the fact that their last name Boleyn (or Bullen, Bulleyn, etc.) was spelled very similarly to the French city of Boulogne.

Author Amy Licence, in her book *Anne Boleyn*, mentions that a fortress named Brie, or Briis-sous-Forges, which lies 40km to the south of Paris, claims a connection with Anne who is said to have stayed in the castle there with Philippe de Moulin, Signeur de Brie, husband of a Marie Boleyn.[1]

By 1283 the Boleyns settled at Salle, near Aylsham, the evidence of which is a John Boleyn recorded as having lived there by the registrar of Walshingham Abbey. Simon de Boleyne, probably the father of John, purchased land at Salle in 1252. Another Boleyn, Nicholas, was a petty thief who robbed a man in Lincoln in 1333. Yet another John Boleyn appears in the records of Salle along with an Emma Boleyn whom, we may presume, was John's spouse. However, the early Boleyns remained inconsequential till Geoffrey Boleyn.

Geoffrey Boleyn, the son of Geoffrey Boleyn I and Alice Bracton Boleyn, left Salle and moved to Norfolk and steadily established himself as a successful trader, initially starting off as a hatter. He may have taken in his sister, Cecily Boleyn, as a brass plate dedicated to her survives in the church next to Blickling Hall. Cecily apparently never married and led a pious life, as her memorial brass depicts. It is also believed that he shared a warm relationship with his other sibling, a brother named Thomas.

Geoffrey Boleyn was a member and later Master of the Worshipful Company of Mercers. He was later promoted to the post of Sheriff of London from 1446-47. He later became a Member of the Parliament of the City of London in 1449 and was then the councilman of the City of London, a post that he held for eleven years. Geoffrey Boleyn's crowning glory was when he was elected Mayor of London in the year 1457.

The London that Geoffrey Boleyn saw was not very different from the one his descendant, Anne Boleyn, presided over as queen a few decades later. The capital city was filthy and the stench from the meat markets and tanneries was overpowering. The sewers were perpetually overflowing and the Hound's Ditch – which stretched from the Tower of London all the way to Blackfriars on the outside of the city walls – encircled the city in its own waste. The timber-framed houses that dominated every lane and alleyway of London were a fire hazard.

All these successful endeavours enabled Geoffrey Boleyn to accumulate great wealth and thereby ensured his initiation into the elite social circles. He married Dionese or Denise about whom virtually nothing is known except for a mention in her husband's will. There is some dispute over whether Geoffrey's son, Thomas III, was born of Denise or his second wife, Anne Hoo. However, a mention by Thomas himself in his own will can safely solve this dispute as Thomas mentions Anne Hoo as his mother and not Denise. We can presume that this was a short marriage.

Geoffrey's marriage to Anne Hoo catapulted him into the higher echelons of society, coupled with a successful career. Already a successful merchant, he began mingling with the great and the good, eventually bringing himself to the notice of Lord Hoo and Hastings. By his marriage to Lord Hoo and Hasting's daughter, Anne, Geoffrey Boleyn took his first steps towards building links with the nobility. Although Anne was marrying someone who was beneath her family in the social ladder, Geoffrey's immense fortune and prosperity more than made up for it.

Geoffrey's love for Anne was evident in the fact that the couple, despite the twenty-years age gap between them, shared a mutual bond of affection, as we can see in Geoffrey's will. Anne bore Geoffrey five children: Thomas, William, Isabel, Anne and Alice.

Geoffrey Boleyn may have also been a philanthropist, a trait that his great-great-granddaughter, Anne, inherited as Queen of England, as certain records mention his contributions to prisons, hospitals and leper houses. He also extended his generosity towards the poor families in London and Norfolk by assisting them monetarily. All this wealth and subsequent charity may have resulted in King Henry VI knighting him, most probably in the year 1461.

Geoffrey purchased a manor house in Blickling from his old friend and benefactor, Sir John Fastolf – a striking personality who inspired one of William Shakespeare's most notable characters, Falstaff. Originally built by Sir Nicholas Dagworth – and once owned by the eleventh-century Saxon king Harold Godwineson – the old manor house was falling into disrepair when Geoffrey bought it and made considerable improvements to the structure and renaming it Blickling Hall. Geoffrey was also instrumental in building the chapel of St Thomas in Blickling Church where the couple's heraldic arms – nestled between beautiful stained-glass paintings – can be seen even today.

In 1462 Geoffrey purchased the estates of Hever Cobham and Hever Brokays from William Fiennes, Lord Saye and Sele. He also acquired the now famed Hever Castle from Sir Thomas Cobham. Enjoying the elevated social status that his new-found prosperity brought him, Geoffrey Boleyn now moved in the same social circles as that of his renowned Norfolk neighbours, the aristocratic Paston family, and even the elite Howards. The comradeship between the Boleyns and the Howards was later cemented by marriage. The Boleyns also made many more advantageous marital alliances like that of William Boleyn to Margaret Butler, the daughter and co-heiress of Thomas Butler, 7th Earl of Ormond.

Geoffrey Boleyn II died in 1463. Prior to his demise he had made a list of demands for his funeral. He stated that as he was a man of simple choices, he wanted to be buried with black candlesticks. He also stated that thirteen torches should be carried aloft by the same number of penurious men, who were to be poor landowners rather than beggars. The torchbearers were to be given a rosary, a gown lined with russet or black, and a black hood. They were also to be given 12 pence each.

He left Anne Hoo a wealthy widow, giving her a substantial share of his goods and effects, including half of his silver plate. He also left Anne her own clothes and jewels, an unusual move during the fifteenth century where women were not authorised to hold any property or personal effects. He made a provision for his clothes and other personal belongings to be sold to provide for items like bedding and clothes, etc. for the needy, thus displaying his charitable side till the very end.

Geoffrey left his sons 300 marks each and his daughters a sum of 1000 marks. He entrusted Anne and his brother, Thomas Boleyn, to distribute the remaining half of the silver plate judiciously between his children. However, he laid the condition of reaching the age of twenty-five or marrying for his children to inherit the said bequests. In a significant move, reasons for which are unfathomable, Anne was not appointed as a trustee for any of her children. Anne never remarried after Geoffrey's death. Instead, she kept herself occupied by managing her husband's vast estates after his passing.

Anne and Geoffrey's eldest son, Thomas, succeeded his father despite being a minor, although some say that he had attained majority at the time of his father's death. However, he did not live long, dying in April 1471, and a will made by him suggested that his health was always on the delicate side. He had asked to be buried with his father and appointed his mother as an executor of his will.

Anne Hoo Boleyn herself died in 1485 at Norfolk. She was buried in Norwich cathedral in a grave that is lost to us today with only an outline on a stone surviving.[2]

Geoffrey Boleyn's successful career as a merchant and his advantageous marriage to Anne Hoo thrust the family into prominent social circles and they befriended their illustrious Norfolk neighbours the Pastons, amongst others. However, it was his son William's marriage to Margaret Butler that truly took the Boleyn name to dizzying heights of fame and success.

Following the demise of Thomas Boleyn, Geoffrey and Anne's eldest son, William, inherited the Boleyn properties and married Margaret Butler. She was the daughter of Thomas Butler, 7th Earl of Ormond. A family with roots in Ireland, the earliest known ancestor of the family was Theobald Butler who lived and died during the reign of Edward I. The earldom of Ormond was granted by King Edward III to Theobald's great-grandson. Thomas Butler, Margaret's father, was the third son of the 4th Earl.

The Butlers were a family who were loyal to the Lancastrians and fought on their side during the Wars of the Roses. Thomas Butler's brother, James Butler, was created Earl of Wiltshire by King Henry VI as a reward for his loyalty before inheriting the family earldom of Ormond. Although forced to flee after the Lancastrians were trounced in the Battle of St Albans, he participated in the Battle of Wakefield[3] where the Lancastrians tasted victory and which led to the execution of Richard, Duke of York.

However, James' luck ran out at the Battle of Mortimer's Cross, where the Lancastrians were routed and James was taken captive. An attainder was passed against him, and his earldom and estates were stripped. James died without issue, despite being married thrice, and it was his younger brother, John, who re-acquired the earldom of Ormond, not

Wiltshire, by making peace with King Edward IV. John died suddenly while on a pilgrimage to the Holy Land in 1478 and the youngest Butler brother, Thomas, Margaret's father, inherited the earldom of Ormond.

The earldom most likely played a vital role in securing the marriage of William Boleyn and Margaret Butler. Besides that, Margaret belonged to an elite ancestry, her maternal grandmother being the daughter of the Earl of Shrewsbury as well as being the great-granddaughter of Lord Bergavenny.

The marriage was a fertile one with Margaret siring four sons and three daughters. Her eldest son was Thomas, born in 1477, followed by James, William and Edward. William Boleyn, a priest, served as the Archdeacon of Winchester and died in 1571. His daughters, Anne, Alice and Margaret, received substantial bequests on their father's death and the three ladies came to the forefront during the reign of their niece, Anne Boleyn.

William Boleyn built up a successful court career, quite unlike his merchant father and grandfather. He was created Knight of the Bath at the Coronation of Richard III in 1483 and hosted a visit of the king at Blickling. This resulted in William being promoted as the Third Baron of the Exchequer. He moved base from Norfolk to Kent, making the picturesque Hever Castle his primary residence. However, he maintained close ties with Norfolk, serving as the mayor of both Norfolk and Kent on two different occasions. He, along with Anthony, Earl Rivers, helped quash a minor riot within the Norfolk gentry.

In the meantime, Henry VII appointed Margaret's father, Thomas, Earl of Ormond, as an emissary to the court of Burgundy. Prior to this appointment, he had served in the King's Privy Council and was also the chamberlain to Queen Elizabeth of York.

The Earl of Ormond died at a grand old age of ninety, quite ancient by medieval standards. His daughter was well into her sixties and already widowed for ten years when her father passed away. He had died an extremely wealthy man, owning over seventy-two manors in England alone, not to mention his properties and estates in Ireland.

Margaret was very close to her son, Thomas, and so was his maternal grandfather, the Earl of Ormond. This preference to his daughter's eldest son was quite obvious when he bequeathed a precious family heirloom – an ancestral ivory horn which was reputed to be the cup from which Thomas Becket, erstwhile Archbishop of Canterbury, drank – to his grandson in his will.

By 1519 Margaret was considered to be of unsound mind; most probably she suffered from what we now know as dementia. Maybe she realised it too and was all too eager to hand over the control of her Ormond inheritance to her son, Thomas.

Thomas Boleyn married Elizabeth Howard of the distinguished Howard family of Norfolk. Elizabeth, the eldest daughter of Thomas Howard, 2nd Duke of Norfolk, was a rare beauty who had paeans written about her by the esteemed John Skelton. Thomas shared a warm camaraderie with his wife's family, taking the help of his brother-in-law, the Earl of Surrey, in securing the Irish inheritance of his mother and aunt, Anne, probably by mediating between the sisters and the Butler family. To put an end to the dispute, the Earl of Surrey suggested a marriage between Piers Butler's eldest son, James, and Thomas Boleyn's daughter, Anne, the future Queen of England, which was conveyed to Cardinal Wolsey. However, despite Anne being recalled from France, the negotiations fizzled out, presumably because the match wasn't a propitious one for the up-and-coming Boleyn family.

Eventually, after Henry VIII was betrothed to Anne Boleyn in 1527, an agreement between Margaret Butler Boleyn, her sister, Anne St Leger and Piers Butler was drawn up by Cardinal Wolsey wherein they placed the earldom of Ormond at the king's disposal. The estates were then divided equally between the sisters and the Irish lands were leased to the Butlers. Henry further showed the benevolent side to his betrothed's family by making Thomas Boleyn the Earl of Ormond.

The tables weren't really turned after Anne Boleyn's spectacular fall from grace and subsequent execution as there is no hint of Thomas Boleyn losing the two earldoms that he acquired during his rise to fame in the English court – that of Ormond and later Wiltshire. Thomas, though, withdrew from court life and lived a quiet existence until his death on 12 March 1539 at Hever, just three years after his daughter's and son's executions. Elizabeth Boleyn had died a year prior to her husband, on 3 April 1538.

The Boleyn Family

Mary, Anne and George Boleyn were the three surviving children of Thomas Boleyn, Earl of Wiltshire, and Elizabeth Howard. Amongst a probable many other children, two sons, Thomas and Henry, lost their lives early. While Thomas is buried at Penshurst Church in Kent, Henry is buried near his father at Hever.

Anne's year of birth has long been a subject of dispute; as is the claim of which of the two Boleyn sisters is the older one. For a long time it was believed that Anne was the eldest. However, in a letter to Thomas Cecil, Lord Burghley, Mary Boleyn's grandson, George Carey, 2nd Baron Hunsdon, in the year 1597, petitioned for the earldom of Ormond in the right of his grandmother, stating that 'my grandmother was the eldest daughter and sole heir' of Thomas Boleyn. He never followed up with the petition, but through the above mentioned letter, George Carey has left enough evidence for us to safely assume that Mary was the oldest sibling. Surely Carey would not have taken on his grand-aunt, Queen Elizabeth I, over a claim to the earldom.

There have been different views on this topic, however. John Weever referred to Anne Boleyn as the eldest Boleyn sibling in his *Ancient Funeral Monuments*, which was later found to be an inaccurate, and in some parts plagarised piece of work. Moreover, Weever wasn't born till 1576. Another red flag in Weever's declaration appears when he refuses to name his source.

Yet another evidence of Mary being the eldest sibling is the fact that she was the one to be married first. It was usual in Tudor England for the oldest sibling to be married first, and however liberal Thomas Boleyn may have been in his views and beliefs, we can be sure that this is one convention he would not have wanted to flout.

Now, let's look into the dispute over Anne's year of birth. Henry Clifford gives 1507 as Anne's year of birth in his memoir of Jane Dormer, Duchess of Feria, which was published in 1643, many years after it was written. This makes Anne 'not quite twenty-nine' when she was executed on 19 May 1536. This would place Anne's year of birth sometime after 19 May 1507 or 1508. Jane Dormer, born two years after Anne's execution, may have obtained this information from the ladies of Queen Mary I's household, where she served as a maid of honour and was a close confidante of the queen herself.

An excavation carried out in 1876 at the royal chapel of St Peter ad Vincula at the Tower of London, where Anne and her brother lay buried, revealed a skeleton of a woman aged between twenty-five and thirty years which the archaeologists believed to be Anne's, based on her year of birth being 1507. Another skeleton of a woman, maybe that of Jane

Parker, Lady Rochford and Anne's sister-in-law, aged around thirty years to forty years, was reburied without further examination.

Assuming the common theory that Mary was older than Anne and George, we can say that she was born by 1500 or 1501. She was named after the Virgin Mary, as was common practice in those days. Anne may have been named after St Anne or one of her ancestors, Anne Butler, Anne Hoo or Princess Anne of York. George was certainly the youngest of the three surviving Boleyn siblings, their two other brothers, Thomas and Henry dying young, and many have been named after England's patron saint, St George.

All the surviving Boleyn siblings may have been born at Blickling Hall in Norfolk. The county traces its history back to pre-Roman times when a Brittonic tribe, the Iceni, rebelled against the Romans when the latter invaded the former's lands. The Iceni's second rebellion, led by Boudica in AD 60, was crushed mercilessly and thus opened the gates of the area to the Romans. Farming and trade flourished at this time as the Romans built roads, ports and waterways. By the fifth century Germanic people from the North Sea area, known as the Angles, took control the region and later became the 'north folk' or Norfolk' and 'south folk or 'Suffolk'. By the time of the Tudor reign, Norfolk grew into a wealthy county on account of the wool-cloth trade with the Low Countries. Norwich, the county's main city, was second in size only to London and boasted of more churches than anywhere else in the kingdom

To the northwest of Aylsham stood Blickling Hall, the exquisitely beautiful residence of the Boleyn family. The Blickling Hall that the Boleyn family knew and lived in does not exist today. According to the various descriptions of the manor house by the contemporaries of Thomas Boleyn, we can assume that Blickling Hall had no defensive features. Sir William Boleyn and Thomas Boleyn were said to have carried out many improvements in the manor which was surrounded by yew hedges that still survive today.

Thomas Boleyn soon found a place at the court of King Henry VII, probably due to the influence of his wife's family, the Howards. Through his knowledge and intelligence, Thomas soon made a name for himself and by November 1501, the year he debuted in the court, he attended the marriage of the king's oldest son, Prince Arthur, to the Spanish princess, Katharine of Aragon, at St Paul's Cathedral in London.

After Arthur's tragic death and the subsequent betrothal of Katharine's to King Henry VII's younger son, Prince Henry, Thomas had made a mark at the court and was chosen to escort Princess Margaret to Scotland when she left England to marry King James IV of Scotland. By 1507, the year of Anne's probable birth, Thomas was appointed 'Yeoman of the Crown' at the port of King's Lynn in Norfolk.

However, there are no surviving records of Mary, Anne and George's childhood. As their parents were busy with court duties it is very likely that the three Boleyn siblings were brought up by their retinue of servants, meeting their parents only on certain occasions. The siblings may have befriended their neighbours, the Wyatts, who lived close to Hever where the Boleyn children spent much of their childhood.

The three siblings must have shared the same tutors and it is believed that Anne and George excelled in their studies. Sir Thomas Boleyn, recognising the potential in Anne early on, ensured that she received a quality education that would have helped her to make a name for herself, proving himself to be quite a progressive man at that time. Anne and George were especially close, a bond that stayed till the very end, and were said to have been intellectually superior to Mary. As daughters of a high ranking official in the royal court, Mary and Anne were expected to make advantageous marriages and Sir Thomas was determined to do just that.

Anne goes abroad

By 1513, recognising the potential in Anne, Sir Thomas sent her to one of the finest courts of Europe, in Brussels, where Margaret of Austria was the regent of the Netherlands. Thus was he working towards providing Anne, his favourite daughter, a glorious future. A position with Margaret of Austria, formerly the daughter-in-law of King Ferdinand of Aragon and Queen Isabella of Castile and the former sister-in-law of Queen Katherine of Aragon, was highly sought after, a fact that Sir Thomas Boleyn may have stressed to his daughters as a subtle warning against doing anything to damage their reputation.

Having had three short, failed marriages, Margaret of Austria swore off any more proposed marital unions and instead headed one of the most cultured courts in all of Europe in Brussels. Being a special acquaintance of her father, Anne quickly found a special place in the heart of Margaret, impressing her with her quick mind and her eagerness to learn. She mastered the French language very quickly and often corresponded with her father, whose French language skills were par excellence.

King Henry VIII, at the time of Anne's arrival at Brussels, had allied himself with King Ferdinand of Aragon and Maximilian I against France. Being married to Ferdinand's daughter, Katharine of Aragon, Henry naturally aligned himself with the two monarchs – who shared a common interest for their grandson and Katharine's nephew, Charles, the future Holy Roman Emperor – against France and personally sailed out for war with his troops. He tasted victory, capturing two French cities, and met Margaret and Maximilian at Lille. It is highly likely, though not recorded, that Anne may have met Henry for the first time there.

However, a small yet vital incident soured Henry's victorious French campaign. Henry's sister's betrothal to Charles, Margaret's nephew, was pre-decided when their fathers were alive. After the defeat of the French, Netherlands and Brussels were ready and eager to welcome the English princess but were unable to pay her a dower without the consent of King Ferdinand of Aragon. This incident infuriated Henry and may have played a role in the initial deterioration of his marriage to Katharine. Subsequently, to Margaret's dismay, the marriage alliance failed after Netherlands and Maximilian spurned Princess Mary once again. Seething with anger, Henry renewed his search for a new husband for his sister. This time, seemingly oblivious to Margaret's attempts to maintain relations with England, he sought a French alliance, having learned of Ferdinand joining hands with the French and Maximilian, and considering a French alliance.

King Henry was quick to secure a match between his sister and the French king, Louis XII. Louis was quite old – he was previously married to Anne of Brittany until her death – at the time of his marriage to Mary. Rumours suggested that Louis tried to marry Margaret of Austria herself despite having spurned her once before. However, giving no credence to such rumours, King Louis XII went on to marry Mary Tudor, much to Margaret of Austria's dismay.

To add to her woes, Anne was recalled home to England from the court of Margaret of Austria to accompany Princess Mary Tudor to France. Margaret, clearly agitated over the new English and French alliance, may have been even more upset on losing Anne (with whom she may have shared a close bond considering the fact that she was good friends with the latter's father). Moreover, France and the Netherlands did not share a cordial relationship.

Therefore, in 1514, with a heavy heart, Anne left the service of Margaret of Austria and returned to England. From there, she and her sister, Mary, proceeded to France, accompanying the Princess of England who was soon to be Queen of France.

Princess Mary Tudor must have been sorely disappointed with her bridegroom. In his fifties, Louis XII was riddled with gout as well as other health problems. Being the youngest of King Henry VII's children, Mary was always petted and spoilt by her parents and older siblings. When her marriage to the French king was fixed, she managed to extract a promise from her brother that she would marry the man of her choice after the death of Louis XII. Her condition agreed to, she finally left England on 2 October 1514 from the port at Dover. Mary Boleyn was reportedly a part of the princess' entourage.

Anne must have soon joined her sister in France. The date of her joining is unclear, though it must have been after the marriage of Princess Mary as her name does not feature in the list of ladies that was maintained by Louis XII. However, after she had joined the household of the now Queen of France, she was retained in her service, along with her sister, Mary, while most of the English ladies-in-waiting were sent back to England.

Anne and Mary quickly settled down into a quiet life along with the queen in Paris. Despite the age difference between the queen and her husband, the marriage was a peaceful one, although some eyebrows were raised at the character of the new French queen, especially on her closeness with the husband of her stepdaughter. However, it was short-lived as Louis XII died on 1 January 1515, barely three months after their marriage.

Anne joined the now widowed queen in mourning, but, along with the other ladies in Mary Tudor's service, she had no inkling of what would happen next.

*****

Charles Brandon, a childhood companion of King Henry VIII and newly created Duke of Suffolk, had quite a reputation as a ladies' man. Mary Tudor, as she embarked the ship at Dover which would take her to France, had already singled him out for her second marriage. She had not forgotten the promise that she had extracted from her royal brother as she bid him goodbye. The two of them, Charles and Mary, were attracted to each other long before her marriage to the French king was arranged and Henry was well aware of it. Despite this knowledge, Henry sent Charles to France to bring his sister back, but not before extracting a promise of his own from his friend: that he would not seek to marry Mary.

The ladies and Mary herself were glad at the break of the monotony of the mourning period with the arrival of the English lords. Being young, good-looking and a royal, Mary Tudor was a prize catch and was being showered with unnecessary and unwanted attention of late. The arrival of her old flame, the Duke of Suffolk, provided much relief and a chance of escape to the widowed Queen of France from the unwarranted attentions of Francis, the husband of her stepdaughter.

Perhaps stung by the rebuff of his young stepmother-in-law, Francis accused Charles Brandon, Duke of Suffolk, of wanting to marry Mary Tudor the minute the duke set foot in France. Mary, in turn, was afraid that Francis would marry her to Charles V and urged the Duke of Suffolk to marry her in haste before Francis could act. Brandon, having no choice, married Mary Tudor.

Predictably, Henry flew into a terrible rage on learning of this secret marriage between his sister and his closest companion. However, on being presented a *fait accompli,* Henry had no choice but to accept the union and the couple were married publicly at Greenwich in the latter half of May 1515, just a few weeks after they landed at Dover.

Most of Mary Tudor's ladies who had accompanied her to France returned with their mistress, except for one. Anne Boleyn, using her knowledge of the French language, quickly secured for herself a place in the household of the new Queen of France.

Anne in France

Queen Claude, the wife of the new king Francis I of France, was only fifteen when her father, King Louis XII, died. The Salic Law prevented Claude from inheriting the throne on the death of her father; however, she was the Duchess of Brittany on her own right on the death of her mother. Continually overshadowed by her enigmatic mother-in-law, Louise of Savoy, Claude headed a rather plain household which was something the gregarious Boleyn girls were not used to. Extremely religious, Claude also suffered from a number of physical ailments that were likely to have been caused due to her yearly pregnancies.

Although always respectful to his queen, Francis I was quite a ladies' man and was known for his roving eye. He loved chasing women and soon set his eyes on Mary Boleyn.

Nicholas Sanders, an Elizabethan writer who had no love lost for Anne, wrote that she was known as 'the English mare' in the French court. However, it seems that Sanders got the two sisters mixed up as it was Mary who was infamous for her promiscuous behaviour in the French royal court, which was infamous for the profligate behaviour of its inhabitants.

Francis soon got bored with Mary and set her aside. Mary did not seem perturbed by this and carried out affairs with the other courtiers, quickly building up a notorious reputation for herself. Anne, however, seemed to have a squeaky-clean image. She must have breathed a heavy sigh of relief when the decadent Mary was recalled to England to protect her reputation.

Devoid of her salacious sister's presence, which threatened to spoil her name, Anne flourished in the court of Queen Claude, occasionally meeting her father, Thomas Boleyn, when he visited France on numerous occasions on important missions. Although unrecorded, Anne must have clearly attended the Field of Cloth of Gold – the meeting between King Francis I of France and King Henry VIII of England – as a part of Queen Claude's entourage. It is quite likely this was the first time King Henry laid his eyes on her, though what he thought of her is not known. Probably he saw her just as one of the many ladies in the French queen's retinue. She also may have seen Queen Katharine of Aragon during one of the many jousts, though again, Anne's opinion about her is unknown.

Amongst the many festivities during the Field of Cloth of Gold, a day was set aside for a meeting between King Francis I and Queen Katherine of Aragon at Guisnes and King Henry VIII and Queen Claude at Ardres. Anne certainly would have been present at this event as an attendant of the French queen. King Henry brought his troubadours and singers along and they danced with the French ladies. At Queen Claude's signal, the dancers removed their masques to reveal their faces to the ladies – most likely including Anne – with whom they were dancing. It is quite likely, though not recorded, that she must have danced with Henry. Being an Englishwoman in the French court, Anne would likely have served as Queen Claude's interpreter for the Field of Cloth of Gold event.

A temporary chapel was set up at the Field of Cloth of Gold where, on 23 June, Cardinal Thomas Wolsey, King Henry VIII's chief minister, conducted a Mass in which Anne was certainly a participant. She may have been impressed by the cardinal's personality and stature, but little did she know that they would be each other's arch nemesis in the near future.

The Field of Cloth of Gold was indeed a glittering event wherein, apart from the historic treaty between France and England, Anne must have had an opportunity to meet her family. She also must have had a chance to show off her Burgundian and French training to her English compatriots. However, she was always aware of the fact that she couldn't stay in France forever, and that the time to return to her homeland was fast approaching.

Anne returns to England

Nine years after she left England as a young girl, Anne Boleyn returned to her homeland in early 1522. Hardly had she had some time to reconnect with her parents, siblings and other family members than she joined the household of Queen Katherine of Aragon as one of her ladies-in-waiting.

After witnessing the sophistication of the Burgundian and French royal courts, Anne must been exasperated and bored with the drabness of the English court. She sought to bring in the urbaneness of the Burgundians and the French by imitating them in their dress and mannerisms. By this, she did manage to stand out from her peers although she may have been a subject of ridicule at times.

Anne's beauty was unconventional by the existing standards. In an age where blond or light-coloured hair and fair and pink skin were considered the appropriate ideals for a woman's looks, Anne, with her dark hair and sallow complexion, did manage to attract looks, albeit some unfavourable ones as well.

Nicholas Sanders, who was incredibly hostile towards Anne, did concede that there was something quite extraordinary about her. However, he does provide a very unflattering description of her:

> Was rather tall of stature, with black hair, and an oval face of a sallow complexion, as if troubled with jaundice. She had a projecting tooth under the upper lip, and on her right hand six fingers. There was a large wen under her

> chin, and therefore to hide its ugliness she wore a high dress covering her throat. In this she was followed by the ladies of the court, who also wore high dresses having before seen in the habit of leaving their necks and the upper portion of their persons uncovered. She was handsome to look at, with a pretty mouth, amusing in her ways, playing well on the lute, and was a good dancer. She was the model and mirror of those who were at court. For she was always well dressed and every day made some change in the fashion of her garments.[4]

In the above account, we can clearly see that although Sander starts off on a disparaging note, he slowly displays his grudging admiration towards Anne. Through Sander's account, we can see that men clearly admired her grace and poise whereas women imitated her fashion sense. Thus, Anne was already becoming something of a trendsetter. However, the existence of her sixth finger is highly doubtful.

Almost immediately on her return to England, Anne was selected to take part in a masque at Greenwich. It was a grand celebration wherein a castle was built in one of the rooms, and right at the pinnacle stood eight ladies bedecked in precious jewels. The ladies represented the virtues of Beauty, Perseverance, Honour, Bounty, Constance, Kindness, Mercy and Pity. Anne played the role of Perseverance and her sister, Mary, played Kindness. There were other women who played the vices, and eight lords, along with the ladies dressed as virtues, defended the castle with rose water and comfits. The eight ladies playing the virtues then danced with the lords. Although we do not know for sure the identity of the lord who partnered Anne in her dance, it is more or less likely that King Henry VIII must have danced with her at some point during the masque.

Meanwhile, Mary Boleyn was slowly becoming infamous as Henry's mistress, and her parents hurriedly arranged her marriage to William Carey in early 1521 to protect her reputation in case she got pregnant with the monarch's child. Even though her father may not have approved of this affair, he must have been pleased with all the rewards and honours that were being heaped on him and his family due to this liaison. He was made the Controller of the Household in 1520 and by 1522 he was promoted to the position of Treasurer of the Household, an envied appointment. Thomas Boleyn's star reached its peak on 16 June 1522 when he was created Viscount Rochford.

Mary, however, was simply discarded when the king tired of her. This appalling treatment of her sister by Henry may not have sat well with Anne and might explain the reasons behind her behaviour during her courtship period with the king.

Anne did not wish to suffer the same fate as her sister and began looking for propitious marital alliances for herself. Due to a dispute between the Boleyn and Butler families, a match between Anne and the Butlers' scion, James Butler, was suggested by Anne's uncle, the Duke of Norfolk, to Cardinal Wolsey.

James Butler was an Irish cousin of the three Boleyn siblings. His father, Sir Piers Butler, the cousin of the old Earl of Ormond, Anne's great-grandfather, had claimed the title after the latter's death. The inheritance of the Ormond earldom followed the female line and Anne's grandmother, Margaret Butler, inherited a part of her father's English possessions. Thomas Boleyn challenged Sir Piers Butler's claim on the earldom and pointed out that he had no legal right to it. Not wishing to antagonise a powerful and influential Irish lord, King Henry VIII and Cardinal Wolsey offered a compromise by way of proposing an alliance between Anne and the Butler descendant.

Thomas Boleyn may not have been very happy with this proposition, and Anne, who was abroad at that time, certainly had no say in any of these negotiations. It is quite likely that Anne met James Butler on her return to England, however, no records survive of the details of any such meeting or whether they had any feelings for each other. In any case, the proposal was eventually mooted.

Not very long afterwards, Anne developed feelings for the young Henry Percy, the heir of the Earl of Northumberland. Henry Percy was a member of Cardinal Thomas Wolsey's household and the relationship progressed quite fast. To the chagrin of his father, the duo fell deeply in love with each other and were rumoured to have become engaged to be married. However, keeping Anne's ambitious nature in mind, we cannot really gauge the extent and the genuineness of her feelings towards Henry Percy. She probably saw him as a stepping stone to a respectable position in society as the Countess of Northumberland and to a vast fortune.

However, her happiness with Henry Percy was short-lived thanks to the interference of Cardinal Thomas Wolsey. Wolsey, probably acting on the instructions from the Earl and Countess of Northumberland, denounced the relationship. The earl and the countess also got him married forcibly to Mary Talbot, the daughter of George Talbot, 4th Earl of Shrewsbury. It was an unhappy marriage and the couple separated after Mary delivered a stillborn son. Mary is rumoured to have declared that her husband was betrothed to another (probably referring to Anne) while he married her (Mary). Wolsey, too, is said to have placed his men in Henry Percy's household in order to control him.

The Henry Percy incident brought out the ruthlessness of Cardinal Thomas Wolsey towards Anne. And she never forgave the cardinal till his very end for this perceived insult towards her. Wolsey had not only told off Henry Percy in the strongest terms but also informed the Earl of Northumberland who immediately put a stop to the affair and got him married to Mary Talbot.

Whether the relationship between Anne and Henry Percy was consummated or not is a matter of debate. A letter written by Anne to a certain Lady Wingfield, in which Anne appears almost desperate to retain her friendship, hints towards a past relationship of Anne's. Also, a deathbed confession by Lady Wingfield also incriminated Anne during her trial later in life.

When Anne began a relationship with King Henry VIII, Henry Percy, sensing danger, purposely distanced himself from this issue by strongly denying any precontract or betrothal. During Anne's fall and subsequent trial, Percy even wrote to Thomas Cromwell denying any sort of engagement with Anne lest he fall with her. This makes us doubt whether the couple genuinely loved each other. Was the relationship a mere ploy to rise up and reach the upper echelons of society?

Whether their feelings towards each other were genuine or not, we shall never know, but the man to bear the brunt of Anne's legendary anger was Cardinal Thomas Wolsey. After her separation from Henry Percy and in disgrace, Anne returned to Hever Castle waiting to be forgiven and invited back to court. Accustomed to the hustle and bustle of the court, life at Hever must have been quite staid for the vivacious Anne. She befriended a neighbour, Thomas Wyatt, who was said to be quite taken by her.

Thomas Wyatt came from an old Kentish family and his father, Sir Henry Wyatt, along with Thomas Boleyn, was created Knight of the Bath during King Henry VIII's coronation. The Wyatts and the Boleyns were probably very close and Thomas Boleyn may also have been Thomas Wyatt's godfather. Although we don't know much about Anne's early friendship with Thomas Wyatt, it is quite possible that the two families socialised frequently with one another.

Thomas Wyatt was a star in King Henry VIII's court. He was a poet of great esteem and was handsome and athletic. Thomas Wyatt is said to have been quite taken with the elegant Anne and is quoted to have said: 'I would gladly yield to be tied for ever with the knot of love.' Wyatt was clearly head over heels in love with her and Anne, too, given her Burgundian influence, may have flirted with her Kentish friend, but there are no records that exist that tell us the true nature of their relationship. Wyatt was already a married man, and despite his declarations of love, it wouldn't have been prudent to pursue a relationship with Anne. However, going by his various poems dedicated to her, he must have certainly hoped for the relationship to be consummated.

It is quite evident that Wyatt's marriage was an unhappy one and the feelings that he never had for his wife were ignited when he saw Anne. By 1526 he charged his wife with adultery and abandoned her, though whether this move was prompted by Anne is not known. After Anne's execution he was openly living in, or as the people of that era would term it 'living in sin', with a maid of Queen Katharine of Aragon's household, Elizabeth Darrell.

Elizabeth Norton's book on Anne Boleyn tells us about an anonymous Spanish chronicler who claimed that Wyatt tried to dissuade King Henry VIII from marrying Anne by terming her as a 'bad woman'. This claim gives us a hint that Wyatt may have harboured hopes of marrying her himself. According to the chronicler, Wyatt apparently wrote: 'Your Majesty knows that before marrying Queen Anne, you said to me, "Wyatt, I am going to marry Anne Boleyn, what do you think of it?" I told your Majesty then that you had better not do so, and you asked me why; to which I replied that she was a bad woman, and your Majesty ordered me to quit your presence for two years.'[5]

It is quite surprising that Wyatt readily denounces Anne as a 'bad woman' – even going to the extent of claiming that she readily gave in to Wyatt's demands to kiss her – when he was so in love with her. Clearly the king, who held Wyatt in high esteem and considered him close enough to share such a personal piece of information with him, was unaware of Wyatt's feelings towards Anne.

As mentioned earlier, whether Wyatt and Anne consummated their relationship isn't known, although Wyatt would have certainly hoped for that. Many chroniclers believed that Anne harboured several lovers before Henry and the rumours gained credence after Wyatt was arrested during Anne's downfall, although he was one of the two whose life was spared.

It is believed that it was Wyatt's admission of his relationship with Anne before her royal marriage that saved him from the executioner's block.

Despite the flirtatious nature of their friendship and Wyatt's admission that saved him from execution, it is highly unlikely that Anne, who was aiming for a prestigious position in the royal court and hoping to ensnare the king, would ever entangle herself in an illicit affair with a married man. She was aiming for the throne of England and would have destroyed her chances by getting involved with Wyatt. On his part, after Anne's trial and subsequent execution, it is highly unlikely that Wyatt would have regained King Henry VIII's friendship and goodwill after his admission of a past relationship with the defamed queen.

There was a minor tiff between the king and Wyatt over a couple of jewels that both the men took in order to claim Anne's affection. Wyatt, probably frustrated at Anne's casual flirting, stole a gem from Anne whereas Henry took a ring from her little finger as a sign of her love. A little misunderstanding at a game of bowls led to a fight between the two and Wyatt managed to diffuse the situation by proclaiming Anne's innocence. This incident made Henry realise that his love for Anne was serious and not just a passing fancy.

Following this incident Wyatt was sent away from the royal court, and in 1528 he was appointed as Marshall of Calais, a prestigious position. Certainly, the king still held Wyatt in high esteem, even though by this time he was in a serious relationship with Anne.

The start of Henry and Anne's relationship

With Wyatt's stand on his relationship with Anne cleared following the game of bowls incident, Henry embarked on a full-fledged pursuance of Anne. His relationship with her sister, Mary, had ended some time in 1526 and he was on the lookout for a new paramour. Anne fit the bill perfectly with her exquisite looks and refined manners that she had learnt from her trysts at the sophisticated courts of Burgundy and France.

In the beginning it seems that Henry was simply looking for a new mistress, having tired of Mary Boleyn. We cannot point out the exact moment when Henry became serious about Anne, but with time, noticing the king's intense feelings for Anne, the people in the court who vied for Anne's attention and affection slowly backed away, allowing Henry to pursue her.

Anne did not waste any time in noticing Henry's feelings towards her. Basking in the attention and affections of two of her suitors, Thomas Wyatt and Henry Percy, she was quite aware of her charm and was certainly flattered when the king began eyeing her.

Anne sought to play it safe by keeping a considerable distance from Henry but flirting back at him all the same. She was well aware of her sister, Mary's, fate as Henry's mistress and certainly did not wish to end up unceremoniously discarded. It seemed that she was entertaining the king's attention merely to attract an influential suitor for herself. Henry was already married to Katharine of Aragon and Anne was aware of it. Also, keeping the reputation of her powerful extended family in mind, she initially kept up a mild flirtation with him in the hope of an influential position in the royal court and a suitable marriage.

King Henry VIII pursued Anne intensely and the latter soon tired of her efforts of keeping him at arms' length as well as keeping up appearances all the while. Henry, though, was smitten with her and poured his heart out in several love letters. Seventeen such love letters from Henry to Anne survive and the words written in them show how deeply in love was the king. Anne's replies, though, are lost to us but we know through Henry's desperate pleas for her attention that she kept a safe distance from him. Not accustomed to women refusing him, Anne's signals confused and sometimes frustrated him.

Anne was very clear about not ending up as Henry's mistress. She did not bow down to his pleas – he offered to make her his permanent mistress – nor was she intimidated by his subtle threats in his letters. However, with time, Anne seemed to have softened her stance and was responding to his letters with considerable warmth. Henry knew that she had nothing else but marriage in mind.

Having run out of options, Henry must have sent a messenger to Hever, where Anne had temporarily retired for the time being to escape the attention, with his proposal of marriage. Although Thomas Boleyn was ecstatic at this turn of events and his fortune, Anne took her time in sending her reply to the king as she weighed up her options. She must have felt triumphant as her plans had finally come to fruition, and maybe a little nervous as she was set to replace the much-beloved Katherine of Aragon whom the citizens of London considered their rightful queen.

Henry was very much in love with Anne and was prepared to fight any number of battles for her. His youthful love for Katherine of Aragon had waned after she failed to give him a son and heir and it seemed that he had regained his passionately romantic nature all over again: this time for Anne.

Anne, however, was determined to keep the king's interest in her alive. Although she replied to Henry's love letters with equal passion, she stopped short of consummating their relationship before marriage. They did write quite a number of explicit love letters to each other though. In one such letter Henry wishes for a moment 'in my sweetheart's arms, whose pretty duckies [breasts] I trust shortly to kiss.'[6] Little did either of them imagine that the wildly passionate love affair would last a mere five years.

On 5 May 1527, in a banquet organised in the honour of the French ambassadors, Anne was led out publicly as King Henry VIII's partner for the very first time. Twelve days later Henry began taking steps to pave the way for his marriage to Anne by setting up a secret canonical court in London to investigate the validity of his marriage to Katharine of Aragon, a matter that he assumed would be done with in no time. He was to be proved very wrong.

The Divorce Saga: The King's Great Matter

Katharine of Aragon was first married to King Henry VIII's older brother, Arthur, Prince of Wales on 14 November 1501. Their nuptials were solemnised at St Paul's Cathedral in a glittering event, which was unusual during the reign of Henry's father, the apparently miserly King Henry VII. The young couple soon left for Ludlow Castle in Arthur's principality of Wales. However, the newlyweds' happiness did not last long as Arthur died of the dreaded sweating sickness in 1502, just a few months into their marriage. With the heir to the throne dead, Henry, Duke of York, King Henry VII's younger son, was now Prince of Wales and the next in line to the throne of England. Unwilling to break the alliance between England and Spain, Katharine was quickly betrothed to Henry. In order to validate his marriage to his brother's widow, a papal dispensation was sought for and readily granted by Pope Julius II and Henry and Katharine tied the knot in 1509.

By 1525 it was clear that Katharine of Aragon, who had just turned forty, would bear Henry no more children. With only one surviving child, Henry thought that the idea of him taking on a younger and more fertile wife would be accepted wholeheartedly. In the Bible, Leviticus states that a brother shall not marry his dead brother's wife, and if he does, the couple shall remain childless, whereas the Book of Deuteronomy claims – in fact commands – that a man marry his brother's wife if his brother dies without producing a child. Henry and Katharine went through a painful series of stillbirths and miscarriages. The marriage resulted in only one living child, a girl, Mary. Henry needed a male heir to keep the Tudor line alive.

By this time, Henry was determined to put his marriage to Katharine of Aragon aside to pursue and then marry Anne.

Cardinal Thomas Wolsey, on 18 May 1527, convened a meeting with a church council at Westminster to discuss the validity of the king's marriage to Katharine of Aragon. Aware of the power and influence of Charles V, the Holy Roman Emperor, who was also Katharine's nephew, Wolsey wished to keep this ecclesiastical meeting confidential. He and Henry hoped to conclude the matter and obtain a divorce quickly so that the king could be free to marry Anne at the earliest opportunity.

However, Katharine and her powerful nephew got wind of this and soon started taking measures to prevent the separation. Katharine appealed to Charles V for help and he responded by writing to the Pope to bring the proceedings to a halt before Wolsey pronounced a verdict. Consequently, on 31 May, Wolsey was forced to adjourn the matter as the news that King Henry VIII sought a divorce from his wife of nearly twenty-five years started becoming common knowledge. Anne, still a part of Queen Katharine's household at this point of time, must have found it quite unnerving to deal with all the unwanted and unwarranted attention and rumours. She was well aware of Katharine's popularity and did not underestimate her; she tried to keep away from the court as much as possible so as to avoid being in her company.

Katharine, for her part, began watching Anne closely now that they were rivals in claiming the king. The queen maintained a dignified silence but could not resist in showing her displeasure towards Anne in many other ways. Never a fan of the queen, Anne spent most of her time now at Hever to escape the unpleasantness.

King Henry VIII, on hearing of the Pope's imprisonment by Charles V, immediately sent Wolsey to France to secure an alliance. Unaware of his king's intention to marry Anne, Wolsey left England confident in his abilities to secure a divorce for Henry.

By mid-June King Henry VIII finally broke the news to his queen, Katharine of Aragon, who, despite having an inkling of the proceedings, broke down. She recovered quickly and immediately wrote to Charles V for help.

The Holy Roman Emperor took this development as a stain on his family's honour and stood up for his aunt, whom he barely knew. Henry, recognising this hurdle, immediately thought it imperative to send an ambassador to Rome.

Henry and Anne underestimated the emperor's support for Katherine. When the Bishop of Worcester, and Dr Lee, Henry's chaplain, tried to coax Charles V in supporting the English monarch's cause, the latter flatly refused.

This was a huge blow to Henry, nevertheless, he decided to send his secretary, Dr Knight, on a secret mission to Rome to not only secure his divorce from Katharine but also a dispensation to marry Anne. The dispensation was necessary considering that Anne's sister, Mary, was Henry's former mistress. Although the Pope granted the dispensation, he did not grant a divorce. Henry quickly dispatched Edward Foxe and Stephen Gardiner to persuade the Pope for a divorce. Gardiner reported the happenings directly to Anne who followed the case keenly. Apparently the two English emissaries found the Pope in a pitiable state when they sought to meet him. He requested more time to consider the matter.

Finally, as Foxe returned to England on 28 April 1528, he brought in a small ray of hope for Henry and Anne. He mentioned that Pope Clement VII was preparing to send his delegate, Cardinal Campeggio, to England to hear the case and would be prepared to confirm a divorce if it were granted by Campeggio.

Cardinal Campeggio, the Bishop of Salisbury, was a favoured choice of a papal legate of both Henry and Anne. However, this time the cardinal's instructions from the Pope were clear: delay the matter as much as it was possible. Therefore, in accordance with the Pope's wishes, the cardinal proceeded at a snail's pace towards England while Henry and Anne were almost beside themselves in anticipation.

However, their fate took a turn for the worse as the dreaded sweating sickness engulfed England in June 1528. This was a dangerous disease that, more often than not, proved fatal to the unfortunate person who caught it. A person could go from being absolutely healthy in the morning to dead by the evening. The sickness began with a headache and a chest ache and quickly graduated to profuse sweating. No amount of remedies worked as the patient either slowly recovered from the illness or passed on in no time. Henry, a known hypochondriac, immediately prepared to keep himself safe from the sweat and thought nothing of sending Anne, who showed signs of the illness, back to Hever until she recuperated completely. He wrote her a number of love letters during this period professing his undying love and devotion. He also sent across his best physicians to help her get back to her feet and into his arms.

Anne stayed at Hever till she recovered completely and Henry sent desperate missives to her pleading with her to ask her father to send her to court. Pleased with all the attention, Anne finally returned to court, much to the king's joy.

Anne retired from court once again before Cardinal Campeggio arrived in England in October 1528, in accordance with Henry's wish of not bringing her to the forefront during the divorce proceedings. He kept her updated, though, on Campeggio's arrival in London, and informed her when the cardinal immediately took to bed due to his gout. This piece of news disappointed Anne and she returned to court. This time, wishing to avoid any kind of confrontation with Katherine, Anne had her own apartments.

Finally rising from his sickbed by early 1529, Cardinal Campeggio got down to work. Unbeknownst to Henry and Anne, Campeggio had further secret instructions from the Pope: to persuade Queen Katharine for a divorce and to dissuade King Henry from one. This seemed like another delaying tactic from the Pope.

Cardinal Campeggio then tried to coax Queen Katherine to give up her marriage to Henry and retire to a nunnery. This move would have enabled Henry to marry Anne while his first wife was still alive. It also meant that the legitimacy of Princess Mary, Katharine and Henry's daughter, could not be challenged.

However, Katharine, who was still in love with Henry despite his unceremonious behaviour towards her, was not ready to give him up at any cost. Being a God-fearing person, she also did not wish to change or pretend to change her profession. She stood her ground, but Henry, too, was unbending in his beliefs and would not be dissuaded. Cardinal Campeggio now found himself in a sticky situation and realised that the matter now would go to trial.

Cardinal Thomas Wolsey, on his part, tried to find arguments in favour of the divorce. While studying the papal dispensation which enabled Henry and Katherine to marry, Wolsey found a loophole. The wording in the dispensation mentioned that Katherine's first marriage to Prince

Arthur, Henry's older brother, had 'perhaps' been consummated. This was all that Henry needed. He grabbed this opportunity to argue that if her earlier marriage had been consummated, despite Katharine's claim that it wasn't, then his [Henry's] marriage to Katharine was not valid.

Katharine claimed that her marriage to Arthur had never been consummated and that she was a virgin when she married Henry after Arthur's death, but there were many witnesses to refute this claim. Sir Anthony Willoughby's testimony, for instance, was pretty damaging to Katharine's claim as he recollected that Prince Arthur spoke to him on the morning after his wedding saying, 'Willoughby, bring me a cup of ale, for I have been this night in the midst of Spain.'

However, Katharine stuck to her claim of her first marriage being unconsummated. Her stubborn stand alarmed and incensed Henry and Anne who were eager to finish this matter once and for all. Katherine also produced another papal bull that countered all of Wolsey's concerns with the earlier one.

Surprised at this latest development, Henry ordered a search for an English copy, but none could be found. Henry immediately declared it a forged document and ordered Katherine to procure the original document from Spain. On receiving the orders, Katharine agreed to write to her nephew, the Holy Roman Emperor, but also sent her chaplain, Thomas Abel, with secret instructions that the emperor should, under no circumstances, part with the document.

Finally, the trial commenced in June 1529 at Blackfriars. Henry and Katharine were both summoned to appear before Cardinal Campeggio, and on arrival were seated opposite each other in the hall. In a seemingly dramatic move, once the court was opened, Katharine rose, walked up to Henry and kneeled at his feet. She also appealed for the case to be heard in Rome as she understood that the trial at Blackfriars wouldn't be an unbiased one.

Katharine kneeled at the king's feet and said:

> Sir, I beseech you for all the love that hath been between us, and for the love of God, let me have justice and right, take of me some pity and compassion, for I am a poor woman and a stranger born out of your dominion. I have here no assured friends, and much less impartial counsel. I flee to you as to the head of justice within this realm. Alas! Sir, wherin have I offended you, or what occasion of displeasure have

> I deserved against your will and pleasure – now that you intend (as I perceive) to put me from you? I take God and all the world to witness that I have been to you a true, humble and obedient wife, ever comfortable to your will and pleasure, and never said or did anything to the contrary therof, being always well pleased and contented with all things wherein you had any delight or dalliance, whether it were in little or much. I never grudged in word or countenance, or showed a visage or spark of discontent. I loved all those whom ye loved only for your sake, whether I had cause or no, and whether they were my friends or my enemies. This twenty years or more I have been your true wife and by me ye have had divers children, although it had pleased God to call them out of this world, which hath been no default of me.[7]

She spoke eloquently and with passion while the king looked on, mortified as Katharine continued to speak. Finally, after finishing her impassioned plea, she stood up and walked out of the court, her head held high, ignoring the calls asking her to come back.

As Katharine refused to return to the court, King Henry VIII forced Cardinal Campeggio to reach a decision. However, Campeggio had come to England armed with the Pope's instruction of not reaching a definite decision. Instead, he revoked the case to Rome amidst much uproar. Finally, Henry and Anne placed the blame of the Blackfriars debacle on Cardinal Thomas Wolsey's shoulders.

Anne nurtured an intense dislike of Wolsey ever since he had tried to meddle in her affair with Henry Percy, Earl of Northumberland. She recognised his influence over the commoners and the fact that the king always listened to him. She knew that Wolsey was the only one who could help her achieve her goal and that he was trying to obtain this divorce more for the king rather than her. She kept up the pretence of cordiality though it must have pained her to do so. She kept up the pressure on Wolsey and on one occasion took it upon herself of writing directly to the cardinal on the matter of the divorce, later adding a postscript by the king. Even if Wolsey did not desire the king's marriage with Anne, he had no choice after reading the postscript:

> The writer of this letter would not cease till she had caused me likewise to set to my hand, desiring you, though it be

> short, to take it in good part. I ensure you, there is neither of us, but that greatly desireth to see you, and much more joyous to hear that you have scaped this plague so well; trusting the fury thereof to be passed, specially with them that keepeth good diet, as I trust you do. The not hearing of the legate's arrival in France, causeth us somewhat to muse; notwithstanding, we trust by your diligence and vigilancy (with the assistance of Almighty God) shortly to be eased out of that trouble.[8]

Wolsey, on his part, recognised the hold Anne had over the king and tried to gain her goodwill by working hard towards their ultimate goal. But if he thought that Anne had forgiven him for their earlier altercations – she had acknowledged a present sent to her by the cardinal with a seemingly warm letter – he was grossly mistaken. Anne was cordial to the cardinal only while she thought he could help her out in 'The King's Great Matter'. Now, though, following the Blackfriars fiasco, she was aware that Wolsey was not as infallible as the couple believed him to be. Wolsey, too, was aware that his influence over the king was slowly waning.

Katharine of Aragon and Anne Boleyn, in a way, were united in this one matter: their mutual dislike for the cardinal. When the two cardinals, Wolsey and Campeggio, visited Katherine at Bridewell after the Blackfriars trial to persuade the queen to agree to a divorce, the queen refused to speak to them in private thereby causing much embarrassment. She embarrassed Wolsey further when she refused to converse with him in Latin, speaking to him in English instead.

Anne Boleyn, though, was instrumental in bringing about Cardinal Wolsey's ruin. By the time of the Blackfriars trial, Anne's household was no less than the queen's. She felt that Wolsey was past his prime and she was now in a position to display her dislike towards the cardinal openly. In the wake of the Blackfriars debacle, she penned a letter of utmost hatred to Wolsey:

> My Lord,
> Though you are a man of great understanding, you cannot avoid being censured by everybody for having drawn on yourself the hatred of a king who had raised you to the highest degree to which the greatest ambition of a man seeking his fortune can aspire. I cannot comprehend, and the king still

> less, how your reverent lordship, after having allured us by so many fine promises about divorce, can have repented of your purpose, and how you could have done what you have, in order to hinder the consummation of it. What, then, is your mode of proceeding? You quarrelled with the queen to favour me at the time when I was less advanced in the king's good graces, and after having therein given me the strongest marks of your affection, your lordship abandons my interest to embrace those of the queen. I acknowledge that I have put much confidence in your professions and promises, in which I find myself deceived. But, in future, I shall rely on nothing but the protection of Heaven and the love of my dear king, which alone will be able to set right again those plans which you have broken and spoiled, and to place me in that happy station which God wills, the king so much wishes, and which will be entirely to the advantage of the kingdom. The wrong you have done me has caused me much sorrow but I feel infinitely more in seeing myself betrayed by a man who pretended to enter into my interests only to discover the secrets of my heart. I acknowledge that, believing you sincere, I have been too precipitate in my confidence; it is this which has induced, and still induces me, to keep more moderation in avenging myself, not being able to forget that I have been.
>
> Your servant[9]

Through this letter it is clear that Anne, secure in Henry's affection for her, was now working actively to bring down the cardinal. She and her cronies worked hard to keep the king, who seemed to have retained a soft spot for Wolsey, away from him. When Wolsey arrived at the court to meet the king, Anne deliberately kept the latter busy with a picnic and ensured that he didn't return till the cardinal had left. Wolsey left the court not knowing that this would have been the last time he would have met Henry had Anne allowed it. Cardinal Campeggio, too, returned to Rome on the same day.

Cardinal Campeggio's journey to Rome was interrupted at Calais where his possessions were searched on the suspicion of him trying to buy Wolsey's safe passage to Rome. Although nothing was found on Cardinal Campeggio, this piece of news shattered Wolsey and frightened him. He certainly had a good reason to be scared; on 9 October 1523 he was charged with taking orders from a foreign power and was forced to give up his post as the royal chancellor and surrender his seal. He was ordered to retire to Esher although he wasn't arrested.

In 1528 the sweating sickness broke out with great severity. In London the mortality rate was high and the court was dispersed. Henry left London, frequently changing his residence; Anne retreated to the Boleyn residence at Hever Castle, but contracted the illness; her brother-in-law, Mary Boleyn's husband, William Carey, died. Henry sent his own physician to Hever Castle to care for Anne, and shortly afterwards she recovered.

Henry was soon absorbed in securing an annulment from Katharine. He set his hopes upon a direct appeal to the Holy See, acting independently of Wolsey, to whom he at first communicated nothing of his plans related to Anne. In 1527 William Knight, the king's secretary, was sent to Pope Clement VII to sue for the annulment of Henry's marriage to Katharine, on the grounds that the dispensing bull of Pope Julius II permitting him to marry his brother's widow had been obtained under false pretences. Henry also petitioned, in the event of his becoming free, a dispensation to contract a new marriage with any woman even in the first degree of affinity, whether the affinity was contracted by lawful or unlawful connection. This clearly referred to Anne.

Clement was at that time a prisoner of Charles V, as a result of the Sack of Rome in May 1527, and Knight had some difficulty obtaining access. In the end he had to return with a conditional dispensation, which Wolsey insisted was technically insufficient. Henry then had no choice but to put his great matter into Wolsey's hands, who did all he could to secure the annulment for the king.

The years 1527-28 were indeed a testing time for Cardinal Thomas Wolsey. Anne was already beginning to go against Wolsey, blaming him for the disintegration of her previous relationship with Henry Percy. Wolsey, recognising Anne's hostility, went out of his way to ingratiate himself with the king's new mistress. However, Anne and Henry were frustrated with the cardinal over the case that was dragging along at a languid pace. What irked the king even more was that his argument based on Leviticus (which mentions that it is sinful to marry a deceased brother's widow) fell flat in front of papal legate. A desperate Wolsey even thought of blackmailing the Pope into granting the divorce.

Wolsey was astute enough to throw himself at the king's mercy rather than arguing against the unfairness of the situation. He quickly summoned his staff and took an inventory of all his belongings, keeping only the bare minimum for himself. He had already given away his prized Hampton Court Palace to the king when the latter asked for it, but he was unaware of a secret trip undertaken by Henry and Anne just a few days after his retirement to Esher to view their new belongings.

Although he was currently in disgrace, the chances of him returning to his power and position of glory were high as Henry's heart hadn't yet hardened against his former chancellor. The king even sent his own physician to Wolsey when he fell ill in December 1529 and insisted that Anne send a Christmas gift, a request that she fulfilled by sending Wolsey a gold tablet. But this stance by her husband must have scared Anne; she may have contemplated that Henry might show mercy towards Katharine and Mary as well.

Eric Ives, Anne's biographer, quite correctly points out that it is very difficult to pinpoint a singular reason for Wolsey's fall from power. After Campeggio's report, Wolsey, in an extremely realistic manner, said: 'I speak freely with his lordship to know his mind, and he generally ends by shrugging his shoulders and has nothing else to say but that the only remedy is to satisfy the king's wish in some way or the other, and let it stand for what it is worth.'[10] Caught between the Holy See and his monarch, Wolsey seemed to be fighting a losing battle for his survival. He feared that the Pope might think that he was working for Anne whereas he was clearly working in line with the law and he made it clear that he bore no grudges towards Queen Katharine of Aragon.

The case dragged on at the legatine court and King Henry VIII and Anne Boleyn left Bridewell for their summer progress, their first as a couple. They went to Durham Place where they visited Anne's father, Thomas Boleyn, and then proceeded towards Greenwich. From there they then travelled northwards towards Waltham Abbey in Essex. At this time, Henry shared his predicament with Stephen Gardiner, Edward Foxe and Thomas Cranmer, all of whom were clerics from Cambridge. During the progress, Henry visited two of Wolsey's properties, namely the Manor of Barnet and Tyttenhanger House, keeping Stephen Gardiner beside him all the time along with Anne's uncle, Thomas Howard, Duke of Norfolk.

After visiting and staying in many castles, Henry and his entourage finally lodged at Grafton, a place he had bought from his Grey relatives. Grafton was the erstwhile home of Henry's maternal grandmother, Queen Elizabeth Woodville.

It was at Grafton where Wolsey accompanied Cardinal Campeggio when he arrived to take leave of the king before returning to Rome. Apparently, although Campeggio was granted an audience with Henry, Wolsey, incredulously, was not. King Henry VIII's erstwhile favourite was not even provided a room for his stay and it was a sympathetic Sir Henry Norris who permitted the fallen cardinal to use his rooms to change his clothes, although he had to find lodgings elsewhere. However, when Henry met a kneeling Wolsey, he picked him up by his shoulders and led him to a corner to speak in private, a move that did not go down very well with Anne who made her displeasure known to the king.

Wolsey's position at that time was a confusing one. Henry continued to extend numerous comforts to his former chancellor, but constantly refused to meet him. Anne and her family kept up the pressure on Henry to exile Wolsey and finally, in 1530, Wolsey received his marching orders. He was ordered to retire to his diocese of York in the north, away from the court and King Henry VIII.

Wolsey was at his home at Cawood when a warrant for his arrest arrived at his doorstep. In a twisted sense of revenge for thrusting her aside when she needed his help, bringing his arrest warrant was Henry Percy, Earl of Northumberland, Anne's former suitor, and a Mr Walsh. However, Percy did not share Anne's ruthlessness and was uncomfortable carrying out the deed that he had been entrusted with.

Unaware of Percy's role, Wolsey took Percy to his bedchamber where the latter conveyed the purpose of his visit. He refused to show the commission of arrest to Wolsey who then declined to be arrested by him, allowing Mr Walsh to do so. Although not an impactful move, this small defiance by Wolsey must have angered Anne.

Cardinal Thomas Wolsey was taken to London in disgrace with his legs tied to his horse. Broken and remorseful, he is said to have remarked: 'had I serv'd God as diligently as I had done the King, hee would not have given me over, in my gray haires; but this is my just reward.'[11]

Facing a trial and possible execution, Wolsey's convoy trudged along towards London, but the cardinal never made it. He died at Leicester on 29 November 1530. Whether the death was due to natural causes or a suicide is debatable. However, it must have brought immense satisfaction for Anne to see her old adversary defeated completely.

A year later, Katharine of Aragon was banished from the court and her old rooms were given to Anne Boleyn. A distraught Katharine wrote to her nephew, Charles V, Holy Roman Emperor: 'My tribulations are so great, my life so disturbed by the plans daily invented to further the king's wicked intention, the surprises the king gives me, with certain persons of his council, are so mortal, and my treatment is what God knows, that is enough to shorten ten lives, much more mine.'[12]

When Henry decided to annul his marriage to Katharine, John Fisher became her most trusted counsellor and one of her chief supporters. He appeared in the legate's court on her behalf, where he shocked people with the directness of his language, and by declaring that, like John the Baptist, he was ready to die on behalf of the indissolubility of the marriage. Henry was so enraged by this that he wrote a long Latin address to the legates in response to Fisher's speech. Fisher's copy of this still exists, with his manuscript annotations in the margin which show how little he feared Henry's anger. The removal of the cause to Rome ended Fisher's role in the matter but Henry never forgave him. Other people who supported Katharine's case included: Sir Thomas More; Henry's own sister, Mary Tudor, Queen of France; Maria de Salinas; Charles V, Holy Roman Emperor; Pope Paul III; and Protestant reformers Martin Luther and William Tyndale.

Anne saw an opportunity in Henry's infatuation and the convenient moral quandary. She determined that she would yield to his embraces only as his acknowledged queen. She began to take her place at his side in policy and in state, but not yet in his bed.

In 1532 Thomas Cromwell brought before Parliament a number of acts including the Supplication against the Ordinaries and Submission of the Clergy which recognised royal supremacy over the Church, thus finalising the break with Rome. Following these acts, Thomas More resigned as Chancellor, leaving Cromwell as Henry's chief minister.

During this period Anne played an important role in England's international position by solidifying an alliance with France. She established an excellent rapport with the French ambassador, Gilles de la Pommeraie. Anne and Henry attended a meeting with the French king at Calais in winter 1532, at which Henry hoped to enlist the support of Francis I of France for his intended marriage. On 1 September 1532 Henry made her the Marquess of Pembroke, an appropriate peerage for a future queen and as such she became a rich and important woman. The three dukes and two marquesses who existed in 1532 were Henry's brother-in-law, Henry's illegitimate son and other descendants of royalty; she ranked above all other peeresses. The Pembroke lands and the title of Earl of Pembroke had been held by Henry's great-uncle, and Henry performed the investiture himself.

Anne's family also profited from the relationship. Her father, already Viscount Rochford, was created Earl of Wiltshire. Henry also came to an agreement with Anne's Irish cousin and created him Earl of Ormond.

The conference at Calais was something of a political triumph, but even though the French government gave implicit support for Henry's remarriage and Francis I had a private conference with Anne, the French king maintained alliances with the Pope that he could not explicitly defy.

Soon after returning to Dover, Henry and Anne married in a secret ceremony on 14 November 1532. She soon became pregnant, and to legalise the first wedding considered to be unlawful at that time, there was a second wedding service, also private in accordance with The Royal Book, in London on 25 January 1533. Events now began to move at a fast pace. On 23 May 1533, Cranmer (who had been hastened, with the Pope's assent, into the position of Archbishop of Canterbury, recently vacated by the death of William Warham) sat in judgement at a special court convened at Dunstable Priory to rule on the validity of Henry's marriage to Katherine of Aragon. He declared it null and void. Five days later Cranmer declared the marriage of Henry and Anne good and valid.

Anne as Queen

Katherine of Aragon was formally stripped of her title as queen and Anne was subsequently crowned queen consort on 1 June 1533 in a magnificent ceremony at Westminster Abbey with a banquet afterwards. She was the last queen consort to be crowned separately from her husband. Unlike any other queen consort, Anne was crowned with St Edward's crown, which had previously been used to crown only monarchs. On the previous day Anne had taken part in an elaborate procession through the streets of London seated in a litter of 'white cloth of gold' that rested on two palfreys clothed to the ground in white damask, while the barons of the Cinque Ports held a canopy of cloth of gold over her head. In accordance with tradition, she wore white, and on her head a gold coronet beneath which her long, dark hair hung down freely. The public's response to her appearance was lukewarm.

Meanwhile, the House of Commons had forbidden all appeals to Rome and exacted the penalties of praemunire against all who introduced papal bulls into England. It was only then that Pope Clement at last took the step of announcing a provisional excommunication of Henry and Cranmer. He condemned the marriage to Anne and in March 1534 declared the marriage to Katharine legal and again ordered Henry to return to her. Henry now required his subjects to swear an oath attached to the First Succession Act, which effectively rejected papal authority in legal matters and recognised Anne Boleyn as queen. Those who refused, such as Sir Thomas More, who had resigned as Lord Chancellor, and John Fisher, Bishop of Rochester, were placed in the Tower of London.

The Church in England was now under Henry's control, not Rome's. In 1534, in one of the realm's first official acts protecting Protestant reformers, Anne wrote a letter to Thomas Cromwell seeking his aid in ensuring that English merchant Richard Herman be reinstated as a member of the merchant adventurers in Antwerp and no longer persecuted simply because he had helped in 'setting forth of the New Testament in English'. Before and after her coronation, Anne protected and promoted evangelicals and those wishing to study the scriptures of William Tyndale. She had a decisive role in influencing the Protestant reformer Matthew Parker to attend court as her chaplain, and before her death, entrusted her daughter into Parker's care.

After her coronation Anne settled into a quiet routine at the king's favourite residence, Greenwich Palace, to prepare for the birth of her baby. The child was born slightly prematurely on 7 September 1533. Anne gave birth to a girl who was christened Elizabeth, probably in honour of either, or both, Anne's mother, Elizabeth Howard, and Henry's mother, Elizabeth of York. The birth of a girl was a heavy blow to her parents who had confidently expected a boy. All but one of the physicians and astrologers had predicted a boy and the French king had been asked to stand as his godfather. Now the prepared letters announcing the birth of a prince had to be changed hastily and the traditional jousting tournament for the birth of an heir was cancelled.

The infant princess was given a splendid christening but Anne feared that Katherine's daughter, Mary, now stripped of her title of princess and labelled a bastard, posed a threat to Elizabeth's position. Henry soothed his wife's fears by separating Mary from her many servants and sending

Elizabeth to Hatfield House, where she would live with her own staff of servants. Anne frequently visited her daughter at Hatfield House and other residences.

The new queen had a larger staff than Katherine. There were more than 250 servants to tend to her personal needs, from priests to stable-boys, and more than sixty maids-of-honour who served her and accompanied her to social events. She also employed several priests who acted as her confessors, chaplains and religious advisors.

Henry and Anne enjoyed a reasonably happy accord with periods of calm and affection. Anne's sharp intelligence, political acumen and forward manners, although desirable in a mistress, were, at the time, unacceptable in a wife. She was once reported to have spoken to her uncle in words that 'shouldn't be used to a dog'. After a stillbirth or miscarriage as early as Christmas 1534, Henry was discussing with Cranmer and Cromwell the possibility of divorcing her without having to return to Katherine. Nothing came of the matter as the royal couple reconciled and spent the summer of 1535 on progress. By October she was again pregnant.

Anne presided over a court. She spent lavish amounts of money on gowns, jewels, head-dresses, ostrich-feather fans, riding equipment, furniture and upholstery, maintaining the ostentatious display required by her status. Numerous palaces were renovated to suit her and Henry's extravagant tastes. Her motto was 'The most happy', and she chose a white falcon as her personal device.

Anne was blamed for Henry's tyranny and called by some of her subjects 'the king's whore' or a 'naughty paike [prostitute]'. Public opinion turned further against her after her failure to produce a son, and sank even lower after the executions of her enemies More and Fisher.

Anne Boleyn and the Early Reformation

Anne Boleyn and the Early Reformation in England have now become almost synonymous. It was for her that King Henry VIII broke the Church of England's ties with Rome and proclaimed himself as its Supreme Head. But what exactly were Anne's personal religious leanings? And what was her role in this movement? For the Reformists and Lutherans, she was their role model, whereas for the staunch Catholics like Nicholas Sander, or Sanders, she was just a dark-eyed, six-fingered hag who resorted to sorcery to snare the man she loved.

Scholars and historians hold various opinions as to how deep Anne's commitment to the Reformation was, how much she was perhaps only personally ambitious, and how much she had to do with Henry's defiance of papal power. There is anecdotal evidence, related to biographer George Wyatt by her former lady-in-waiting Anne Gainsford, that Anne brought to Henry's attention a heretical pamphlet, perhaps Tyndale's *The Obedience of a Christian Man* or one by Simon Fish called *A Supplication for the Beggars*, which cried out to monarchs to rein in the evil excesses of the Catholic Church. She was sympathetic to those seeking further reformation of the Church, and actively protected scholars working on English translations of the scriptures. If Cavendish is to be believed, Anne's outrage at Wolsey may have personalised whatever philosophical defiance she brought with her from France.

Downfall and Execution

Anne's fall from power began on the day her rival, Katharine of Aragon, died. King Henry VIII and Queen Anne Boleyn were at Eltham Court on Christmas in 1535 when the news of the former queen's deteriorating health reached them. Katherine rallied through for a few more days before eventually breathing her last on 7 January 1536, shut away at Kimbolton Castle. Her dearest friend, Maria de Salinas, now Countess Willoughby, was at her side when she met her maker.

Henry's callous reaction to Katharine's death has been summed up by Eustace Chapuys, the Imperial ambassador, who visited Katharine during her last days:

> On the following day, Sunday, the King was clad all over in yellow, from top to toe, except the white feather he had in his bonnet, and the Little Bastard was conducted to mass with trumpets and other great triumphs. After dinner the King entered the room in which the ladies danced, and there did several things like one transported with joy. At last he sent for his Little Bastard, and carrying her in his arms he showed her first to one and then to another. He has done the like on other days since, and has run some courses at Greenwich.[13]

It is common knowledge that Chapuys had a deep dislike of Anne, but he had a semblance of respect towards Henry despite facing his mood swings time and again. He clearly disapproved of this new romance which saw his queen being discarded unceremoniously. Hence, it is not surprising that he was quite scathing in his opinion on Henry's reaction to Katharine's death. Moreover, whilst yellow signified mourning in Spain, it signified joy in England. However, if we are to go by Chapuys' account, Henry and Anne may have breathed a sigh of relief at the news of Katharine's passing.

Anne was an astute politician, and instead of antagonising her step-daughter, Mary, extended a hand of friendship towards her. She sent a message to Mary through her aunt, Anne Shelton, inviting her to court and even stating that she [Mary] would be exempted from carrying her train if she became more amenable. It is difficult to deduce whether this was indeed a heartfelt letter or just one of Anne's shrewd political moves. Mary, though, in a show of loyalty towards her mother, stuck to her guns and refused to consider Anne's pleas.

Anne's position at this time in the court and in her husband's life was a tenuous one. Having already miscarried, Anne was pregnant again, and going by the contents and the earnest tone of her letter to Mary, it seemed as if she wished to make amends. One can also see it as a desperate move by Anne to keep her position and her daughter's inheritance secure as Henry's roving eyes had rested on Jane Seymour.

Discovering her sitting on Henry's lap, Anne lost her temper despite Henry trying to pacify her. To make Anne's situation even worse, Henry met with an accident on 24 January while jousting when he was thrown off, trampled and pinned under his horse. He was unconscious for over two hours and rumours of his death were abroad. On hearing of her husband's injury and the rumours, a shocked Anne must have given the succession a thought. Would the nobles back Mary or would they side with the infant Elizabeth? Or would they wait till Anne reached the end of the current pregnancy to see if she gave birth to a male child?

King Henry VIII recovered but was now disillusioned by his current marriage. He is believed to have said to someone in greatest confidence that he considered his marriage to Anne null as he claimed that he was seduced into matrimony through witchcraft, which was not a serious offence during Henry's reign. Despite these misgivings, Anne and Henry seemingly ironed out their differences and settled down in an uneasy peace.

That all changed on 29 January 1536, the day that Katharine of Aragon was laid to rest at Peterborough Cathedral, when Anne miscarried her child which was purportedly male. The couple was devastated and Anne laid the blame on her uncle, the Duke of Norfolk, saying that he frightened her into miscarrying by bringing her the news of Henry's fall. But the damage was done. She was now scared that Henry would treat her the same way he had treated Katharine – put her aside for a new paramour, in this case Jane Seymour.

Anne recovered quickly enough to console her ladies and assured them that she would soon be with child again. And this time, it would be a boy. However, as Anne recovered from her miscarriage at Greenwich, Henry left the palace in early February and proceeded towards Whitehall. While there, he continued to woo Jane Seymour before summoning Anne back beside him by the end of February.

The wheels of time were slowly beginning to turn against Anne and history was about to repeat itself. The power in the royal court was slowly shifting from the Boleyns to the Seymours – exactly how it had played out when Henry serenaded Anne under the same roof as Katharine. It was believed that Jane was being coached by her brother, Edward Seymour, and her kinsman, Sir Francis Bryan, to capture and hold the king's attention. Support for Jane slowly gained pace as Eustace Chapuys readily sided with her against Anne.

Anne thought of a novel way to try and bring Henry back to her. On 2 April John Skip, Anne's almoner, delivered a sermon which was a little controversial by nature. He depicted Henry as the Old Testament's Ahaseurus and Thomas Cromwell as his wicked minister, Haman. He also depicted Anne as the good Queen Esther and through this sermon tried to convey the message to the king that he should put away his ministers who were poisoning his ears against his good queen.

Unfortunately for Anne, this plan of hers backfired spectacularly. Henry, who had declared himself as the Supreme Head of the Church of England, saw Anne's intervention through Skip as a question mark on his divine faith. Henry and Cromwell both regarded this as a public chastisement and were immensely displeased. In reality, Anne was a philanthropist who regarded her queenship as a means to help the needy.

John Skip was arrested and interrogated for 'preaching seditious doctrines'. He stuck to his story, stating that he intended the sermon to be a sort of a warning to Henry and Cromwell to go easy on the monasteries. And thus began Anne's downfall.

With Katharine of Aragon no more, the Boleyns understood that they needed an alliance with the Holy Roman Emperor and invited Eustace Chapuys, the Imperial ambassador, to Greenwich. He was welcomed enthusiastically at the gates by George Boleyn who expressed a desire to befriend the emperor. He was then invited by Cromwell for an audience with Anne, but Chapuys was hesitant. Nevertheless, he went and was caught in an uncomfortable situation where he was compelled, much to the chagrin of Mary and her faction, to bow to and acknowledge Anne. Embarrassed, he refused to dine with the king, choosing to dine with George Boleyn instead.

Being groomed in the French court in her childhood and adolescence, it is quite surprising to see Anne trying to forge a relationship with the emperor. One can assume that she was trying to secure an advantageous marriage for her daughter, Elizabeth, so as to guarantee her future lest anything happen to her. Clearly, she was aware that her star was waning.

While a trip to Calais with Henry and Anne was being discussed, an uneasy development put everything and everyone on tenterhooks. On 20 April Thomas Cromwell withdrew from the court, citing ill health. In reality, as he mentioned to Chapuys, he was asked by Henry to gather evidence against Anne. Seemingly the only person other than Chapuys who Cromwell had confided in was Thomas Wriothesley the First Earl of Southampton. The signs were there to see long before Cromwell's withdrawal, though. There were families, such as the Courteneys and the Poles, who were working actively with Chapuys to bring Anne down. On 14 April 1536 the Order of the Garter was granted to Sir Nicholas Carew and not George Boleyn, who was expecting it.

On 24 April Henry officially permitted Cromwell to investigate the 'treasonous conspiracies' against him and Sir Thomas Audeley, the Lord Chancellor, set up the oyer and terminar courts and ordered the concerned men to do as the king wished. Anne must have had her misgivings as she summoned her chaplain, Matthew Parker, and entrusted him with the care of Elizabeth. Henry maintained a show of normalcy and Anne toed the line as she made the payments for some buttons, a damask cowl, tassels and a cap, amongst other things, for Elizabeth.

On 30 April Anne momentarily let her guard down in a conversation with Sir Henry Norris. A widower, Norris was courting Anne's cousin, Margaret 'Madge' Shelton. Norris had been avoiding Anne of late, and, increasingly frustrated, Anne reprimanded him for this. The increasing rumours about Henry planning to put aside Anne for another wife did not help in lessening the queen's stress. Consequently, she snapped at Norris and said: 'You look for dead men's shoes, for if ought came to the king but good, you would look to have me.'[14] She must have realised her folly immediately; it was treasonous to even imagine the death of the king and Anne had spoken out aloud. As soon as the words left her mouth, a terrified Norris immediately tried to distance himself from her. He hurried away and sought out Anne's almoner, John Skip, and swore that the queen was a good woman. This move may have been orchestrated by Anne herself who was aware and fearful of the repercussions.

On the same day, Mark Smeaton, a lute player, was arrested. He was in his early twenties and had worked for Cardinal Wolsey before joining Henry's Chapel Royal. From there, Anne, a good judge of another's talents, brought him into her own household. He then rose to the position of Groom of the Privy Chamber, a move that disconcerted many. Smeaton, by nature, was known to be quite brazen and had rubbed many people up the wrong way. Due to his class and social standing, he never gained a place in the inner circle remaining a mere official at the royal court.

Smeaton was taken to Thomas Cromwell's house at Stepney and interrogated about his relationship with the queen. There is a possibility that he may have been tortured and forced to confess to adultery with the queen. He was then sent to the Tower as preparations for May Day celebrations got underway at Greenwich. Francis Weston, William Brereton, Sir Henry Norris and George Boleyn along with Sir Thomas Wyatt had all participated in the tournament. Towards the end of the tournament, Henry left abruptly, and according to George Constantine, sought Henry Norris to ride back with him to Westminster. He may have promised a pardon if he confessed but Norris desisted from telling Henry anything, especially about the awkward conversation he had with Anne a few days previously.

Abandoned, an anxious Anne tried to maintain a façade of normalcy as she went about her duties. She was still treated like a queen and it is testimony to the strength of her character that she did not break down after Henry's departure from Greenwich. She had her dinner and offered her prayers before settling into bed not knowing the storm that awaited her, or that she had seen her husband for the last time. The next day, 2 May, she was summoned to appear before the King's Council at Greenwich. Her brother George, Francis Weston, Sir Henry Norris and William Brereton were arrested on the same day and sent to the Tower of London.

The panel that Anne faced consisted of Sir William Paulet and William Fitzwilliam, Treasurer of the Household, and they were headed by Anne's own uncle, the Duke of Norfolk. She was familiar with these men who were an integral part of her husband's household. Her uncle informed her that she stood accused of adultery and incest and that three men, Sir Henry Norris, Mark Smeaton, and a third unknown man, were under suspicion. The judges, with the exception of Paulet, were especially rude to Anne and Norfolk tut-tutted as the charges against her were read out.

She was then rowed in a barge downriver to the Tower of London, accompanied by her uncle and two other men, entering the dreaded prison through the infamous Traitor's Gate. It is not known whether Cromwell accompanied them or met them at the Tower but there are correspondences from the constable that indicate that he must have been present when Anne was brought in. She was met by the Constable of the Tower, Sir William Kingston, at the Byward Tower, the same place where her coronation procession had arrived a mere three years ago. The irony did not end there for Anne; she was lodged in the same room as three years previously and not in a dungeon as she had feared. An incredulous Anne still was in a state of disbelief at the sudden turn of events and may have hoped that it was all a big mistake and that Henry would come back to her. Anne's Vice-Chamberlain, Edward Baynton, and her close friend, Archbishop Thomas Cranmer, found it difficult to believe the charges levelled against their queen and wrote to Henry about it. However, they worded their letters carefully lest they found themselves in the ring of suspects. They owed utmost obedience to Henry and did not wish to jeopardise their positions.

The supporters of Katharine of Aragon and the Holy Roman Emperor were overjoyed at the fall of Anne. Chapuys mentioned that Henry was seeking to annul his marriage on the basis of a precontract between Anne and Henry Percy, Earl of Northumberland. Henry Percy submitted his statement in which he mentioned that no such precontract existed, but that would mean Henry admitting that his first marriage was valid, something that he had denied vehemently before marrying Anne. In the meantime, the goods and estates of all the accused were seized and reverted back to the Crown.

Meanwhile, in her rooms in the Tower, Anne was served by a handful of women who did not particularly like her. That included Margaret Coffin, Mrs Stonor, Lady Kingston, and her aunts, Lady Elizabeth Boleyn and Anne Shelton. The women must have discussed amongst themselves about the charges levelled against Anne and this may have added to her discomfort. Anne may have been kept with them on the assumption that they might spy on her, which could be likely. Her mood kept fluctuating;

at times she wished to die, and at others she raged against the injustice that had been meted out to her. While contemplating the reasons for her arrest and imprisonment, Anne revealed her conversation with Sir Henry Norris to Mrs Coffin who dutifully reported it to Sir William Kingston, who in turn reported it to Thomas Cromwell. Anne was also surprised at Mark Smeaton's arrest as he had visited her chamber once during the summer progress of 1535 when the royals were at Winchester.

Anne then wrote a final letter from her prison to her husband, King Henry VIII. It read:

> Your Grace's displeasure and my imprisonment are things so strange unto me as what to write or what to excuse I am altogether ignorant.
>
> Whereas you sent unto me, willing me to confess a truth and so to obtain your favour, by such an one whom you know to be my ancient professed enemy, I no sooner received this message by him than I rightly conceived your meaning; and if, as you say, confessing a truth indeed may procure my safety, I shall with all willingness and duty perform your command. But let not Your Grace ever imagine that your poor wife will ever be brought to acknowledge a fault, where not so much as a thought thereof proceeded. And to speak a truth, never Prince had wife more loyal in all duty, and in all true affection, than you have ever found in Anne Boleyn, with which name and place I could willingly have contented myself, if God, and your Grace's pleasure had been so pleased. Neither did I at any time forget my self in my exaltation, or received Queenship, but that I always looked for such an alteration as now I find; for the ground of my preferment being on no surer foundation than your Grace's fancy, the least alteration, I knew, was fit and sufficient to draw that fancy to some other subject. You have chosen me, from a low estate, to be your Queen and companion, far beyond my desert and desire. If then you found me worthy of such honour, good your Grace let not any light fancy, or bad counsel of mine enemies, withdraw your princely favour from me; neither let that stain, that unworthy stain of a disloyal heart towards your good Grace, ever cast so foul a blot on your most dutiful wife, and the infant princess your daughter.

Try me good king, but let me have a lawful trial, and let not my sworn enemies sit as my accusers and judges; yea, let me receive an open trial, for my truth shall fear no open shame; then shall you see, either mine innocency cleared, your suspicion and conscience satisfied, the ignominy and slander of the world stopped, or my guilt openly declared. So that whatsoever God or you may determine of me, your Grace may be freed from an open censure, and mine offence being so lawfully proved, your Grace is at liberty, both before God and man, not only to execute worthy punishment on me as an unlawful wife, but to follow your affection already settled on that party, for whose sake I am now as I am, whose name I could some good while since have pointed unto: your Grace being not ignorant of my suspicion therein.

But if you have already determined of me, and that not only my death, but an infamous slander must bring you the enjoying of your desired happiness, then I desire of God, that he will pardon your great sin therein, and likewise mine enemies, the instruments thereof; and that he will not call you to a strict account for your unprincely and cruel usage of me, at his general judgement seat, where both you and my self must shortly appear, and in whose judgement, I doubt not, (whatsoever the world may think of me) mine innocence shall be openly known, and sufficiently cleared.

My last and only request shall be, that my self may only bear the burden of your Grace's displeasure, and that it may not touch the innocent souls of those poor gentlemen who (as I understand) are likewise in strait imprisonment for my sake. If ever I have found favour in your sight; if ever the name of Anne Boleyn hath been pleasing to your ears, then let me obtain this request, and I will so leave to trouble your Grace any further, with mine earnest prayers to the trinity to have your Grace in his good keeping, and to direct you in all your actions. From my doleful prison the Tower, this 6 of May.

Your most loyal and ever faithful wife
Anne Boleyn[15]

*****

On 8 May Thomas Wyatt, Anne's former admirer, was arrested along with Sir Richard Page, a gentleman of the Privy Chamber, and were interrogated on the charges of adultery. It is quite possible that Henry recollected his earlier altercation about a jewel with Wyatt when the former was courting Anne which may have led to his arrest. Sir Francis Bryan was also summoned by the council but wasn't arrested. He may have been summoned to simply give evidence against Anne.

King Henry VIII called a grand jury at Westminster to address the case and commanded Thomas Cromwell to be present as well. The jury, which was headed by Thomas More's son-in-law, Giles Heron, presented their verdict to the judges. They had come to a conclusion that there was enough evidence to put Anne, along with George Boleyn, Sir Francis Weston, Sir William Brereton, Sir Henry Norris and Mark Smeaton on trial. They accused her of adultery, incest and treason. They mentioned that she solicited the attention of the men by using her guile and giving them gifts. They also accused her of plotting the king's death, a crime that carried a severe punishment.

Eric Ives, Anne's biographer, however, has proven that the adultery charges were trumped up. The accused had iron-strong alibis on the dates mentioned by the jury. If we go by the jury, Anne is said to have solicitated Sir Henry Norris merely a month after giving birth to Princess Elizabeth. On many of the dates, the court wasn't even in the location that was mentioned. Again, if we go by what the jury said, Anne would have been pregnant when she is said to have slept with Mark Smeaton. Again, Anne would have been at least two months pregnant when she committed incest with her brother, George Boleyn. Many such discrepancies were discovered by historians like Eric Ives, Alison Weir and G.W. Bernard as they tallied the dates with Anne's movements. The only valid charge seemed to be the danger to the king's life if they proved the charges of Anne plotting her husband's death to be true.

Francis Weston, Mark Smeaton, Henry Norris and William Brereton stood trial at Westminster on 12 May. They stood before a panel of peers consisting of Thomas Boleyn, the Dukes of Norfolk and Suffolk, Thomas Cromwell, William Fitzwilliam, the Duke of Exeter and Henry Percy, the Earl of Northumberland. The panel also had in attendance many religious conservatives and many supporters of Cromwell. Mark

Smeaton pleaded guilty to 'violation and carnal knowledge of the Queen' while the other three pleaded not guilty. Notwithstanding, all four of them were proclaimed guilty and were sentenced to be hung, drawn and quartered.

Anne and George Boleyn stood trial on 15 May in the Tower of London. Anne was brought into the King's Hall by Sir William Kingston as a crowd watched a queen stand trial. Anne had dressed in a black velvet gown with a red damask petticoat. She wore a cap on which perched a black and white feather. The Duke of Norfolk presided over the panel that consisted of his son, the Earl of Surrey, Charles Brandon, the Duke of Suffolk, Chancellor Audeley, her former paramour Henry Percy, Earl of Northumberland, and most importantly, Thomas Boleyn. Anne stood stoically as the charges against her were read out but her true feelings were reflected on her face.

Those charges were the same as the ones that were read out to the four men: that Anne was following her carnal lust for the men through conversations and kisses, solicitating them with gifts, and provoking her brother to lay with her, mentioning that she never loved the king and would marry one of the men once he was dead. Eustace Chapuys also mentions that Anne had, on several occasions, ridiculed the king and laughed at his poetry.

A brilliant orator and an astute politician, Anne responded to the charges with alacrity, her replies so convincing that it seemed that her freedom was imminent. However, doing the king's will was the ultimate duty of every subject, and they pronounced Anne guilty of all charges. George Boleyn, too, was said to have defended himself splendidly, impressing many with his knowledge and confidence to stand up to the mighty dignitaries. But the tables were turned on George and Anne when George's wife, Jane Boleyn, Lady Rochford, testified against them as the only witness to provide evidence for the charges of incest. Whether she did it out of her own free will due to jealousy at their closeness or was coerced we do not know until later when, in a sense of poetic justice, she met the same fate as her husband and sister-in-law. Thomas Wyatt and Sir Richard Page were acquitted of all charges and were freed.

George and Anne Boleyn were condemned to death, with the former begging for his debts to be settled through his properties. As they were escorted back to the Tower, Anne still hoped that the death penalty would be overturned and she would be sent to a convent instead.

Execution

George Boleyn, along with Sir Henry Norris, Sir Francis Weston, Sir William Brereton and Mark Smeaton, were brought to the scaffold at Tower Hill on 17 May to be executed while Anne was made to watch through the window. Given his rank, George was the first to die and he declared that he had sinned and deserved death. He also implored the crowd to 'trust not the vanity of the world and especially in the flattering of the court'. Norris was executed after George, then it was Francis Weston's turn. Finally William Brereton and Mark Smeaton were put to death. Neither of them proclaimed their innocence but accepted their sentence with utmost grace and urged people to pray for their souls.

The next day, Anne sent for her almoner, John Skip, to pray along with her. She may have thought that she was to die that day but that was not to be. Her husband had granted her one last mercy of being executed by an experienced swordsman rather than by the axe. Execution by the sword was quick and painless compared to an axe. However, the executioner hadn't yet arrived from St Omer and would arrive only later that day. The delay must have added to Anne's anxiety.

Anne made her final confession that night in which she proclaimed her innocence, declaring that she had never been unfaithful to the king during their courtship and marriage. To be on the safe side lest her words be misinterpreted, Anne requested Sir William Kingston, Constable of the Tower, to be present as she expressed her pain at her execution being delayed: 'for I thought to be dead by this time and past my pain'.[16] Kingston may have felt sorry for her at that time as he attempted to console her by assuring her that the execution would be 'subtle' and quick to which Anne replied: 'I heard say the executioner was very good and I have a little neck,'[17] earning the Constable's admiration for being strong in the face of her imminent death.

The morning of her execution, 19 May 1536, dawned and Anne heard Mass for one last time. Her ladies then dressed her in a gown of black or deep grey damask which they put over a red kirtle. It is not clear whether Anne wished to portray herself as a martyr with her choice of the colour red, but it is unlikely that she would try and ruffle feathers at this point. To honour her French legacy, she wore a French gable hood. She was led to the scaffold where she delivered her now famous last speech:

> Good Christian people, I have not come here to preach a sermon; I have come here to die. For according to the law and by the law I am judged to die, and therefore I will speak nothing against it. I am come hither to accuse no man, nor to speak of that whereof I am accused and condemned to die, but I pray God save the King and send him long to reign over you, for a gentler nor a more merciful prince was there never, and to me he was ever a good, a gentle, and sovereign lord. And if any person will meddle of my cause, I require them to judge the best. And thus I take my leave of the world and of you all, and I heartily desire you all to pray for me.[18]

It had all the elements of the pitch-perfect last speech that condemned prisoners gave in those days, but it is quite interesting to note that she may have had an inkling that her case might be re-examined in the future as she implored people to judge her with care.

She then removed her cloak and coif and tucked her hair under her cap so that her neck was exposed as she was watched by Thomas Cromwell, Charles Brandon, Chancellor Audeley, Henry Fitzroy and a crowd of over 2,000 people. Her discarded clothes would be a part of the executioner's payment.

She then knelt on the straw – a block wasn't needed in the case of execution by the sword – as her ladies blindfolded her. As she murmured her prayers, the executioner distracted her and cut off her head in one clean stroke. No coffin was arranged and her ladies wrapped her head in a white cloth and packed her body in an elm arrow chest and carried her away.

On the same day, after Anne's execution, Archbishop Thomas Cranmer, one of Anne's greatest supporters, passed a disposition that allowed King Henry VIII to marry Jane Seymour. They were betrothed the very next day and even Chapuys, who never thought highly of Anne, was not pleased.

*****

This brings us to a vital question: Did Henry really love Anne? On one hand, he disbanded the Church of England to secure his divorce from his wife of twenty-five years to marry her. He sent his faithful ministers and friends – Sir Thomas More and Bishop John Fisher – to the block for having opposed his union with her. Yet, he planned Anne's execution with clinical precision, as revealed in an entry in a warrant book that was recently discovered. In it he mentions that although Anne was condemned to die either by burning or decapitation, he was 'moved by pity' to spare her the painful death by burning. He continued: 'We however command that […] the head of the same Anne shall be [...] cut off.'[19] This discovery also refutes the belief of some people that Henry would have settled for an annulment and banishment to a nunnery but Cromwell would have none of it, and that it was Cromwell who was determined that she should die. The failure of Anne to beget sons only strengthened Cromwell's case.

Anne's only crime was to be born in the wrong era. Her beliefs and her talents were way ahead of the time. The only thing King Henry VIII wanted was an heir to the throne and he would have loved that wife unconditionally, the case in point being that he is buried next to Jane Seymour, the wife he loved best.

Anne Boleyn is buried at the Chapel of St Peter ad Vincula in the Tower of London where she lies alongside her brother, George Boleyn.

7

Elizabeth Barton: The Holy Maid of Kent

Nestled in the sleepy town of Aldington in the county of Kent, one comes across a stone structure, ruins of a bygone era, overlooking the Romney Marsh. These ruins of an ancient chapel stand in mute testimony to one of the most odious legends of the Tudor reign. The story of Elizabeth Barton – more famously, or infamously, monikered 'The Mad Maid of Kent' – has gone down in the annals of history as one of the most poignant executions by King Henry VIII[1]. Elizabeth Barton, a servant girl turned nun, was the only executed woman during the reign of Henry VIII to have her head spiked on London Bridge for all to gaze at. Surely, an ignominious end for a seemingly simple peasant girl.

But what were the events that led the twenty-eight-year-old to such a gruesome end? Was Elizabeth Barton genuinely receiving visits from the Almighty or was it all a sham?

Life of a Servant in Aldington and Elizabeth's early life

Elizabeth Barton was born in 1506, probably in the village of Aldington in Kent. During Elizabeth's time it was an idyllic village overlooking the Romney Marsh and the English Channel. Among the half-timbered Tudor houses was an archiepiscopal palace of William Warham, the Archbishop of Canterbury. The Court Lodge Farmhouse was especially frequented by Archbishops John Morton – the previous Archbishop of Canterbury – and Warham.[2]

Farming was the main occupation of the residents of the village and the wealthier people appointed servants – usually adolescents – to assist them in the agricultural and household work. Often seen as a stepping stone to more fruitful careers and/or successful marriages and not as a career, it was usually the parents who negotiated and secured jobs for their children. Once the deal was finalised with the prospective employer, the servant moved into the latter's house. Most of the servants were unmarried; married servants were extremely rare.[3]

The employer was required to maintain their household help for the term of their service, irrespective of the nature and volume of work and the capability of the servant in carrying out their assigned jobs.

On their part, the servants were obliged to adhere to the terms of the agreement between them and their employer. They were not free to leave the employment before the said term ended, and absconders were dealt with strongly. They were ordered back into the household of their master unless the servant could prove that he/she had been mistreated. The wealthy merchants and householders usually employed more than one servant which meant that illicit relationships were common. Although the girls were warned against the beguiling ways of certain men 'of flattering tongues' and 'crocodile tears', undesired pregnancies happened frequently. Usually the pregnant servant was dismissed, and most probably left to fend for themselves. This in turn contributed to the rise of infanticides.

Rape was a common accusation levelled at employers by their servants. However, proving it in the fifteenth century was especially tough as the crime usually happened behind closed doors, which was why the conviction rate was extremely low. More often than not it ruined the reputation of the servant girl and consequently rendered her jobless.

Diligent workers built useful social connections which helped them further their careers. Some even sought to start their own households by entering into a marital alliance with a well-connected man. There are cases of servants who were fortunate enough to share a lifelong bond of friendship with their fellow servants, as in the case of Elizabeth Cooper of Norwich who befriended Thomas Sutton, her co-worker, who went on to become the Sheriff of Norwich and helped Elizabeth out when she found herself at the wrong end of the law. And in certain cases, some especially fortunate servants even received a small bequest in the event of their employer's death.

Elizabeth Barton's life as a servant girl was not too different from the above examples. Described as a 'poor wench without learning', Elizabeth was employed in the household of Thomas Cobb, a gentleman in the parish. Cobb was a man who held immense sway in the village, being the Archbishop of Canterbury's most senior manager who looked after his estates in Aldington. She joined Cobb's household at the age of nineteen – it was quite common for the servants to start working in their adolescence – probably working as a farmhand and a house help, as was usual with the servants of wealthy householders.[4]

Illness and Visions: 1525, The Holy Week

The churches were being cleaned and the altars were being swept in preparation for Palm Sunday. The Holy Week, leading up to Easter Sunday, had just begun and the priests in the various churches and cathedrals all over medieval England were gearing up to narrate the story of Christ's triumphant return to Jerusalem. A special shrine was also being prepared with the Holy Sacrament representing Christ along with the particular church's own relics. This would be taken in a procession around the church while another procession in the opposite direction would meet them at the church doors.

Over the next few days during Holy Week, the priest would read out the passage about the veil in the temple of Jerusalem while the veil separating the chancel and the nave would be dropped and put away. This ceremony took place on the Wednesday of Holy Week. On Maundy Thursday the church and the altar were prepared for Easter Sunday by washing them with water and wine.

The celebrations took a serious turn on Good Friday with the ceremony of 'Creeping to the Cross' wherein the priests would crawl on their hands and feet up to a crucifix on the altar to experience Christ's suffering.

Finally, on Easter Sunday, the candles that were lit in the sepulchre would be extinguished, the candles in the church re-lit and the sepulchre opened to rejoice and celebrate the Resurrection of Christ.[5]

Elizabeth had barely adjusted to the humdrum of the Cobb household when she fell ill. And not just the usual fever or the 'quickening' of the womb – as was common with servants living in close quarters – but deathly ill. The infirmity rendered her bedridden and unable to contribute to the household and farm chores. It also made her throat swell as she struggled to breathe.

Cobb, known to be a conscientious master, fulfilled his part of the terms agreed with Elizabeth despite her not working. He probably would have relieved her of her duties at the end of her one-year tenure, but till then he paid for her upkeep and treatment.

Very soon, an ill Elizabeth began experiencing strange visions along with lengthy seizures that resulted in her face contorting. She also suffered periodically from paralysis. During these moments of feverishness, she often spoke of the Seven Deadly Sins, the Ten Commandments and other such scriptures, which she had probably learned in Church.

Concerned, Cobb summoned Richard Masters, a well-read rector, and a local gentleman, Edward Thwaites,[6] to examine Elizabeth. Initially, Thwaites reckoned that her illness, her seizures and the resulting hallucinations was nothing but epilepsy, but he took back his claims for reasons unknown. There were allegations levelled against the two men for using Elizabeth's illness for their own means – Thwaites had a stronger financial motive – but this seemed unlikely and therefore were never proven. Rather, the two men, in all probability, began regarding the simple servant girl as a clairvoyant. During her trances, Elizabeth accurately predicted the death of a child, which she claimed was revealed to her by the Virgin Mary in a dream. In her delirious state she also claimed that the Virgin Mary had led her to a secluded chapel to pray after which she was cured of her illness.

Such claims made the seemingly simple servant girl turned soothsayer into an infamous celebrity, and people arrived in droves to catch a glimpse of Elizabeth. Her visions persisted even after her health was restored. The apparent accuracy of her predictions brought her many followers and pilgrims began visiting the chapel on the hillside.

Her master, Thomas Cobb, was also convinced of his employee's divine declarations and extended to her a rare honour by inviting her to dine with him and his wife in the dining hall of his home.

Along with her many followers, however, Elizabeth also attracted her share of naysayers. William Warham, the Archbishop of Canterbury, supposedly found the case interesting, but nevertheless, he asked Masters to keep a close watch on Elizabeth and make careful notes of her trances and subsequent claims. Warham was even granted a personal interview with Elizabeth. Finding her supposed claims credible, he resolved to investigate further and sent for Dr Edward Bocking, a highly educated man with a doctorate in divinity, and William Hadley, a university graduate from the monastery of Christ Church in Canterbury. They travelled to Aldington to examine Elizabeth and the nature of her visions, along with another monk and a priest from the Observant Friars.

Meanwhile, Elizabeth apparently suffered from bouts of sickness as she waited for Masters to return. According to a source, Elizabeth suddenly began to throw up before recovering miraculously quickly. Her seemingly eccentric behaviour included her supposedly pretending to be unwell despite being in perfect health.

The trances showed no signs of abating and Elizabeth now spoke about religion and visitations to Heaven during these periods. She spoke often about an image of the Virgin Mary in a tiny, ancient chapel on the hill overlooking Romney Marsh. Enveloped in a mystical aura, the almost ruined chapel was home to a bedraggled monk, the origins of whom are yet unknown. Elizabeth then proclaimed that she had a vision wherein the Virgin Mary had commanded her, in order to be cured of her malady, to light a taper at the chapel. Her claim that she was also required to ring a bell raised a few eyebrows as there weren't any bells in the chapel, as Thomas Cobb explained to her. However, this failed to deter Elizabeth and she made more, seemingly accurate, claims based on her 'visions', much to the astonishment of the people who had gathered there.

The slip-up about the bells sowed the seeds of doubt in the minds of some people who thought her claims, predictions and visions were just the ramblings of a sick mind. She complicated the situation further by declaring, on reaching the dilapidated chapel, that her cure would be delayed instead of being instantaneous. The reason for this remains a mystery. Were her visions genuine or was she simply trying to avoid accusations of repeating other, similar miracle cures at that time?

The men sent by William Warham, after much investigation into her faith, declared Elizabeth of sound mind and also said that they believed her. She even prophesised the time and date of one of the commissioners, Mr Bocking's, death. Elizabeth Norton, in her book *The Hidden Lives of Tudor Women*, mentions that this was Elizabeth's preferred way to ensure that people with authority over her obeyed her and accepted and acted on her demands.

When the day of the miracle, as prophesised by Elizabeth, arrived, massive crowds gathered at Aldington and outside Thomas Cobb's house to find out if it would come to pass. Elizabeth was carried out on a bed, escorted by Mr Bocking, Cobb, Masters and Thwaites.

She led the procession to the chapel where she fell into a trance-like state on hearing the Mass being sung. It is believed that she seemed warped and deformed, with her tongue hanging out and her eyes bulging and staring unblinkingly into the distance as she lay prostate on the floor.

Edward Thwaites, who was recording the happenings in the chapel, watched in wonder as Elizabeth's lips moved in a silent prayer sometimes in a melodious prayer and sometimes in a harsh rebuke. The spectators watched awestruck as Elizabeth spoke about various visions, one of which was to retire as a nun. Whether it was true or an elaborate ruse, Elizabeth certainly knew how to hold a crowd's attention.

The Mass over, Elizabeth got up and declared herself finally cured, much to the rejoicing of the onlookers. Soon enough, the news – and the rumours – of the 'Maid of Kent' spread through the country like wildfire, finally reaching the ears of King Henry VIII who asked his friend and humanist, Sir Thomas More, for his opinion.

Although largely unimpressed, More did not dismiss Elizabeth as a fraud. It seemed that Henry, too, did not care much for the simple maid turned prophetess. However, he would soon start thinking differently.

*****

At that time the court of Henry VIII in London was in an uproar. The king was planning to discard his queen of twenty-five years for a daughter of a mere courtier. Anne Boleyn had returned to England from France in 1522 and was already creating quite a stir in the court by introducing French fashions amongst the ladies and impressing one and all, including the king, with her refined manners that she had learnt in the sophisticated courts of Burgundy and France.

Henry VIII was enamoured by his queen's new lady-in-waiting and the fact that her sister was his former mistress did not deter him from pursuing her. Much to Katharine of Aragon's dismay, the affair that she may have presumed to be just a passing fancy was now gaining steam and her validity of her marriage to Henry was being questioned. Anne's affair and the supposed rumour of a secret wedding to Henry Percy, the son and heir of the Earl of Northumberland, was quickly forgotten as Henry cast aside her sister, Mary, to seek Anne's attention.

With the support of many factions as well as the citizens of London behind her, Katharine underwent a series of questionings and trials to no avail. Despite vehemently denying that she had slept with Henry's older brother, Arthur, to whom she was married briefly, the marriage between Henry and Katharine was pronounced illegal and was annulled, bastardizing their daughter, Mary Tudor, the future Mary I of England. The trial of Katharine of Aragon caused an immense religious upheaval and resulted in King Henry VIII breaking away from Rome and proclaiming himself as the Head of the Church of England.

Back at Aldington, Elizabeth Barton proclaimed her desire to become a nun as the Virgin Mary had instructed her. William Warham, the Archbishop of Canterbury, agreed to her request and she was inducted in the Benedictine House of St Sepulchre's which was quite close to Canterbury.

The monastery was headed by Philippa John, a winsome prioress. It was a modest little place housing not more than five nuns, not including the prioress, who welcomed Elizabeth warmly into their fold. They may have heard of Elizabeth's fame, which had spread far and wide, and may have been curious about her.

However, very close to where Elizabeth was confined in her nunnery was Hever Castle, the Boleyn residence. Anne, we presume, may have heard about Elizabeth on one of her many visits home. During one such visit, in early October 1528, William Warham wrote to Cardinal Thomas Wolsey, England's papal legate and the man who had King Henry VIII's ear, informing him about Elizabeth and also mentioning that she had sought an audience with him. Warham was suitably impressed with Elizabeth to petition Wolsey for a meeting. In the meantime, she stayed put in the monastery, claiming inoffensive visions of angels and confessors amongst many other things. She helped the people who lost loved ones and may have offered to contact the recently deceased person's spirit to offer solace. What those people thought about Elizabeth's visions and proclamations is not known to us.

Elizabeth also began healing people who seemed to experience similar visions. Slowly but gradually, her fame spread, yet she remained humble even when Sir Thomas More was made aware of her 'talents'. She lived quietly and chastely without drawing much attention to herself and this was evident in her unassuming living quarters which consisted of a mattress, a few sheets, a couple of pillows and a bolster. She preferred to donate the gifts that she received to the nunnery's church and even donated the money that she received in return for her prayers for the needy to charity, keeping only a bare minimum amount for herself.

A desperate Dr Bocking, flustered by the lack of visions ever since Elizabeth joined the nunnery, kept pressurising her to reveal something or make a prediction. Elizabeth, on her part, felt the need to return to the little derelict chapel, which had now become a place of pilgrimage with ardent devotees flocking there in droves, whenever there was a need for a revelation.

These occasional visions or revelations were tolerated by the sceptics so long as Elizabeth mainly kept to herself, but things started changing when Elizabeth met Cardinal Thomas Wolsey in 1528. This meeting, facilitated by William Warham, brought to fore her ambitious side. An ambitious and immensely wealthy clergyman, Wolsey was King Henry VIII's closest confidante and was currently in the midst of the 'King's Great Matter', trying a secure an annulment for King Henry's marriage to Katharine of Aragon for the latter to marry his current paramour, Anne Boleyn, despite the former despising her.

No evidence of Elizabeth's meeting with Cardinal Wolsey survives but what we know is that she told the cardinal that she had seen a vision of three swords being pressed into Wolsey's hands. The first sword symbolized the power of him being a man of God, the second symbolized the power he held over the king and the third symbolised his interference in the annulment of the king's marriage to Katharine of Aragon and his role in trying to elevate Anne Boleyn to queenship.

This was quite a dangerous move as Elizabeth had now spoken directly against the king's decision to end his marriage to Katharine and marry a courtier's daughter. Wolsey was suddenly wary of her and so was Warham. Thanks to Wolsey, she gained access to King Henry VIII who was himself intrigued by this peasant girl turned prophetess.

Henry met Elizabeth several times although he was cautious and discreet in his dealings with her. Each time they met, Elizabeth spoke out against his marriage with Anne Boleyn. It is not known whether Henry suspected Katharine's involvement, not that there was any, but it may have perturbed the discarded queen to know someone was speaking out so openly against the whole episode and further antagonising the king against her.

Elizabeth received unstinting support from one of Henry's fiercest critics, Bishop John Fisher, who thought her no less than a saint. When she met him on her way home to Kent after meeting the king, the Bishop of Rochester thought that she was an angel from Heaven. He drew courage from her words, describing her as 'the person that by many probable and likely conjectures, I then reputed to be right honest, religious, and very good and virtuous.' So enthusiastic was he in his admiration of Elizabeth that he did not bother to check her background or credentials.

However, it appeared that Anne Boleyn was insouciant towards the prophetess and her proclamations saying on one occasion that she has decided to go ahead in pursuing the marriage and queenship regardless of her detractors.

Elizabeth then claimed that an angel had appeared to her, persuading her to visit the king again to warn him against his union with Anne Boleyn. Her revelations and subsequent warnings about the king's 'Great Matter' were getting more dire with each passing day, with Elizabeth, on one occasion, warning Henry to take back Katharine or suffer the consequences.

Henry, however, paid no heed to Elizabeth's warnings and proceeded to take the matter of the annulment of his marriage to Katharine to a legatine court at Blackfriars which was presided by Cardinal Wolsey and Cardinal Campeggio, the absentee Bishop of Salisbury.

The case was then revoked to Rome by Cardinal Campeggio, leaving Henry, Anne and Henry's brother-in-law, Charles Brandon, Duke of Suffolk, seething in rage. Wolsey's star fell rapidly as he lost his master's goodwill and was accused of colluding with the Pope and defying Henry's orders. He was exiled to his diocese at York in disgrace. He was formally arrested from Cawood Castle by Henry Percy, Anne's former suitor, in a sort of poetic revenge by his nemesis. The cardinal, once the most important man of the country, died a broken man at Leicester while on his way to meet King Henry VIII and stand trial in London.

Elizabeth Barton claimed to have foreseen the death of Cardinal Thomas Wolsey, revealed to her by the Virgin Mary, but was off by some fifteen years to the day. She seemed to have salvaged the situation by claiming that due to the Cardinal dying earlier than his appointed time (i.e., her miscalculation) his soul was in a limbo. She also claimed that she witnessed the devils fighting for his soul in Purgatory and had saved it from further damnation. With public feeling rising against Anne, Elizabeth was being believed more and more, and her influence grew, even outside England. She met with two of the Pope's ambassadors and even corresponded with the Pope himself, warning him of deadly diseases such as the plague if Katharine of Aragon was not reinstated as the Queen of England and King Henry VIII's rightful wife. She even predicted the end of Pope Clement if he ruled against Katharine.

Pope Clement denied the king his divorce, though however, we cannot say whether the judgement was of his own volition or due to Elizabeth's dire predictions, which gained credence mainly due to her austere lifestyle in her nunnery.

Sir Thomas More, Lord Chancellor and an ardent critic of the king's 'Great Matter', finally met Elizabeth Barton at Syon Abbey after hearing glowing accounts of her visions and healing powers from one of Elizabeth's associates, Father Rich, who was an Observant Friar of Richmond. Ever the pragmatist, More did not completely dismiss Elizabeth; however, he was not ready to believe her fully either. He steered clear of the controversial topics, asking her to pray for him instead. He also exhorted her not to speak further on the Great Matter. This, however, wasn't the version of events that Elizabeth told when she was interrogated. She claimed that More rejoiced on hearing her words. She also claimed that she had several conversations on the same topic with Gertrude Courtenay, Marchioness of Exeter and Henry's kinswoman.

Bolstered by this so-called encouragement from some of the king's closest associates, Elizabeth now started speaking about a civil war. She also predicted the king's death within six months if he married Anne.

Now positively alarmed, Henry and Anne tried bribing Elizabeth into silence by offering the post of an abbess while on their way to Calais in 1532. Elizabeth Boleyn, Anne's mother, also offered her a post in Anne's household in return for her silence. Elizabeth refused both offers. She claimed that while the king was away she had a vision wherein she found herself in Henry's chapel, watching him reach out for the bread of the host which was then magically carried away by an angel for Elizabeth herself.

However convincing Elizabeth may have been, her delaying tactics did not work and King Henry VIII married Anne Boleyn in a private ceremony at Whitehall on the morning of 25 January 1533. Now it was time to see whether Elizabeth's prophecy of the king's death would really come true or if it was merely a hoax.

Anne was formally crowned Queen of England in a glittering coronation ceremony at Westminster Abbey on 1 June 1533, five months after her marriage. Her detractors, however, were out on the streets with their caps firmly on their heads as a mark of disrespect to their new queen who, they believed, had usurped the rightful queen, Katharine of Aragon. They also mocked Henry and Anne's initials 'HA', much to Anne's distress.

King Henry VIII continued to be in good health and spirits, thus casting doubt on Elizabeth's predictions about his demise. Despite this, the nun from Kent remained largely popular and some of her contemporaries, including Dr Bocking, even wrote books about her. She was described as a 'spiritual virgin' and as someone who represented the 'benignity and kindness of God.'

In reality, despite these fantastical claims by one of her ardent supporters, Elizabeth was in a bit of difficult position. Her prophecy about King Henry VIII's death having come to naught, she was understandably nervous. Henry was furious and asked his chief minister, Thomas Cromwell, to inform Archbishop Thomas Cranmer to initiate an inquiry into Elizabeth's claims.

On the king's and Cromwell's instructions, Cranmer, who was always doubtful about Elizabeth, summoned her to his manor of Oxford. Having been pampered by all and sundry, even by the Pope, Elizabeth was feeling pretty complacent as she made her way to the Archbishop's manor, along with the prioress of the nunnery where she lived.

However, she was taken by surprise as Cramner and Cromwell's associates, far from being impressed by the prophetess, began firing a volley of questions at her, questioning her visions, her foretellings of disaster and many more such incidents that Elizabeth claimed to have witnessed through her visions.

Elizabeth may have been taken aback at the sudden show of hostility, but maintained that all her visions and prophecies were true, despite finding it difficult to interpret them. She asked for leave to go back to the little chapel at Kent to understand and interpret her visions.

Unimpressed, but maintaining a cool façade, Cranmer bided his time, playing along with Elizabeth's claims about the authenticity of her prophecies while at the same time intending to pack her off straight to Cromwell's doorstep as soon as he got the answers he was seeking.

Oblivious to Cranmer's veiled hostility, Elizabeth was confident of the fact that the interview went well. She was soon to be proved very wrong. After he had finished questioning the nun, Cranmer sent her to the Tower of London.

Meanwhile, a pregnant Anne Boleyn went into her confinement on 26 August 1533 and gave birth to a healthy daughter, Elizabeth, in the afternoon of 7 September. Despite the disappointment on the birth of another girl child, Henry may have still held hopes of siring a son with Anne.

Elizabeth Barton's star, however, was on the wane. In what we may consider an unusual yet rash move, Elizabeth wrote a letter to Katharine of Aragon, assuring the exiled former queen of her prosperity and her daughter Mary's success and glory. She sent this missive through Henry Gold, one of Katharine's supporters.

Not wanting to stir up any more trouble, the exiled Katharine kept quiet, refusing to entertain the prophetess of Kent and her lofty claims. The discretion demonstrated by Katharine in this matter impressed Thomas Cromwell. The queen's chaplain, however, threw caution to the winds with his support of Elizabeth Barton and earned himself an attainder.

In the Tower, Elizabeth's confidence began to crack. The suddenness of the arrest and the grim condition of her prison cell, despite Cromwell's orders of treating her as a 'high-born' lady, contributed to her loss of composure and she finally admitted that she had not been entirely truthful about her visions and proclamations. She said that those dire predictions of doom in the life of the king and her other visions were all a figment of her imagination.

However, Elizabeth was not going down without a fight. When her supporter, Thomas Gold, visited her at the Tower, she mentioned to him that she was forced to say that she had faked her visions. She asked him to convey the same to her supporters and Thomas Gold's brother, Henry Gold, wrote to Dr Bocking to stand by Elizabeth's revelations.

However, time was running out for the Holy Maid of Kent. The men who had first examined her, Dr Edward Bocking and William Hadley, were arrested and their houses were searched. Certain damning papers were found in the possession of Dr Bocking, but the search at Hadley's house revealed nothing that could link him to this matter. Both men were sent to Cromwell in London while another one of Elizabeth's supporters, Richard Masters, was arrested the next day. By the end of September 1533 Edward Thwaites was apprehended as well. Thwaites' papers, wherein he had written a flowery and glowing account of Elizabeth and her visions along with Dr Bocking's book and papers, were burned immediately.

In November 1533 King Henry VIII called upon his council along with the principal judges in England and many other eminent English nobles to discuss the case of the Holy Maid of Kent. However, the charge of treason could not be pinned on her as she had spoken to the king directly of all the things that she was accused of promulgating.

Although her pluckiness saved her momentarily, she was to be soon undone by her own words. Towards the end of the third day of the meeting, Elizabeth, along with her supporters, Dr Bocking and Henry

Gold, were summoned to the elite council. On learning that Elizabeth had 'confessed' to Gold that her confession was false, the council wished to hear from the lady herself that even her last proclamation was untrue.

Much to Dr Bocking and Henry Gold's anger, Elizabeth declared that she was 'the falsest woman that ever God gave life unto' and dissolved into tears. A smug Cromwell then took over and enlightened the council of the maid's misdeeds, claiming that she meant to rally the public against the king through her visions and proclamations. Rumours circulated in London that Elizabeth not only confessed to treachery but also to the more serious charge of heresy.

The public, who had once revered Elizabeth, now shunned her. The monks of Dr Bocking's monastery wrote a letter to the king asking for forgiveness for their 'miserable brother's' dereliction, even going to the extent of offering money to obtain the king's forgiveness.

The Marchioness of Exeter, too, gave up on Elizabeth, writing an obsequious letter to King Henry VIII, denouncing her as 'most unworthy, subtle and deceivable' woman.[7]

The game was finally up for Elizabeth Barton. By 16 November 1533 she confessed to being a traitor and a heretic. With nearly all her erstwhile supporters now distancing themselves from her, she was backed into a corner and had no way out.

By January 1534 Elizabeth and thirteen of her supporters were implicated and accused of treason. A bill of attainder was passed against them. It is interesting to note that Sir Thomas More and Bishop John Fisher were amongst the arrested men. More escaped punishment by producing a letter in which he warned Elizabeth to stay away and not meddle into state affairs. Bishop Fisher was imprisoned along with five others, and Elizabeth, along with two Franciscan monks, Richard Risby and Hugh Rich, and her two erstwhile ardent supporters, Edward Bocking and Richard Masters, were sentenced to death. Elizabeth was subjected to a public humiliation when she was forced to confess her wrongdoings in front of a crowd of 2,000 people at St Paul's Cross and was taken around the country to repeat the same.

She was then dragged to Tyburn, the infamous execution site, and hanged until her life was snuffed out of her. Further humiliation and degradation waited for Elizabeth as her head was chopped off and impaled on a spike at London Bridge.

One can easily dismiss Elizabeth as a foolish maid who played a joke on the country and paid for it with her life. In an age where even imagining the death of the monarch was considered treason, Elizabeth had actually voiced her opinion on matters of state and whether she was in a trance or not is beside the point. The Tudor age did not welcome women with a voice of their own, whether they were intentional or masked behind divine voices, and such women ended up paying a heavy price for their 'sins'.

Elizabeth Barton is buried at the Greyfriars Church at Newgate. One can also visit the ruins of the little chapel at Aldington, Kent, which overlooks Romney Marsh. While there, spare a thought for the poor servant girl turned nun who went down in the annals of history as the only woman who suffered the ignominy to have her head impaled at London Bridge.

8

Katheryn Howard

Sunday, 12 February 1542, Tower of London

The guards at the Tower stood flummoxed at the morbidly strange request by the prisoner. Scheduled to be beheaded the next day, young Katheryn Howard, former Queen of England, had asked for the execution block to be brought to her cell so that she could 'practise' laying her head upon it. She wanted to appear dignified on the scaffold, she said to her guards, and not lose her nerve at the final moment.

This was perhaps not out of character for a girl who, though still a teenager, had experienced a tumultuous and tragic life. Famously touted as 'the rose without a thorn' by her husband, the ageing King Henry VIII, Katheryn's reign as the Queen of England was a brief one, second only in brevity to her predecessor and former mistress, Anne of Cleves.

A vivacious personality who was but a mere pawn in the cut-throat world of the Tudor court, Katheryn was thrust mercilessly into the life of King Henry VIII – who was well into his dotage – and just as easily disposed of when her seemingly scandalous past came to light. But was she really guilty of the crimes she was alleged to have committed? Or was she just in the wrong place at the wrong time, and in the company of the wrong people?

The Howards: A History

Sola Virtus Invicta (Only Virtue Unconquered)[1]

The Howard family are sometimes aggrandised as a noble family of yore who were said to have been more aristocratic than the Tudors themselves. We can safely say that they were a noble family belonging to the higher echelons of the society in Norfolk – much like their neighbours, the

Pastons – who enhanced their financial and social standing through their instinct for self-survival and advantageous marital unions.

The Howards traced their ancestry back to Robert Howard (1385-1436) of Tendring who married Margaret de Mowbray (1388-1459) who was a descendant of Thomas de Brotherton, Edward I's son by his first marriage to Eleanor of Castile. Thomas was on good terms with his half-brother, Edward II, who granted him the earldom of Norfolk, a title that was heritable through the female line. Due to this clause, the title of Earl of Norfolk passed on to Margaret de Mowbray's son, John Howard (1425-1485).

John Howard was an affluent gentleman from Norfolk, who, being a supporter of the Yorkists, had several altercations with the de la Poles, Dukes of Suffolk, who were staunch Lancastrians. Sir John was a firm supporter of Edward IV, and later of Richard III, who helped restore the earldom of Norfolk to the Howards from Anne Mowbray, the child bride of Richard, Duke of York, Edward IV's son, whom we also know as one of the Princes in the Tower. Sir John first married Katherine Moleyns, with whom he had six children, and was later married to Margaret Chedworth who bore him a daughter.

Sir John extended his loyalty to King Richard III right till his monarch's end at Bosworth, where it is believed that the words 'Jack of Norfolk, be not too bold, for Dickon thy Master is bought and sold'[2] were pinned in his tent. He probably did not pay any attention to these words of caution as he found himself dead with his king on the battlefield. His son, Thomas Howard, Earl of Surrey, was badly wounded but was saved by his opponent, Sir Gilbert Talbot, who carried him off the battlefield instead of killing him.

Thomas Howard swore loyalty to King Henry VII after a brief stint in the Tower of London, and proved it by declining an opportunity to escape during the rebellion of Lambert Simnel in 1487. Pleased with this and wanting to start his reign on a positive note, King Henry VII restored the earldom of Surrey and sent him to subdue a rebellion in Yorkshire. He also made Thomas Howard lieutenant of the North of England.

By 1501 he was a part of Henry VII's Privy Council and he, along with Richard Foxe, Bishop of Winchester and Lord Privy Seal, and William Warham, Archbishop of Canterbury and Lord Chancellor, formed an 'executive triumvirate' closest to the king. He was also associated with the negotiations of the marriage between Katherine of Aragon and Arthur, Prince of Wales.

Thomas Howard, Earl of Surrey, repaid this trust shown to him by his king by leading a force against James IV of Scotland when he invaded and ravaged Norham Castle. James challenged him to a one-on-one combat which Surrey declined stating that, being just an emissary for his king, Henry VII, it would be improper to duel with another king.

Whether this won over either monarch is not known, but later, when relations between England and Scotland took a turn for the better, Surrey was one of the English mediators of the Treaty of Perpetual Peace which was sealed with the marriage of James with Henry VII's daughter, Margaret Tudor in 1503. Henry VII, ever mindful of his public image, selected Surrey and his countess to lead the princess's train of ladies as they journeyed through the north-east on their way to Edinburgh.

Surrey managed to charm James as well, as Margaret wrote to her father, stating that the nobleman was always seen in the company of the Scottish king. When he decided to return to his native land, he was laden with precious gifts and was full of effusive praise for James.

Surrey was succeeded by his son, Sir Thomas Howard, and his second son, Sir Edward, was a favourite of King Henry VIII. Sir Edward was accorded the honour of wearing King Henry VII's armour at the latter's funeral. The two Howard brothers are also remembered for their battle, and subsequent defeat, of Sir Andrew Barton, a Scottish seafarer turned pirate.

Surrey, however, wasn't faring too well. His appeal to maintain peace with France was met with fierce criticism from the royal court and eventually it was quashed when the English navy invaded in 1512. His own son, Sir Edward, was appointed Admiral in command of a fleet of eighteen ships. The navy, under Sir Edward's command, won a decisive victory off Brest, but lost one of King Henry VIII's closest companions, Sir Anthony Knyvet.

In 1513 Henry VIII personally decided to attack France, leaving Surrey and his son, Sir Thomas, behind to guard the north and support Queen Katharine of Aragon, who was the regent in Henry's absence.

This turned out to be Surrey's moment of glory as the English army, led by Queen Katharine, won a rousing victory against Scotland at Flodden, where King James IV was killed. Surrey used his knowledge of James' character to help the English best him on the battlefield.

To honour him for this victory, the dukedom of Norfolk was restored to him with Surrey now becoming the 2nd Duke of Norfolk. The earldom of Surrey was now inherited by his eldest son, Sir Thomas. However, Sir

Edward wasn't so lucky. In order to avenge Sir Anthony Knyvet's death at Brest, he led an imprudent mission against the French fleet and was killed in the attempt.

In the meantime, Sir Thomas's family was growing by leaps and bounds with the Earl of Surrey having twenty-one children from his two wives. The 2nd Duke of Norfolk, given his high social standing, arranged advantageous marriages for his numerous offspring with prestigious families such as the Boleyns, Carews, Stanleys and many more, resulting in a vast and somewhat confusing family tree.

Amongst his vast brood, the two marriages that stand out are that of his eldest son, Sir Thomas, who first married Anne of York, sister to Queen Elizabeth of York, and then Elizabeth Stafford, the daughter of Edward Stafford, 2nd Duke of Buckingham, and of his eldest daughter, Elizabeth Howard, who married Sir Thomas Boleyn, a courtier whose star was on the rise in the court of Henry VIII. Elizabeth produced three surviving children, Mary, Anne and George, who would go on to become famous (or rather, infamous) in history.

The new Earl of Surrey and Elizabeth Stafford, seemingly in love despite a twenty-five year age gap, produced four surviving children: Katherine, Henry, Mary and Thomas.

With Sir Edward dead, Norfolk's younger son, Lord Edmund, was made the Admiral. He married a widow, Joyce or Jocasta Culpeper, and produced, apart from his many children and stepchildren, Katheryn Howard, the fifth wife and queen of Henry VIII.

Katheryn Howard's Early Life

For many years, the date of Katheryn Howard's birth varied from anywhere between 1521 to 1527. However, new research by historian and Katheryn's biographer, Gareth Russell, the author of *Young and Damned and Fair*, concludes that she was probably born in the year 1522 or 1523, meaning that she would have been eighteen when she first came to the court of King Henry VIII[3]. Katheryn, being the fifth child of an inconsequential courtier, wasn't important enough to have her birth recorded.

Katheryn's father, Edmund, born in 1478, wasn't, as Conor Byrne describes in his *Katherine Howard: A New History*[4], 'comparatively less successful in his ability to equal, or surpass his eldest brother's achievements at court and his closeness to the king on which much depended in the way of attaining prestige and preferment.' He took part in the jousts commemorating the birth of a son, albeit a short-lived one, to King Henry. Despite the fact that he led a force of 1,500 men from Cheshire, Yorkshire and Lancashire at the Battle of Flodden Field in 1513, Edmund could never make it big in the royal court of King Henry VIII and his economic woes plagued him throughout his life. His situation briefly took a turn for the better when he was appointed the Comptroller of Calais in 1513, presumably through the influence of his niece, Queen Anne Boleyn. However, King Henry VIII's feelings towards him hadn't changed one bit and this was evident in his appointment as a mayor of Calais by the assembly in 1537, only for the position to be revoked by Thomas Cromwell Lord Privy Seal.

Edmund Howard married Joyce or Jocasta Culpeper, daughter of Sir Henry Culpeper of Oxen Hoath, Kent, in 1515. Previously married to Ralph Leigh at the tender age of twelve, Joyce brought a considerable amount of wealth, along with five children – John, Ralph, Isabel, Joyce and Margaret – into her marriage with Edmund Howard. She bore Edmund six children: Henry, Charles (Sir Charles Howard), George (Sir George Howard), Margaret Howard, Katheryn (future Queen Consort of England) and Mary.

Joyce died sometime between 1527 and 1528, probably due to childbed fever. Edmund's financial woes, already on the edge due to fact that he supported his stepchildren along with his own, compelled him to approach Cardinal Thomas Wolsey for aid. Immediately after Joyce's death, Edmund married again, this time to Dorothy, widow of Sir William Uvedale of Wickham. This marriage brought in a little money and may have been instrumental in Edmund's appointment to the commission of peace for Wickham. Edmund married for the third time after Dorothy's death, this time to Margaret Jennings, daughter of the Mundys of Markeaton Hall in Derbyshire.

Meanwhile, Katheryn and her siblings were most likely being brought up by their stepmother at Oxen Hoath as their father served the king in Calais. Some believe that she lived with her maternal aunts either at Oxen Hoath or Teston, but this arrangement seems a little unlikely. It is not known whether Edmund's children and stepchildren (from Joyce's previous marriage) shared a warm relation with Dorothy and Margaret or not.

Katheryn joined the household of her stepgrandmother Agnes Tilney, Dowager Duchess of Norfolk, at Chesworth in Horsham approximately by 1531 as her father was now in too dire a financial situation to help his children live together as a family. Also, Edmund may have wanted his daughter to receive quality education and prepare her for a career in the royal court. The dowager duchess did exactly this for Katheryn and a few more grandchildren.

Her education at the duchess's household comprised of basic household skills, music and dancing. She may have been made aware of the importance of maintaining good and chaste behaviour at her stepgrandmother's household so as not to bring disgrace and dishonour to the esteemed name of the Howards. She must have also been told about the various women in her family who upheld the family honour with their virtuous behaviour and their sense of duty.

Women in the medieval era who used their feminine charms and guile to satisfy their desires were described as lascivious. However, women belonging to the most influential noble families were able to play a huge part in advancing their families' status and fortune by using their intelligence, knowledge and wisdom. Agnes Tilney, the Dowager Duchess of Norfolk and second wife of the Earl of Surrey, took the status of the Howard family to new heights when she was appointed godmother to Princess Mary. She was also the chief lady of the queen's household and second only to Mary Tudor, Queen of France and the sister of Henry VIII. She managed her time effectively between her houses at Horsham and Lambeth, and also attended to her duties at the royal court. The Howard family star rose to its zenith when their kinswoman, Anne Boleyn, ascended the throne of England, though just three years later her spectacular fall from grace undermined the Boleyn and Howard names for quite a long time.

The various duties of the dowager duchess resulted in a negligent approach towards the girls who were boarding with her. Her lax attitude towards them resulted in the girls indulging in sexual escapades nearly every night. The results of these misdemeanours had far reaching consequences for the Howard family, as we will see further in the chapter.

Meanwhile at the court of King Henry VIII, her cousin, Anne Boleyn, was rapidly falling from grace with her erstwhile allies, the Duke of Norfolk and Thomas Cromwell, now turning into her sworn enemies. The faction working against her were doing their best to bring her down and they finally did so with a stunning climax of Jane Parker, Lady

Rochford and the wife of George Boleyn, Anne's brother, providing evidence which implicated her husband and sister-in-law, sending them to the executioner's block.

What Katheryn thought of this entire episode, or whether she was even aware of it and its implications, are not known. While Anne's life story was inching towards its gruesome end, Katheryn was making her foray into the adult world when she began her music lessons. Lessons such as music, household management, needlework, etc., were instrumental in young girls making respectable marriages and helping in the effective running of the household. In Katheryn's case, her family hoped to find her a place in the royal court as a gentlewoman.

The Howards were great manipulators and rose high in the court as well as in the favour of King Henry VIII by building and maintaining a network of various powerful people, solicitating their patronages whenever necessary. Women of the Howard family also played a major role in the ever-changing world of court politics by entering into various advantageous martial bonds with some of the most influential families in the land. Many of the Howard men inherited vast lands and estates through their wives and went on to accrue immense wealth.

It was fairly easy for the Howard women to assume a position in the queen's household, with their kinswoman, Elizabeth Boleyn née Howard going on to work in the household of Katharine of Aragon. Katheryn Howard had many such women in her family to look up to.

The Howards gained a massive advantage in their influence in the court of Henry VIII when Anne Boleyn, daughter of Elizabeth Howard Boleyn, caught the eye of the king and went on to become the Queen of England, ousting Katharine of Aragon. It is not known what Katharine thought of her cousin ascending upon the throne of England, but we may assume that she may have been filled with pride on seeing the Howard star rise. Neither is it known what her feelings were over Anne's trial and subsequent execution, but it is highly unlikely that she was worried about any backlash she might have had to face due to the brutal character assassination of her royal cousin.

Her kinsman, the Duke of Norfolk, was deeply saddened at his diminishing influence over the king following Anne Boleyn's downfall. Once an extremely influential personality at court who saw the rise of his niece at the cost of eminent men like Bishop John Fisher and Sir Thomas More, he was forced to give evidence against the very same niece whom he helped elevate to the throne of England.

Whether there was any talk about Katheryn joining her royal cousin's household is not known. However, it is an unlikely prospect as by the time Katheryn came to the appropriate age to make her court debut, Queen Anne's star was already on the wane. Her once powerful uncle would not have had enough influence to secure a place in the court for a seemingly inconsequential family member. Neither would he have wanted to antagonise the king and Cromwell further.

Meanwhile, Katheryn continued to live at her stepgrandmother's house. For this very purpose, the dowager duchess arranged for her to have regular music sessions with one of her neighbours, Henry Manox. Manox was the younger son of George Manox of Giffords, who may have been relatives of the duchess. It seemed like a normal arrangement for a girl of her age who was destined for a career as a lady-in-waiting or a maid-of-honour. The surviving court indictments against Katheryn during her downfall suggest that nothing was what it seemed between the young girl and the piano teacher. We must keep in mind, however, that court indictments in that era were often presented in a way to suit the interests of the defamers instead of the victims. Therefore, it is not an easy task to come to a definite conclusion of such events by just studying the court indictments. In Katheryn's case, people at that time would have termed her as a sexual deviant while today we would view her as a victim of sexual abuse and even emotional blackmailing as we will see in her tryst with Francis Dereham. Whether Katheryn was a willing participant or not, Manox certainly took a huge risk in committing this sexual perfidy with a member of the prestigious Howard family; a family that was far above his own in status.

Musical ability was highly prized in the Tudor court. Anne Boleyn, Katheryn's cousin, was believed to be an accomplished musician and a talented lute player. Henry Manox was expected to train Katheryn not only to play the piano but also the virginals and the lute. It is believed that she not only had a musical ear but also was a good dancer.

It is difficult to say whether Manox taught music to Katheryn's companions or not. Evidence suggests that she was the only person in the household to be under his tutelage. Through this, we can assume that her stepgrandmother thought highly of her and her prospects at the royal court.

An uncomfortable exchange between Manox and Katheryn gives us a hint that the latter was an unwilling participant in this whole affair. Manox told the then twelve-year-old Katheryn to allow him 'to perceive by some token' that she loved him, to which she replied: 'What token should I show you? I will never be taught with you and able to marry me you be not.'

This conversation between the music teacher and his young student, with whom he was clearly besotted, shows that Katheryn was fearful about besmirching her and her family's reputation. She also may have been extra careful about protecting her family's honour after the fall of her cousins, Anne and George Boleyn. However, as time passed and Anne became but a distant memory, she may have become less cautious about the same as she grew older as we will see soon.

The only person to protest against Manox's behaviour was Mary Lascelles. She is reported to have told him: 'Man what mean thou to play the fool of this fashion […] know not thou that if my lady of Norfolk knew of the love betwixt thee and Mistress Howard, she will undo thee.'[5] This was clearly a warning not to play around with the reputation of the dowager duchess and her family.

However, Manox seemed to be confident about Katheryn's reciprocation of his love and is recorded in the indictments against her to have said: 'I know her well enough […] she [Katheryn] hath said to me that I shall have her maidenhead though it be painful to her, not doubting but I will be good to her hereafter.' This indictment, one of the many contributing to Katheryn's downfall and eventual execution, clearly shows Manox's arrogance but does not clearly portray Katheryn's absolute willingness to participate in his plans.

Clearly fearful of her and her illustrious family's reputation, Katheryn is said to have allowed Manox to caress her, maybe under duress as Manox kept insisting on it, but stopped him from proceeding any further. Manox, too, is said to have mentioned that he never knew Katheryn carnally.

The dowager duchess, at some point of time, may have had an inkling about the going-ons between Manox and Katheryn. This may be the reason for the abrupt termination of Manox's services in the Howard household. Interestingly, Manox is said to have then married Margaret Munday, widow of Katheryn's father, Edmund.

The indictments, sadly, were drawn up in a manner which made Katheryn look like a promiscuous young woman throwing herself on Manox whereas that was hardly the case. Mary Lascelles, despite her later actions, was just trying to protect Katheryn's reputation at that time, as Manox, who exerted a certain level of control over his student, tried to manipulate the situation by claiming to be so much in love with Katheryn that he was not in control of his actions. Perhaps he had hoped to marry her and make a foray into the royal court and the nobility through the Howards.

Katheryn was at a vulnerable age, an age at which accusations of licentiousness were often levelled at girls in a similar situation. Moreover, the dowager duchess' lack of supervision did not help matters either. She, along with Mary Lascelles, may have tried to dissuade Manox, but already aware of the Howards' damaged reputation at the royal court due to the Anne Boleyn episode, it is entirely possible that Manox may have blackmailed Katheryn into the affair.

Katheryn's affair with Francis Dereham

While Katheryn was still in a relationship with Henry Manox, or immediately after, she met the dashing Francis Dereham at Lambeth. Dereham, who was already in a relationship with Joan Bulmer, one of the dowager duchess' wards, was distantly related to the Howards. Within no time, his attentions were diverted to the fourteen-year-old Katheryn.

Francis Dereham was descended from Nicholas de Dereham and was the Duchess of Norfolk's first cousin once removed from his maternal grandmother's side. He was the second son of Thomas Dereham of Crimplesham and was born between 1506 and 1509. That makes him between twenty-nine to thirty-two when he first met Katheryn in 1538.

Being a second son, there was little to no chance of Francis inheriting any of his family's wealth, but he owned some lands in Norfolk from which he generated an income. He relied on his service to his more illustrious family members to further his career, probably hoping for a position in the royal court. His close connection with the duchess ensured him a position in her household as an usher.

His position in the household meant that he had to supervise the duchess' wards as they went about their duties. Katheryn was required to wait on the duchess and accompany her to chapel every morning. Afterwards, Katheryn would retire till suppertime when she was required to wait on the duchess and, maybe, some visitors. Dereham would be present to notify Katheryn and the other women of the household of the time and place to attend to the duchess. This meant that Dereham was almost always in company with Katheryn and the other women.

The set-up at the duchess' house in Norfolk, and at Chesworth Park (Horsham), was almost the same, with the duchess' wards sleeping in a dormitory, two of them sharing a bed. The doors were locked every night and the key was in the duchess' possession.

Dereham, along with a man he befriended at the Duchess of Norfolk's household by the name of Edward Waldegrave, and a few other men, found ways to sneak into the girls' dormitory every night, despite the keys being in the duchess' bedchamber. He also managed to draw up a plan to escape lest the duchess discover him and his companions in the company of the girls in her keeping.

Dereham soon got tired of Joan and was on the lookout for a new paramour. He was now attracted to Katheryn though she was quite disinterested in him and found his ways lewd and ignorant. Dereham, however, was undeterred. He was determined to win her 'by many persuasions' and nothing that Katheryn would say or do would make him give up on her. He also enjoyed lording over her given her low position in the household. It is not known but quite likely that Dereham may have forced himself on Katheryn using the power of his position in the household and his influential extended family.

Although she may have found the entire situation stifling, Katheryn was left with very little choice other than to reconcile herself with Dereham's unwanted attention. The news of the affair was soon common knowledge in the household. Katheryn's fellow housemate Malyn Tilney remarked that she often came across Dereham sharing a bed with Katheryn and placing his hands on her 'privy place'. Joan Bulmer, too, said that Dereham visited the dormitory to meet Katheryn between four or five 'o clock in the morning. Many more housemates and men reported to seeing Dereham visit Katheryn, sometimes even taking her by surprise by putting his privates in her hands.

It is believed, on the basis of a quote by Katheryn ('a woman might meddle with a man and yet conceive no child unless she would for herself,')[6] that she was aware of contraception. Various methods to prevent an unwanted pregnancy such as sponges, herbs and astringent solutions were known to her and she may have used some of these methods during her trysts with Dereham.

The news of Katheryn's affair with Dereham now spread outside the Duchess of Norfolk's household. Katheryn's fellow housemates Alice Wilkes and Mary Lascelles spoke about her behaviour and were unable to sympathise with her. Mary Lascelles had previously warned Katheryn during her affair with Henry Manox, but her advice fell on deaf ears as Katheryn allegedly repeated the same mistake Mary had warned her against. With no love lost for Katheryn, Mary advised Alice to stay out of the matter.

Katheryn must have eventually fallen in love with Francis Dereham as they began referring to each other as husband and wife. Katheryn, many believe, was quite unaware of the repercussions such a step would have even at that time, although Dereham would have been aware of the same. However, she had no idea that by this stage she and Dereham had entered into a contract of marriage. Apart from referring to each other as spouses, they had consummated the union which made the betrothal even more binding. She even took the liberty of borrowing money from Dereham to buy herself little trinkets and clothes promising to pay it back although Dereham considered it a gift to his beloved.

The Duchess of Norfolk, although aware of Dereham's flirtatious nature, couldn't have known about her niece's liaisons with him. She was away from her home at the royal court leaving the day-to-day management of the household to a Mrs Emmet.

The couple's cover was blown by Katheryn's erstwhile lover, Henry Manox, who watched the growing affection between Katheryn and Dereham with jealous interest. He asked around for details, and not getting a satisfactory response, wrote an anonymous letter to the duchess. The letter stated:

> Your Grace,
> It shall be meet you take good heed to your gentlewomen for if it shall like you half an hour after you shall be a bed to rise suddenly and visit their chamber you shall see that which shall displease you. But if you make any body of counsel you shall be deceived. Make them fewer your secretary.[7]

In an eerie prelude to future events in Katheryn's life, Manox left the letter in the duchess' pew at Lambeth Church. It is believed that Dereham had managed to anger Manox sometime earlier and he was now exacting his revenge. However, because he assumed that the duchess would know the names of the offending parties, he had failed to name them, and his letter did not have the desired effect that he had hoped for.

The duchess instead used the letter as a warning to Mrs Emmet whom she felt was growing rather lax of her charges and duties. She also warned her wards to abstain from any wrongdoings and said that she intended to be more vigilant from then on.

The appearance of the letter sent Katheryn into a panic. She, quite rightly, assumed that the letter implicated her and Dereham and managed to steal the letter from the duchess' bedchamber. She showed it to Dereham who, correctly, suspected Manox to be behind it. He copied out the letter and placed the original back into the duchess' custody.

Dereham confronted Manox, calling him a knave and saying that he neither loved himself nor Katheryn. Katheryn's uncle, Lord William, also threatened Manox and his wife with dire consequences until he left England for France in 1541.

In the meantime, the Duchess of Norfolk kept a closer watch on her wards and on one occasion caught Dereham and Katheryn embracing and kissing each other. The duchess flew into a rage and both received a thrashing, along with Joan Bulmer who just happened to be there.

Despite their declarations of undying love and referring to each other as husband and wife, the affair between Dereham and Katheryn did not last long. Clearly, as we will see later, Katheryn did not take the unwitting betrothal seriously enough, claiming that she was forced into it all along.

Meanwhile back in London, the court of King Henry VIII was plunged into mourning as Queen Jane Seymour died twelve days after giving birth to the much longed for heir, Prince Edward. Barely had she gone cold in her grave, talks of a new marriage for the king were underway and the name of the German Anne of Cleves came up as a potential bride.

For Henry, the physical appearance of his prospective queen was extremely important. While marriage talks were underway, Henry dispatched his court painter, Hans Holbein Jr, to Cleves to paint a likeness of the duke's two sisters, despite his reluctance.

When Holbein returned and presented his paintings to the king, who was on progress at Grafton, the latter liked what he saw and sent his ambassadors to compel the Duke of Cleves into drawing up a marriage treaty. A minor glitch in the negotiations – Anne being precontracted to the Duke of Lorraine[8] – was soon overcome and preparations were underway to bring King Henry VIII's fourth wife and queen to England.

Almost immediately, the positions for the queen's household were opened and many young girls vied for a suitable placement. Some of the women who had served Queen Jane simply transferred to the new household and may have served as a mentor to the new entrants.

Katheryn was now at the perfect age to begin her career at the royal court. She must certainly have been endorsed by her powerful Howard kinsmen to find her name right at the top of the list of the new recruits for the queen's household.

However, the king had the final say in recruiting the women for his new queen's household. Henry needed the English ladies to serve the queen from the moment she set foot in England, which is why he personally interviewed the potential candidates. Katheryn must have impressed Henry sufficiently to secure a place in Queen Anne's household. However, whether Henry fell in love with Katheryn during the interview cannot be determined for certain. Neither did her Howard relatives use her as a bait for the king at that time.

Along with Katheryn, Catherine Carey, Mary Boleyn's daughter, and Mary Norris, the daughter of the late Sir Henry Norris, too found employment in the queen's household.

Katheryn eagerly looked forward to her life at the royal court. However, Dereham did not take the news of her employment well and was disheartened at the thought of her going away. He was no doubt afraid that she might catch the eye of someone at court or her powerful relatives might try to marry her off to a potential suitor once she entered court.

By this time, Katheryn, excited at the prospect of a glittering court life, was tiring of Dereham's possessiveness. Dereham tried to emotionally blackmail her into staying back but Katheryn would have none of it and brusquely told him to do as he wished.

Following Katheryn's departure Dereham, too, quit the Duchess of Norfolk's household and left Lambeth. The duchess understood his predicament and allowed him to leave. Before doing so he gave Katheryn a purse of 100 pounds for safekeeping adding that if something were to happen to him, she was to keep that money. When Katheryn asked about his plans, Dereham remained deliberately vague.

With Dereham out of the way, Katheryn was filled with an ambitious excitement for her new life. She was assigned a room to stay, basic provisions, a daily allowance for food and an annual stipend of 10 pounds. She saved up her money to reimburse Dereham for the money that he had lent her to buy clothes and various trinkets.

Already having served at a noblewoman's house at Horsham and Lambeth, Katheryn applied her knowledge at the queen's household. She found out that she was more than adept in managing household affairs.

However, Henry's interest in Anne did not last long. A mere seven months into his new marriage he claimed that he did not find his new wife desirable and that she emitted foul odours. He quickly had the marriage annulled and bestowed the rather unusual title of The King's Beloved Sister onto Anne of Cleves.

King Henry VIII's roving eye soon fell on Katheryn. It is not known whether he fell in love with her before the annulment of his marriage to Anne of Cleves or after. Although the match was frowned upon – Henry being old enough to be Katheryn's grandfather – they carried on with their courtship. It is hard to tell whether Katheryn ever had any genuine feelings for Henry, who was at that time fat, ill and stinking due to the pus from his injured leg.

The Fall of Thomas Cromwell

On 18 April 1540 Henry granted Cromwell the earldom of Essex and the senior court office of Lord Great Chamberlain. Despite these signs of royal favour, Cromwell's tenure as the king's chief minister was nearing its end. The king's anger at being compelled to marry Anne of Cleves was the opportunity Cromwell's conservative opponents, most notably the Duke of Norfolk, were waiting for.

During 1536 Cromwell had proved to be an agile political survivor. However, the gradual slide towards Protestantism at home and the king's ill-starred marriage to Anne of Cleves, which Cromwell engineered in January 1540, proved costly. Many believed that Hans Holbein contributed to Cromwell's downfall as he had painted a very flattering portrait of Anne which may have deceived the king. When Henry finally met her, he was reportedly shocked by her plain appearance. Cromwell had passed on to Henry some exaggerated claims about Anne's beauty.

Initially, Cromwell was one of only two courtiers with whom the king confided that he had been unable to consummate the union, the other one being Lord High Admiral Southampton, who had escorted Anne from Calais. When Henry's humiliation became common knowledge, Southampton, or maybe Edmund Bonner, Bishop of London, made sure that Cromwell was blamed for the indiscretion. Both men were erstwhile friends of Cromwell and their self-serving loyalty indicated that the minister's position was already known to be weakening.

To add to Cromwell's difficulties, a proposed alliance between the French and the Holy Roman Emperor failed to materialise, leading to events that rendered the support from the Duke of Cleves unnecessary. King Henry VIII was now in a marriage that was not only loveless but now also meaningless. Cromwell was now in a disadvantageous position and his enemies swooped in like vultures. Stephen Gardiner, the Bishop of Winchester, and Thomas Howard, Duke of Norfolk, saw an opportunity to push Norfolk's niece, Katheryn, into the forefront to be the king's new mistress, and maybe one day, his wife and queen.

Thomas Cromwell was arrested on 10 June 1540 and accused of treason, amongst various other charges. His enemies had a field day humiliating him and even tore off his Order of the Garter. Initially defiant, he was quickly overpowered and carted off unceremoniously to the Tower of London. A Bill of Attainder was drawn up, listing many of his crimes, some of which included working towards personal gain, corruption, and supporting Anabaptists. His properties and titles were forfeited but King Henry VIII postponed his execution till the annulment with Anne of Cleves was settled. While imprisoned, Cromwell wrote a pitiful letter to the king pleading for mercy.

Thomas Cromwell was denied a fair trial and condemned to death. He was beheaded – a gruesome one where three blows were needed to sever his head – on Tower Hill on 28 July 1540, the same day that Henry married Katheryn at Oatlands Palace. Cromwell's head was then put on a spike at London Bridge. Henry regretted the execution later in life and blamed his ministers for bringing about the ruination of his favourite minister.[9]

Katheryn as Queen

Katheryn's wedding wasn't a particularly ostentatious one. It was conducted in private at Oatlands Palace in Weybridge, without the customary preceding and succeeding celebrations. Henry then visited his former wife and now sister, Anne of Cleves, on 6 August to see if she was happy and also to break the news of his new marriage.

A former lady-in-waiting and now Queen of England, Katheryn had a retinue of people in her household to cater for her. Many of them had been transferred from Anne of Cleves' household, along with some new but familiar faces such as her half-sister Isabel and her husband, Sir

Above: Pontefract Castle circa 1640. (Wikimedia Commons)

Right: Thomas Howard, Duke of Norfolk by Hans Holbein Jr. Uncle of both Queen Anne Boleyn and Queen Kateryn Howard. (Wikimedia Commons)

Above: An Illustration of Pilgrimage of Grace. (Wikimedia Commons)

Below: Tower of London. (Wikimedia Commons)

Right: Cardinal Reginald Pole from the National Portrait Gallery. (Wikimedia Commons)

Below: Windsor Castle, Henry VIII gate. (Wikimedia Commons)

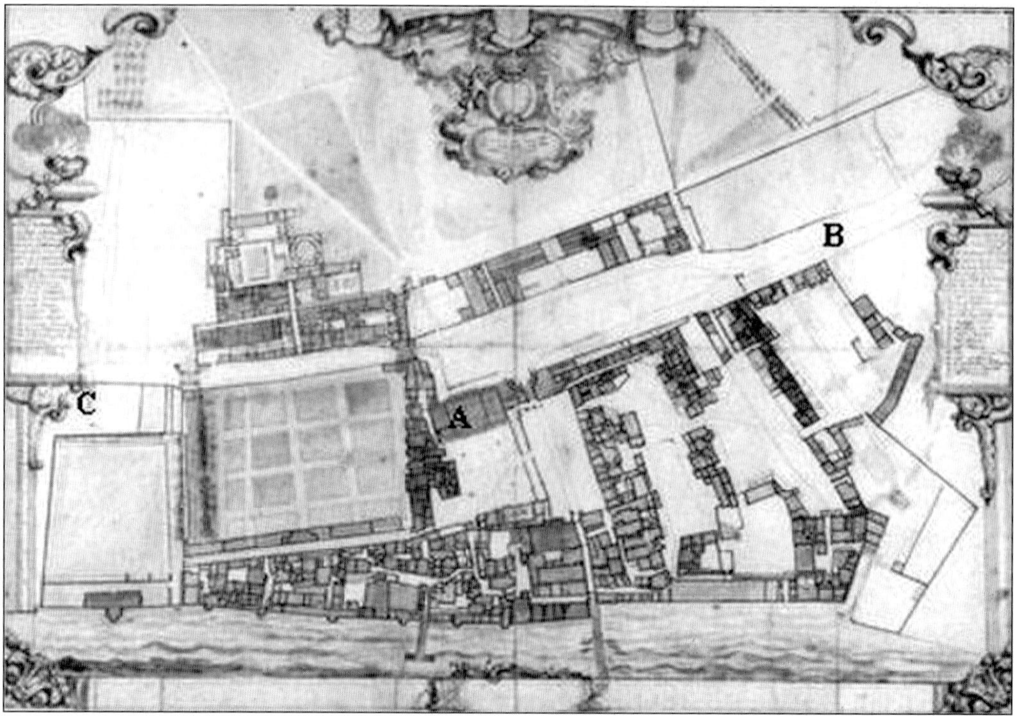

Above: Plan of Whitehall Palace. (Wikimedia Commons)

Below: All Saints Church at Romney Marsh, Kent. (Wikimedia Commons)

Illustration of the torture of Anne Askew by Sir Thomas Wriothesley and Sir Richard Rich. (Wikimedia Commons)

William the Conqueror. (Wikimedia Commons)

Left: A disputed painting said to be of Queen Kateryn Howard by Hans Holbein Jr. (Wikimedia Commons)

Below: Resting place of King Henry VIII and Queen Jane Seymour at St George's Chapel, Windsor Castle. (Wikimedia Commons)

Right: An illustration supposedly showing Elizabeth Barton having one of her visions. (Wikimedia Commons)

Below: Hever Castle in Kent. The Boleyn residence. (Wikimedia Commons)

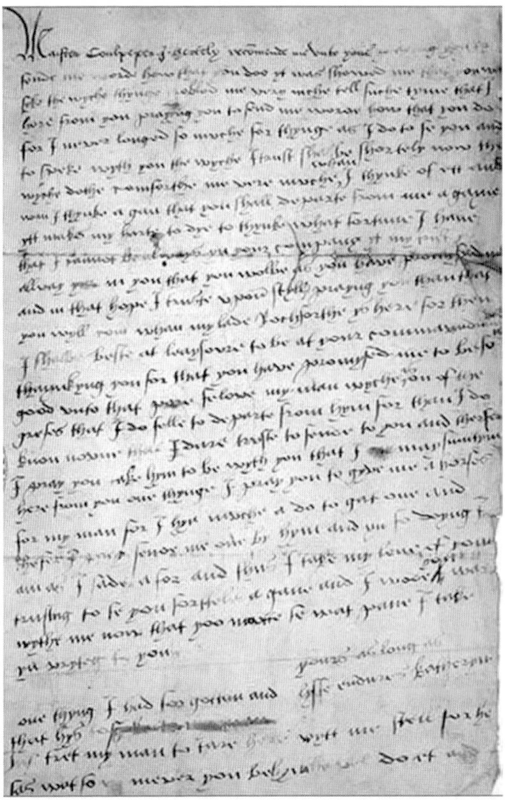

Above: The site of the scaffold at Tower Hill in the Tower of London where the likes of Anne Boleyn, Sir Thomas More and many eminent people were executed. (Wikimedia Commons)

Left: A letter supposedly written by Queen Kateryn Howard to Thomas Culpeper. (Wikimedia Commons)

Queen Anne Boleyn. (Wikimedia Commons)

A portrait of Anne Askew by Hans Eworth. (Wikimedia Commons)

Ruins of Coldharbour Gate. (Wikimedia Commons)

Framlingham Castle, birthplace of Margaret Pole, Countess of Salisbury. (Wikimedia Commons)

Above: An illustration of the execution of Margaret Pole, Countess of Salisbury. (Wikimedia Commons)

Left: Portrait supposedly of Margaret Pole, Countess of Salisbury. (Wikimedia Commons)

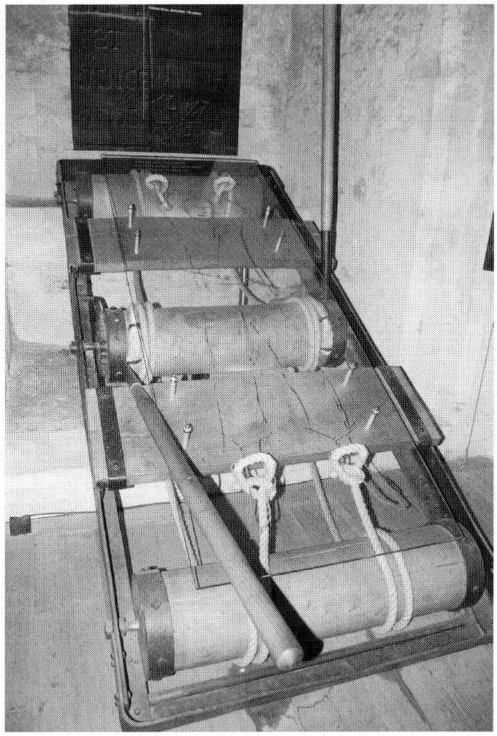

Right: The Torture Rack at the Tower of London. (Wikimedia Commons)

Below: Site of the Tyburn Tree. (Wikimedia Commons)

An 1864 illustration of the execution of Queen Katheryn Howard. (Wikimedia Commons)

Traitor's Gate at the Tower of London from where Queen Anne Boleyn and Queen Katheryn Howard entered the Tower for their imprisonment. (Wikimedia Commons)

King Henry VIII by Hans Holbein Jr. (Wikimedia Commons)

Edward Baynton, and the daughter of her uncle, the Duke of Norfolk, Mary Howard. Also serving her were her former housemates from the duchess' household, amongst them Malyn Tilney. Joan Bulmer, her former bedmate, was absent though. Veterans such as Anne Basset and Jane Boleyn, Lady Rochford, the wife of her deceased cousin, George Boleyn, too, found a place in her household.

A formidable and wealthy widow, Jane had continued to serve Queen Jane Seymour after the execution of her husband and her sister-in-law. However, following Queen Jane's death, Lady Rochford retired to Blickling Hall till she was summoned back to court to serve Anne of Cleves. She then stayed on and joined her cousin-by-marriage in Queen's Katheryn's household.

Katheryn was not an easy queen to please. She was completely unprepared for the mighty responsibility that was thrust upon her so suddenly at such a young age. Moreover, after her liaison with Francis Dereham and her light flirtation with Thomas Culpeper, a gentleman of the king's privy chamber, marriage to an old and ill man did not find much favour with the young girl queen.

Nevertheless, enamoured by the rich jewellery and the fancy gowns that came with the queenship, Katheryn powered along, leaving for a summer progress after a short honeymoon. The couple visited Buckingham, Grafton, Ampthill and St Albans, amongst other places. The French ambassador, Charles de Marillac, who visited the royal couple while they were at Grafton, remarked that the new queen was 'a young lady of moderate beauty, but very graceful.' Marillac also observed that Henry was head over heels in love with Katheryn and 'caressed her more than his other wives'. An anonymous Spanish chronicler also claims that Katheryn made Henry spend a fortune on her dresses and jewels.

Life for Katheryn now consisted of endless hours of enjoyment and being served hand and foot, something that she was slowly getting used to. While at Ampthill in September, a delighted Katheryn received her new jewels along with other gifts such as a gold-enamelled clock in the shape of a book. She also received many books, but they were more of a decoration than to serve their real purpose.

Henry missed no opportunity to show off his young wife to the visiting emissaries and foreigners. He also loaded honours and titles to Katheryn's family.

The couple, after their summer progress, were supposed to go to London but an outbreak of the dreaded plague made them reroute to

Windsor instead. A perpetual hypochondriac, Henry ordered that no one should be allowed inside the castle till they were safely out of an infected area for eight to ten days.

Although King Henry VIII was enjoying his rather long honeymoon with his new queen, he had matters of state to attend to. He was eager to appease the Holy Roman Emperor as well as the Duke of Cleves, especially after his disastrous marriage to his sister. He sent Stephen Gardiner, the Bishop of Winchester, to the emperor in a bid to convince the latter that his views towards his religion hadn't wavered much.

Once the epidemic had abated and Henry deemed it safe enough to step out, the royal couple made their way to Woking Palace, which was previously owned by the king's grandmother, Margaret Beaufort.

Katheryn's idyllic honeymoon came to an abrupt halt at Woking Palace, for her former companion and kinswoman, Katherine Tylney, along with her former amour, Francis Dereham, had arrived at court. Although, Katheryn did not meet Dereham then, she did meet her namesake and appointed her as her chamberer.

A few days later she received a visit from her stepdaughter, Princess Mary. Being the daughter of the aristocratic Queen Katharine of Aragon and educated under her tutelage, grace and dignity came easily to the princess. This resulted in a frosty first meeting between Mary and her rather young stepmother. After an apparent tantrum by Queen Katheryn about Princess Mary's behaviour, King Henry VIII ordered the princess to leave and stay in her own household along with her little stepbrother, Prince Edward. The Imperial Ambassador, Eustace Chapuys, also mentions that two of Mary's maids were taken away from her by Katheryn in an apparent show of displeasure over the lack of respect shown to her by the princess.

Mary's behaviour towards Katheryn can be attributed to the fact that she was yet to be married while her much younger stepmother was not only married but could also be bearing the new Duke of York any time soon (if we are to go by Henry's rather lascivious behaviour with his young wife). Moreover, she was Anne Boleyn's cousin, a fact that may have fuelled her dislike of the new queen. However, the king and Katheryn's anger did not last long and very soon Mary returned to court and stayed on permanently with both their blessings. It is not known, though, whether or not Mary's opinions on Katheryn had changed.

After Woking, the royal couple moved to Oatlands where the golden autumn sun made the place an ideal idyllic retreat for the honeymooning couple. Katheryn usually kept herself away from getting involved in matters of state, preferring to indulge herself in luxuries. She did extend her patronage towards a few minor matters, but apart from that she simply enjoyed her new, opulent lifestyle.

Rumours of Katheryn's pregnancy began to circulate during the Christmas celebrations in 1540 when Marillac mentioned that the queen had grown stout – a usual euphemism for pregnancy. Another rumour – that Henry had finally grown tired of Katheryn and was planning to remarry Anne of Cleves – gained ground at the same time. However, although rumours about Katheryn's pregnancy, or the lack of it, were never confirmed, the almost perpetual show of affection between the royal couple ensured that the remarriage rumours bit the dust.

Henry was an extremely generous husband and gifted Katheryn jewel-embedded clothes, more jewellery, a crucifix, a gold girdle and a gold chain. We are not aware as to what Katheryn gifted Henry although we know that she gifted a cross to her husband's niece, Lady Margaret Douglas. The royal couple also sent gifts of gold, jewels and fine clothes to Anne of Cleves who, in turn, sent them two magnificent horses. The king's former wife and now 'Beloved Sister' also received an invitation to visit them at Hampton Court for New Year which she gladly accepted. Once she arrived, she was received with full honours by several gentlemen including Sir William Howard, the queen's uncle. Special quarters were reserved and prepared for her, where she was received by Anne, Countess of Hertford, and Katherine, Duchess of Suffolk, who conducted her to the queen's chambers.

Anne was shown much respect and kindness by her erstwhile lady-in-waiting and now queen, and to her credit she, too, showed much deference to Katheryn. The two ladies chatted genially till Henry joined them and the three of them proceeded to dine, along with Henry's oldest daughter, Princess Mary. The king retired early to his apartments after which the ladies joined in the dancing and revelry. This was the same routine the next day and when Katheryn received a gift of two lap dogs, she generously gifted one to Anne. The two ladies enjoyed themselves till it was time for Anne to return to her household at Richmond. However, unbeknownst to Katheryn, the wheels of fate were turning and this time not in her favour.

King Henry VIII made plans to visit his ports at Dover in February to inspect his navy. However, he was forced to cancel his plans as the ulcer on his leg was acting up and he fell ill yet again (he had only just recovered in September). The ulcer, which was usually kept open, closed again, causing him much pain and discomfort.

He recovered quickly enough, but this time his illness soured his mood. Already a temperamental person, his temper went from bad to worse. He complained that his subjects were 'unhappy' and declared that he would make them so poor that they would be unable to oppose him. He voiced his regret over the execution of Cromwell, accusing his ministers into brainwashing him to execute his favourite and 'most faithful' servant. As a result, Shrovetide was a dull affair with Henry not willing to receive any visitors.

It was now time for Katheryn to make her first entry into London as queen as the royal couple headed to Greenwich. Travelling together in the royal barge, the couple were met by the Lord Mayor, the aldermen and the nobles of the city. Katheryn was welcomed with full honours and she intervened to release the poet Thomas Wyatt and Privy Councillor Ralph Sadler who had been arrested and imprisoned; the men's only crime was the fact that they were close friends of the now disgraced and executed Thomas Cromwell. The royal pardon was granted albeit with conditions attached. Having fulfilled many more royal duties, the couple proceeded to Greenwich amidst the firing of guns.

Katheryn and Thomas Culpeper

Rumours of Katheryn's pregnancy began afresh during the Holy Week in 1541. Henry had just returned from a tour in Kent and he was overjoyed to hear the news. He immediately began making preparations for his long-awaited Duke of York.

However, the rumours died down as quickly as they had begun and all of Henry's preparations for his future child came to nothing. It is not known or recorded whether Katheryn lost the child or was even pregnant. She carried out her religious duties on Maundy Thursday, and returning to her chambers, sent her servant to her husband's chambers to call a man. That man happened to be Thomas Culpeper.

Thomas Culpeper had been suspected of raping a woman many years ago, but being a favourite of the king, he was soon cleared of any charges. He and Katheryn had flirted earlier when she had first come to court, but he stepped aside when King Henry VIII came into the picture.

Now, though, saddled with an old, infirm and cantankerous husband, Katheryn was seemingly open to some harmless fun. When Culpeper came, the queen gave him some gifts and sent him back. While thanking her, he casually mentioned their past relationship which irked Katheryn.

However, Katheryn couldn't stay angry for long. She soon forgave him and sent him fresh meat and fish when he fell ill. But these meetings were not frequent and, therefore, could not be termed as a love affair.

A letter from Katheryn to Culpeper tells us the reason behind Katheryn sending for him in the first place. It reads:

> Master Culpeper,
> I heartily recommend me unto you, praying you to send me word how that you do. It was showed me that you were sick, the which thing troubled me very much till such time that I hear from you, praying you to send me word how that you do. For I never longed so much for [a] thing as I do to see you and to speak with you, the which I trust shall be shortly now, the which does comfort me very much when I think of it, and when I think again that you shall depart from me again it makes my heart to die to think what fortune I have that I cannot be always in your company, yet my trust is always in you that you will be as you have promised me and in that hope I trust upon still, praying then that you will come when my Lady Rochford is here, for then I shall be best at leisure to be at your commandment. Thanking you for that you have promised me to be so good unto that poor fellow my man which is one of the griefs that I do feel to depart from him, for then I do know no-one that I dare trust to send to you and therefore, I pray you take him to be with you that I may sometimes hear from you one thing. I pray you to give me a horse for my man for I had much ado to get one and therefore I pray send me one by him and in doing so I am as I said afore and thus I take my leave of you, trusting to see you shortly again and I would you was with me now that you might see what pain I take in writing to you.
>
> Yours as long life endures,
> Katheryn[10]

The reason behind writing a letter in such intimate tones to a gentleman who was in close quarters with the king is intriguing. If we look at it through rose-tinted glasses, it will seem as if Katheryn, young as she was, had grown weary of her old and ailing husband and was looking to rekindle her earlier romance with Culpeper. And if we look at it in a more practical way, we may assume that she was merely keeping in touch with her husband's favourite courtier, who had replaced Sir Henry Norris as the Gentleman of the King's Privy Chamber, to keep herself abreast of her husband's health, wellbeing and his ever-changing moods. For Culpeper, too, friendship with the reigning queen had its advantages.

The summer of 1541 saw a frenzy of activity with Katheryn, along with Princess Mary, took centre stage. The princess had asked for a family reunion and Katheryn, too, was enthusiastic about it.

Katheryn first went to Chelsea where she made arrangements for Princess Elizabeth's arrival. She then proceeded towards Barnard's Castle as Elizabeth and her household settled down at Chelsea. The queen returned to Chelsea the following day and she and Elizabeth went to Essex to Prince Edward's residence at Waltham Holy Cross. King Henry VIII had already arrived there with Princess Mary and both of them received Katheryn and Elizabeth, the former meeting her stepson for the first time.

This very private family reunion was a huge success, mainly because Princess Mary and Katheryn seemed to have ironed out their differences. Afterwards, Katheryn returned to Greenwich while Henry proceeded to Westminster to fulfill his royal obligations. However, it was a short visit and he was back at Katheryn's side by the end of May.

Despite the irascible king sharing a warm and loving relationship with his wife, Katheryn wasn't yet crowned. Although she was not as ambitious as her deceased cousin, Anne Boleyn, this thought may have rankled her at some point, along with the fact that she had not yet borne Henry his future Duke of York.

The summer progress of 1541 approached and Henry and Katheryn began preparing for it. They were planning to visit the northern counties where Katheryn's uncle, the Duke of Norfolk, had just put down the rebels of the Pilgrimage of Grace. Katheryn was to be the calming factor for the dissatisfied subjects. She, along with Princess Mary, who wasn't yet legitimised, as per the request of the Pilgrims, would provide reassurance and arbitrate for mercy on behalf of those imprisoned. Katheryn accompanying Henry for the progress also put any rumours of her supposed pregnancy to rest.

However, the execution of Margaret Pole, Countess of Salisbury, on 27 May 1541, merely for being a Plantagenet, just before the royal couple left for the summer progress left a sour taste with those who loved the elderly lady. In the two years that the countess was imprisoned, Katheryn had treated her kindly and even sent her warm clothes and blankets during the winters. The execution, the reason for which was unclear, shocked everyone at court, especially due to the countess' age and the brutal manner in which she was executed.

While Lady Margaret was being hacked to death by an inexperienced youth, Henry and Katheryn went to Westminster while their household proceeded to Eltham in preparation for their summer progress.

The Summer Progress

The summer progress of 1541 was a grand affair with illustrious nobles such as Sir Richard Rich, the dukes of Norfolk and Suffolk, Sir Thomas Wriothesley and Bishop Tunstall joining the entourage amongst others. After three months of preparations, they finally set out on 30 June. Their plans of reaching Lincoln in time were thrown in a disarray due to the bad weather, which meant that the travelling party reached only as far as Grafton by mid-July. The bad weather also resulted in Katheryn falling sick, though but she soon recovered. They then moved to Northampton and from there to Pipewell, where they stayed there till 28 July, after which they proceeded towards Lyddington.

After brief stays at Lyddington and Collyweston, the erstwhile estate of Henry's grandmother, Lady Margaret Beaufort, the couple visited Grimsthorpe, the home of Henry's childhood friend, Charles Brandon, Duke of Suffolk, and his wife, Katherine Willoughby. After spending three nights with them, they went to Sleaford where they prepared for a grand entry into Lincoln.

The royal couple were welcomed in Lincoln by the Archdeacon of Lincoln and they proceeded to meet other dignitaries. After a grand procession, Henry was presented with the sword and the mace of the city. Henry and Katheryn then proceeded towards Lincoln Minster where they were received by the Bishop of Lincoln. The magnificent reception of the king and his queen, and Henry's benevolence, indicated that the Pilgrimage of Grace was forgiven.

Katheryn, though, had her own private matters to take care of. As the night set in, she visited Lady Rochford in her chamber and stayed there until early morning. This happened the next night as well, with Katheryn being accompanied by Katherine Tylney. What transpired between the ladies is not known.

The next stops on their progress, Gainsborough and Nottingham, were uneventful. They then entered Yorkshire and visited Hatfield. It is not known whether Katheryn rendezvoused with Thomas Culpeper during these visits. However, as the royal couple proceeded towards Pontefract, an unwelcome surprise awaited Katheryn: Francis Dereham.[11]

Following his departure to Ireland, Dereham was unable to settle into a fixed job and it was rumoured that he had indulged in piracy. Hearing about Katheryn's rise to queenship, Dereham returned to England with the purpose of seeking a job in her household. He hung around at court doing odd jobs for Duchess Agnes and others whom he knew from Norfolk. However, Dereham mentioned to the duchess a letter pertaining to him and Katheryn, which made her furious at her stepgranddaughter's defiance. She threw Dereham out and Lady Howard and Lady Bridgewater petitioned the queen for a position for Dereham in her household. Katheryn took him into her service, albeit reluctantly.

The meetings between Katheryn and Lady Rochford, though, continued unabated in Pontefract although the former's life had become cumbersome with the reappearance of Dereham. Katheryn had decreed that none of her ladies should accompany her during her nightly sojourns, arousing some suspicion. Meanwhile, Dereham had begun making Katheryn's life even more difficult as he made enemies wherever he went. A braggart, Dereham told whoever would listen that people despised him as the queen held him in such high regard. Katheryn warned him to watch his words, but her warnings fell on deaf ears and Dereham continued to display his arrogance time and again.

The progress continued and very soon the travelling party reached Hampton Court where Katheryn was reunited with another of her former housemates, Alice Wilkes. With her household now filled with her former housemates and her former paramour, Katheryn began to feel nervous lest her dalliance with Dereham before her marriage to Henry came to light. She tried keeping them quiet with expensive gifts, but was constantly worried about a possible betrayal. It was not long before Katheryn's life fell apart.

Downfall

Another former housemate of Katheryn, Mary Lascelles, was now married and living in Sussex. Katheryn and Mary did not exactly see eye to eye and she had refused to join her household when the former married King Henry VIII.

During a meeting with his sister, John Lascelles, Mary's brother and a former servant of Thomas Cromwell, urged her to try for a place in the queen's household. Mary refused again and said that she felt very sorry for the queen. When asked, Mary revealed that the queen was a woman of questionable morals. John was immediately pressed Mary for more details. Mary then told him about Katheryn's liaisons with Francis Dereham and Henry Manox while they were a part of the Duchess of Norfolk's household. Little did she know that this revelation would have far-reaching consequences.

For Lascelles, this was a golden opportunity to avenge his former master, Thomas Cromwell. He was also aware that should he be proved wrong, he stood to lose his life. Being a reformer, John Lascelles was glad that the reformers had stayed back in London while the king and queen were on their progress.

Making up his mind, Lascelles approached Archbishop Thomas Cranmer and told him what his sister had revealed to him. Although Katheryn had been kind to Cranmer on many occasions, the archbishop thought it was his duty to act on this information and ask for permission to launch an investigation. He consulted the nobles in London, most of them reformers like he and Lascelles, and came to a decision to tell the King.

As Archbishop Cranmer awaited King Henry VIII and Queen Katheryn's arrival, word reached him that Prince Edward had fallen dangerously ill with quatrain fever. The king was beside himself and summoned all his physicians to take care of his only legitimate heir. He was even more disconcerted with the fact that Katheryn had not yet borne him a child, the future Duke of York. The prince made a quick recovery though his health remained frail. His relieved father gave thanks to the Almighty and also prayed for Katheryn to bless him with more sons.

His mind now at ease after the recent scare, King Henry VIII headed towards the Chapel Royal at Hampton Court and found Archbishop Thomas Cranmer's letter waiting for him on the pew. He was surprisingly calm as he read Cranmer's damning accusations. Given his love for

Katheryn, he may have assumed that Cranmer had simply acted upon rumours, or that the letter was forged. However, since an accusation had been levelled, he couldn't let it go without investigating. He gathered up a few of his trusted council members – namely, William Fitzwilliam, Earl of Southampton and Lord Privy Seal, Sir Thomas Wriothesley, Sir Anthony Browne and John Russel, Lord Admiral – to launch an investigation into the charges. Henry decided to keep the investigation confidential as he still found the matter preposterous and untrue.

The Investigation

The council started by interrogating Roger Cotes, a tailor in the employ of the Duchess of Norfolk. The results were not conclusive and they proceeded to question John Lascelles.

Lascelles proved to be a mine of information and told the investigators that his sister had mentioned that Dereham had known Katheryn intimately before her marriage to the king and had lain with her on many occasions, much to the disgust of the other housemates. He also revealed Katheryn's affair with Henry Manox, claiming that Manox had knowledge of the queen's private parts.

John Lascelles stood by his claims, and bolstered by this, the Earl of Southampton rode off to Sussex to question his sister, Mary Lascelles, to see if the siblings' statements matched.

Mary's statements tallied with John as she told them about Katheryn's relationship with both Manox and Dereham. She mentioned that she had once accompanied Katheryn to confront Manox and also that Katheryn was deeply in love with Dereham. She revealed that Katheryn would be naked and kiss Dereham, who would slide into her bed in his doublet and hose. She also gave the names of three grooms of the chamber and a chamberer in the duchess' household who were aware of the happenings. The Earl of Southampton was probably in a daze from Mary's testimony as he headed back to Hampton Court to present his findings to the king.

Thomas Wriothesley was in charge of interrogating Henry Manox and arresting Francis Dereham. Manox told him about falling in love with Katheryn, his student, and about the duchess catching them red-handed and giving Katheryn 'two or three blows' and warning her to stay away from Manox. He also said that although he knew Katheryn physically, he never knew her carnally. The former piano teacher also mentioned how he had written an anonymous letter to the duchess warning her of the goings-on in her household, and how, after this incident, Dereham had confronted him and called him a knave.

Dereham was thrown into a cell in the Tower of London following his arrest. On being questioned by Wriothesley, he confessed that he knew Katheryn carnally and that he had lain with her on her bed many times wearing just a doublet and hose. He also confessed that he hung around the fringes of the court when Katheryn married Henry and then joined the queen's household.

The council gathered at Hampton Court once again and sent for the Duke of Norfolk who, despite an outbreak of plague in his household, hurried to try and repair the damage.

The Earl of Southampton informed the king about John and Mary Lascelles' testimonies and Thomas Wriothesley repeated Dereham's confession, thus affirming the fact that Katheryn was a woman of loose morals.

Henry listened to the evidence of his wife's premarital escapades with growing shock and dismay. He ordered his men to confine the queen to her apartments while he made plans to leave Hampton Court.

Katheryn was now a prisoner in her own paradise, and in a last-ditch attempt to save herself, broke free and ran towards the king who was heading towards the Chapel Royal one last time before leaving. Her pleas fell on deaf ears, however, as she was dragged back into her room by the guards. Her uncle, the Duke of Norfolk, was informed by the king as he left Hampton Court. This would the last time Katheryn would see her once adoring husband.

Katheryn was now under house arrest and her entertainments came to an abrupt halt. Although she must have had an inkling of what was going on, no one told her about the investigations and the arrest of Dereham.

On 7 November she received a delegation of councillors, namely Archbishop Thomas Cranmer, Chancellor Audeley, Bishop Stephen Gardiner, Robert Radcliffe, and her uncle, the Duke of Norfolk, in her apartments. They informed her of the charges and wanted her to confess, which, after many denials, she finally did. She pleaded for mercy, imploring them to remember the acts of mercy that she had extended towards others. She also mentioned that her relationship with Dereham ended a year prior to his marriage to Anne of Cleves. When questioned of her motives for concealing this information from the king, she confessed that she had been blinded by the glory and love that she received from him and wanted to keep her past encounters to herself. Again, she pleaded for mercy as she signed her confession.

After Cranmer reported Katheryn's confession to the king, he sent the archbishop back to her to uncover details of her relationships with Manox and Dereham in the hope that his 'rose without a thorn' might not really be guilty.

Cranmer returned to find an extremely disturbed and distressed Katheryn. He assured her of Henry's mercy and coaxed her to talk. A sobbing Katheryn then admitted to knowing Dereham and that he had often spoken to her about marriage. She also mentioned the gifts that they had exchanged. Although she denied gifting him a gold ring, she admitted to asking Dereham to arrange for a French fennel for herself. She also confessed that he often lent her money for various purposes.

Cranmer then asked Katheryn about the money that Dereham had given her before leaving for Ireland and instructing her to keep it for herself lest he failed to return. Cranmer mentioned that such a promise is usually only made by a husband to a wife. He asked Katheryn whether Dereham had made such a promise. Katheryn replied in the affirmative and added: 'I confess as I did before, that diverse times he had lain with me, sometimes in his doublet and hose and two or three times naked, but not so naked that he had nothing upon him, for he had always at the least his doublet, and as I do think, his hose also, but I mean naked when his hose was put down.'[12]

This was all Archbishop Cranmer needed to hear. By confirming that Dereham had a carnal relationship with Katheryn, she had effectively confirmed that a precontract of marriage had existed between them. She gave the archbishop all the details of their life at the duchess' household, and also mentioned that, on coming to the court after she became queen, Dereham had mentioned about reports that she wanted to marry Thomas Culpeper, an allegation that she denied at that time.

Although Katheryn was unaware, her sexual relationship with Francis Dereham made their playful and flirtatious 'mock' marriage into a binding contract. Following his meeting with Katheryn, Cranmer wrote up his report for Henry, mentioning everything that his queen had told him.

Katheryn had never agreed to a relationship with Francis Dereham, but he, on the other hand, had forced himself on her, thereby exploiting her sexually. The damage was already done, however. Whether she liked it or not, she had been in a legally binding marriage with Dereham, and a man could not be accused of raping his wife.

Despite the attempts of maintaining the utmost secrecy, news leaked out and almost immediately old rumours of the king remarrying Anne of Cleves gained new traction. Many even speculated about who would be the next wife, though Henry was far from being even remotely attracted to any woman at that point in time.

On reading Archbishop Cranmer's report, King Henry VIII decreed that Katheryn should be sent to Syon Abbey with haste. He also ordered Chancellor Audeley to reveal the news of the queen's indiscretion. Strangely, he also ordered Audeley not to mention a word about Dereham and the precontract. The fact that Katheryn had confessed to a relationship with Dereham and the latter vouching that it was of a sexual nature confirmed that the queen could be charged with bigamy. Thus, the problem could be solved by merely dissolving her marriage to the king.

Under rigorous questioning, Dereham confessed that he had visited Katheryn's chambers after her marriage to Henry but denied having revived their former romance. Whether he was subjected to the rack or not is not known, but under immense pressure he revealed that it was now Thomas Culpeper who had taken Dereham's place in Katheryn's life.

The royal court was in uproar at this unexpected revelation. Although Katheryn had confessed to Cranmer about her relationship with Culpeper before her marriage to the king, people had assumed that it had come to an end. However, as per Dereham's confession, it was far from over.

Culpeper was arrested and imprisoned in the Tower, though being a gentleman of the privy chamber, he was not subjected to the torture that Dereham faced. However, a shocked Culpeper revealed every detail of his and Katheryn's relationship, implicating Jane Boleyn, Lady Rochford, as well. He mentioned that Lady Rochford had assisted the couple in carrying out their relationship in secret, often allowing them to use her chambers as their place of rendezvous. He also confirmed the nightly escapades of Katheryn and Lady Rochford at Lincoln and Pontefract, as well as mentioning that he and Katheryn exchanged letters and gifts with the help of Lady Rochford.

He stated that their relationship was going strong until King Henry VIII entered the picture. Unable to refuse the king's advances, Katheryn married Henry, but in time rekindled her lost romance with Culpeper. There was no turning back for Katheryn, Francis Dereham and Thomas Culpeper now. The 1534 Treason Act was applied against them.

Katheryn was questioned afresh about her relationship with Culpeper. Despite instructing Lady Rochford not to disclose details of their affair to the investigators, Katheryn did not bat an eyelid before incriminating the former as an insinuator, despite the latter's misgivings. She also mentioned that Lady Rochford stood guard as she and Culpeper met in secret and that she often purchased gifts for her mistress to give to her paramour. Once again, she signed her confession.

Sunday, 13 November was the day that Katheryn was declared an adulteress. Mary Lascelles, along with Alice Wilkes, were ordered to appear in front of the council when summoned. Sir Thomas Wriothesley visited the disgraced queen's gentlewomen and servants at Hampton Court and revealed the offences of their mistress and dissolved her household. The king's niece, Lady Margaret Douglas, who was in a relationship with Katheryn's brother, Charles, was banished from the court and sent to Kenninghall.

Barring a few, her servants were sent away and another round of questioning began with Katherine Tylney who confirmed Katheryn's nightly trysts during the summer progress. She also mentioned that Katheryn had taken her along to one of them though desisted from going into any details, merely stating that she had acted as a chaperone. She also mentioned that the queen had asked her to carry secret missives to Lady Rochford. Another housemate, Marget Morton, mentioned that she had caught Katheryn looking lovingly at Culpeper through the window of her privy chamber at Hatfield. She, too, mentioned that she was ordered to carry secret messages to Lady Rochford.

Finally, Lady Rochford was questioned and flatly denied any knowledge of the happenings at Pontefract. She also said that the conversations between Katheryn and Culpeper had been whispered and that she could hardly hear them. She did, however, admit that she had stood guard as Culpeper and Katheryn met in secret. Lady Rochford also mentioned that Katheryn and Culpeper had a sexual relationship, a strange proclamation as she had earlier said that she couldn't hear them.

Trial and Execution

Leaving behind a life of luxuries, Katheryn arrived at Syon abbey in a barge on 14 November. She was allowed only a handful of servants, her half-sister, Lady Baynton, being one of them. Apart from a few simple pieces of clothing, her fine gowns and jewels were taken away and were now in the care of Thomas Seymour.

She was kept on a suicide watch as Henry began informing his ambassadors about the sordid happenings at court. Lady Rochford, Francis Dereham and Thomas Culpeper were imprisoned in the Tower and their goods and estates were forfeited. Katheryn's uncle, the Duke of Norfolk, admitted to having been hoodwinked by his niece, effectively washing his hands of her. He also declared that he wished for his niece to be burnt alive.

His love now turned into hatred, King Henry's mood swings were now worse than ever. Katheryn's betrayal had emphasised his age and infirmity and he was unable to accept it. He oscillated between forgiving her and condemning her.

The trial of Thomas Culpeper and Dereham began on 1 December. Special commissions of oyer and terminer were established in Lincolnshire, Surrey, Yorkshire, Kent and Middlesex. The council were unanimous in proclaiming the queen, Lady Rochford, Francis Dereham and Thomas Culpeper guilty of adultery and 'conspiring, imagining and compassing the final destruction of the King'. Their indictments were brought to Guildhall where the accused stood on trial before the council, which consisted of Chancellor Audeley, Charles Brandon, and the Duke of Norfolk among others.

The two men pleaded not guilty and Dereham attempted to use his contract with Katheryn (before her royal marriage) in a desperate attempt to save his life. Culpeper merely mentioned that he was forced into the relationship by the queen with help from Lady Rochford. However, they soon changed their plea to guilty. They were then sentenced to death. The trial lasted for six hours.

Katheryn remained at Syon, hoping for a pardon, while Lady Rochford was imprisoned in a cell in the Tower. The latter's mental health began deteriorating and she was sent to the home of Lord Russell. King Henry VIII, in an act of compassion for his erstwhile favourite, decided to commute Thomas Culpeper's punishment to a simple beheading rather than the more gruesome hanging, drawing and quartering.

On 10 December 1541 the two men were led to Tyburn for their execution. Given his official position, Culpeper was the first to be executed. He disposed of the usual formalities of asking the people to pray for the king and his own soul before kneeling down on the stone and having his head chopped off.

It was now Dereham's turn. He was hanged until his last breath was almost squeezed out of him. Then, while he was still alive, he was brought down, his abdomen sliced open and private parts chopped off and his innards drawn out. Finally, he was executed by the axe. His body was then chopped into pieces and sent wherever the king ordered. Dereham's and Culpeper's heads were then parboiled and spiked at London Bridge.

Katheryn was not given the dignity of a trial, unlike her cousin, Anne Boleyn. She was, instead, condemned by an Act of Attainder that was passed against her and Lady Rochford without much fanfare. Despite the exhortations of Chancellor Audeley, she wasn't given a chance to defend herself.

On 10 February Katheryn was visited by Charles Brandon, Duke of Suffolk, the Earl of Southampton and a few other dignitaries, and escorted out of Syon Abbey one last time. She travelled to the Tower in a small boat, passing by some familiar sights such as Norfolk House, where she spent her childhood, and Whitehall, where she reigned as queen, before finally reaching the Tower, where the sight of the heads of her former lovers would have terrified her.

The next day, Chancellor Audeley brought out the new statute that had been passed to allow the execution of a mentally ill person, designed specifically to put Lady Rochford to death.

While at the Tower, Katheryn broke down frequently and it was feared that the execution would be postponed to allow her to recover. However, this was not to be. Sir John Gage visited her on the day before her execution to dispose her soul and prepare her for death. Katheryn then asked for the block to be brought to her so that she could practise dying with dignity. Her request was granted.

The next day, crowds gathered to watch the second queen of England to be executed. Amongst them was John Lascelles who had been instrumental in bringing about her downfall. She was then escorted out of her cell by Sir John Gage, Constable of the Tower, and brought to the same spot where Anne Boleyn had been executed.

Her last line, 'I die a queen but I would rather die a wife of Culpeper', is much disputed, and most likely is a figment of an overactive imagination. It is quite likely that she simply asked for forgiveness and for mercy on her soul. She handed the executioner a purse of coins indicating her forgiveness for his act. She was then blindfolded as she said her prayers. The executioner then beheaded her with a single stroke of the axe. Lady Rochford came next and her insanity, real or otherwise, did not save her from the axe.

Aftermath of Katheryn's arrest

After Katheryn Howard's arrest the Duke of Norfolk, the dowager duchess' stepson, was sent to her house in Lambeth to search for any evidence that might help them prove the charges against the erstwhile queen. Once there, the search party discovered that the duchess had attempted to destroy some letters written by Francis Dereham and his friend, William Damport. Holding her responsible for the loss of this incriminating evidence, the duchess was promptly sent to the Tower. She was interrogated about the goings-on within her household, but being a lax supervisor, could not tell the investigators anything of much value.

The friend of Francis Dereham, William Damport, was also questioned, and quite possibly, tortured, in a bid to extract more information. Damport's fate is unknown but it may be possible that he was freed.

On the day of Dereham's and Culpeper's executions, the duchess was questioned once again, this time admitting to promoting her grand-niece as a prospective bride for King Henry, despite being aware of her past relationships. She also confessed to having urged Katheryn, then queen, to admit Dereham into her household and also to burning the letters written by Dereham and Damport. By mid-December her eldest son, William Howard, his wife, and the duchess' daughter, Anne Howard, were arrested and interred in the Tower. Another daughter, Katherine Daubeney, Lady Bridgewater, was also arrested and imprisoned. Jailed along with them was Katheryn's former housemate, Malyn Tilney. All of them were charged with misprision of treason and with concealment of the 'evil demeanour' of Queen Katheryn which resulted in the 'slander' of the king and hampering the succession. They were all sentenced to life imprisonment but most of them were pardoned after Katheryn's execution. The dowager duchess was not brought to trial, most probably due to her age and that she 'may die of perversity to defraud the King's Highness of the confiscation of her goods', but she was sentenced to imprisonment nevertheless and her goods and estates were seized. She died in May 1545.

Katheryn's mortal remains are interred at the Chapel of St Peter ad Vincula, and, along with Lady Rochford, lie near their kinsmen, Anne and George Boleyn.

9

Margaret Pole

1464, Whittlebury Forest, Northamptonshire

One fine morning, according to legend, a young, blond widow stood underneath an oak tree along with her two sons, waiting for the King of England, the newly coronated Edward IV, seeking justice – the reinstatement of her dowry and jointure by her mother-in-law, the wily Lady Grey of Groby. The widow, Lady Elizabeth Grey, whose husband, Sir John Grey, was killed at the Battle of St Albans fighting for the Lancastrian side, was the eldest daughter of the Duchess of Bedford, Jacquetta Woodville and her 'lowly' husband, Sir Richard Woodville, Earl Rivers.

Legend also has it that King Edward IV was instantly captivated by Lady Elizabeth's beauty and readily accompanied her to her home at Grafton Manor, where she was staying with her parents. The matter easily sorted, King Edward IV apparently suggested that Elizabeth become his mistress, but he was rebuffed. Never having failed with the ladies, the king then married her in secret with only the duchess, the priest who married them, and an altar boy as witness.

Although the secret wedding did take place, the above story of the king coming across a fair maiden under an oak tree may well be a fable. Nevertheless, the secret marriage set in motion a chain of events that would change the lives of the Plantagenet family for generations to come, with many of them meeting a grisly end. One such person is Margaret Pole, Countess of Salisbury.

The Tragic Life and End of George Plantagenet

Farleigh Castle is a medieval castle overlooking the River Frome in Somerset, near Bath. Initially a manor named Ferlegh during the Norman conquests, it was granted to Roger de Courcelles by William the

Conqueror. During the early years of the reign of Edward III the manor passed to Bartholomew de Bunghersh from the Montfort family, the then current owners of the manor whose patriarch, Hugh de Montfort, rechristened it as Farleigh Montfort.

Sir Thomas Hungerford[1], a wealthy courtier who accumulated his riches by being the steward of John of Gaunt, eventually bought the manor in 1369 and made it his principal home. Despite not acquiring the necessary royal permission, Sir Thomas began crenellating the manor to build a castle, thereby having to apply and obtain a royal pardon in 1383.

Years later, his son, Walter Hungerford, inherited the newly renovated and renamed Farleigh Castle in the year 1412 after the death of his mother, Joan. Walter, a close companion of King Henry V, fought at the Battle of Agincourt beside him and was appointed the Steward of the Royal Household. He later prospered even more as he rose up the ranks to become the Treasurer of England. Walter, known by now as Baron Hungerford, amassed many more lands and manors and filled his coffers with immense wealth. He also expanded Farleigh Castle considerably.

Walter's son, Robert, inherited the castle on his father's death. However, due to a series of unfortunate incidents, which later saw Robert's eldest son, Lord Moleyns, and his grandson (Lord Moleyn's son), Thomas, executed, Farleigh Castle reverted to the ownership of the Crown. The Yorkist King Edward IV gave the castle to his youngest brother, Richard, Duke of Gloucester, in the year 1462.

George Plantagenet, Duke of Clarence, may have taken up residence in the castle some time during that period as the place went down in the history books as the birthplace of his daughter, Margaret.

George Plantagenet, Duke of Clarence, is quite a mysterious figure. Born on 21 October 1449 at Dublin Castle[2] in Ireland, George was the third son, after Edward, of Richard Plantagenet, third Duke of York[3] and his wife, the formidable Cecily Neville[4]. His father, Richard, claimed descent from Edmund, 1st Duke of York, Edward III's fourth surviving son. He accepted the authority of Henry VI as his monarch and sought to be recognised as the heir presumptive based on his descent from Edmund of Langley. Years later, during the Readeption of Henry VI in the year 1470-1471[5], George tried to put himself after Edward of Westminster, Prince of Wales, in the line of succession on the basis of the same claim as his father's.

Dublin and Trim Castles were George's homes in the first year of his life while his father, Richard, Duke of York served as the Lieutenant of

Ireland. But in September 1450, just a month prior to George turning one, Richard decided to return to England as he feared the growing influence of his arch-enemy Edmund Beaufort, Duke of Somerset, in the court of Henry VI. Also, Richard was hard-pressed for funds to consolidate England's position in Ireland and money wasn't forthcoming from the royal court, perhaps due to the machinations of Somerset. Moreover, to Richard's anger, Somerset was high in favour with Henry VI and saw himself as a potential heir to the throne of England. Fearful of Somerset's authority over the still childless English king, Richard marched on to England, determined to do away with the Beaufort faction inheriting the throne.

By the time Richard and his family, his wife Cecily Neville and sons, Edward and George, reached England, William de la Pole, now Duke of Suffolk and a former friend of Cardinal Beaufort, was the mastermind behind the throne, on which sat a meek and timid Henry VI. The war with France was not going too well and the English army were in disarray. Public anger towards the monarchy was growing and accusing fingers were pointed at de la Pole for the repeated defeats against the French army. To cut a long story short, fed up with the repeated losses, the English public took matters into their own hands and captured and executed de la Pole. It is quite possible that Richard was behind these actions.

It was in this volatile environment that George and their new brother, Richard, along with their sisters, Anne, Elizabeth and Margaret, grew up. Their two eldest sons, Edward and Edmund, were at Ludlow Castle. It is presumed that the York children grew up in the care of their mother, but no records have survived to attest to this.

On their father's front, things weren't going too well. In the summer of 1451 Richard, Duke of York, put forth a formal proposal to be recognized as the heir presumptive to the English throne. This move incensed Henry VI and Edmund Beaufort, Duke of Somerset, and they sent formal summons to Richard to answer for his perfidy. He ignored the summons and retreated with his family to Ludlow Castle where his two eldest sons lived. This may have been George's first meeting with his two older brothers.

The relationship between the three (not including Edmund) York brothers was certainly very interesting. While Richard, the youngest brother, idolized the eldest brother, Edward, Earl of March, George viewed him more or less as an equal and a potential adversary. Richard, meanwhile, due to the relative absence of the Duke of York, looked upon Edward as a replacement for their father. We can safely assume, judging by the brothers' future actions, that George did not share the same feelings and sentiments as Richard.

George enjoyed a healthier relationship with his sisters. Certain records exist which show a close bond between George and his sister Margaret, and he was said to be quite close to Anne who, later in life, expressed concern over her brother's well-being.

As for their father, matters took a turn for the worse when he was taken captive and separated from his family. After extracting a promise to not rebel again, he withdrew to Fotheringhay Castle[6] where they may have stayed till their youngest brother, Richard, was born in late 1452.

The family may have stayed for longer at Fotheringhay after Richard's birth as the Duke of York spent much time in the vicinity. He built a strong bond with the Nevilles, who were his kinsmen. The friendship continued as we see Edward giving the wardship of Richard to Richard Neville, Earl of Warwick, after their father's death.

What is surprising is that nothing of this sort was done for George. We can only presume that the Duke of York and his two eldest sons were too preoccupied with warfare to spare a thought for George and his training.

Richard, Duke of York, tasted a rousing victory at the Battle of St Albans which led to the death of his arch-rival, the Duke of Somerset, and the capture of the Lancastrian King Henry VI. Now having the upper hand, the Duke of York and the Duke of Warwick separated King Henry VI from his queen, Margaret of Anjou, and their son, Edward of Westminster, who took refuge at Kenilworth.

Although the already mentally damaged Henry VI was crowned at St Paul's Cathedral by Richard, he remained a puppet in the hands of the duke, now Lord Protector, and his cronies. And though Henry's mental health remained unstable he was declared fit and opened the new Parliament in 1455.

By the end of the year, however, he started showing signs of mental instability yet again and the duke was restored to his position as the Lord Protector. However, this time the king was one step ahead of him and handed the governmental authority to the royal council. By 1456 the king turned the tables on the duke and stripped him of his post as he took over the royal authority, consigning the duke to being a mere royal councillor.

King Henry VI may have been prompted to take this step on learning of the imprisonment of his half-brother, Edmund Tudor, by the Earl of Warwick, a close associate and friend of the Duke of York. He then left for Kenilworth[7] to join his wife and son.

Henry VI was now united with his wife and son, who was reportedly developing an evil streak himself. She apparently tried to persuade her husband to abdicate in favour of their son. Despite a very public show of reconciliation between Richard, Duke of York, and Margaret of Anjou, they were soon once again baying for each other's blood. The duke came to a decision to move to Ludlow Castle[8] where his wife, along with their children, were lodged. George had last met his brothers when he was one year old and may have resented them. This would have major repercussions during the reign of his brother, King Edward IV.

Richard, Duke of York's fall from grace resulted in the Lancastrians pillaging and ransacking Ludlow Castle where his family was staying. His wife, Cecily, and children, Margaret, George and Richard, were taken prisoner and were sent to Coventry. Prevented from passing a Bill of Attainder against the duke, his estates were confiscated and turned over to the Crown instead. His wife received 1000 marks for hers and her children's upkeep and was ordered to go and live with her sister, Anne Neville (not to be confused by Queen Anne Neville, Richard III's wife), Duchess of Buckingham and a Lancastrian supporter.

By the end of June 1460 the earls of Warwick and Salisbury returned and declared war. At the Battle of Northampton the earls managed to defeat the Lancastrian army and captured King Henry VI, thereby taking control of the monarchy. However, the Duke of York was still in Ireland and probably did not think it safe to return immediately. He bided his time, returning in September 1460. Cecily Neville promptly left her sister's household, taking her children with her, and camped at the Paston's house in Southwark. Later, she proceeded towards Hertford after receiving summons from the duke, leaving the children at Southwark where their elder brother, Edward, now Earl of March, visited regularly.

They probably missed their father's grand entry into London on 10 October 1460. It was now clear that the duke had his eyes on the throne of England rather than being just a Lord Protector of the realm. After some legal wrangling, Parliament decided that while Henry VI retained the throne, York would succeed him rather than Henry's own son, Edward of Westminster, Prince of Wales, after his death, in what we can assume was a peace-making effort.

Predictably, Margaret of Anjou was furious and she headed to Scotland to seek military help. Her supporters began rounding up an army in the north of England and two Yorkist armies, one led by the Duke of York himself, accompanied by his second son, Edmund, Earl of Rutland, and another led by Edward, Earl of March, who headed towards Wales, met them in the north. The Earl of Warwick was left behind in London to protect the duchess and the younger children. George and his parents were probably at Baynard's Castle awaiting news from the north, which seemed to have been trickling in at painfully short intervals.

The Duke of York, meanwhile, was residing at Sandal Castle and was taken by surprise when the Lancastrian army landed at his doorstep. His overconfidence with regards to the size of his army was compounded by a fatal mistake by John Neville, brother of the Earl of Westmorland, and resulted in a sound defeat of the Yorkists and the death of Edmund, the duke's son. Richard was beheaded and his head sent to York where it was displayed on top of Mickelgate Bar[9] with a paper crown stuck on it, which was Margaret of Anjou's way of mocking the duke's temerity to attempt to claim the throne.

At Baynard's Castle, the Duchess of York, Cecily Neville, must have been devasted by the news of her husband and son's deaths, though much has been written about her calm in the face of the storm. George was only eleven years old when he was sent to Utrecht in Burgundy along with his youngest brother, Richard, for safekeeping.

The death of his father and the subsequent yet sudden separation from his immediate family must have been a harrowing experience for young George. Without someone to look up to with regards to his education, coupled with the absence of a guiding presence in the form of his mother and older brothers, he must have felt lost and probably angry, and may have carried this feeling of resentment throughout his adolescence and adult life. This is evidenced by his erratic behaviour and mood swings after his eldest brother, Edward, became King Edward IV of England.

Suddenly thrust into the limelight, George was clearly unprepared for the role he had to play in the deadly political game. He found it difficult to comprehend the sudden shift in the political atmosphere surrounding his family. He was especially close to his mother, a bond that was quite evident later in his life when she unsuccessfully pleaded against the death penalty imposed on her favourite son. This time, fearing for the safety of her young children, she had George and Richard sent away to Burgundy, which was ruled by Philip the Good, Duke of Burgundy. However, he was less than enthusiastic in his welcome of the two English children as he had no intention to oppose the Lancastrians. He ordered the boys to be sent to Utrecht, which was ruled by one of his bastard sons, David of Burgundy. Not much is known about George and Richard's lives in exile at Utrecht, but they must have received some sort of education.

In the meantime, the Yorkists, under the leadership of Edward, Earl of March, won a decisive victory at the Battle of Mortimer's Cross, where Owen Tudor was killed. The upstart Welshman had dared to enter into a union with the Queen of England, Catherine of Valois, after a sound defeat by the Lancastrians at the Second Battle of St Albans. George and Richard's brother was then proclaimed King Edward IV on 4 March 1461.

Keeping in mind the sudden elevation in the status of the two young brothers under his care, a possible match between one of the princes, most likely George, and Marie of Burgundy, was proposed. However, it did not materialise.

By April 1461 George and Richard were on their way to England, lauded as the new king's brothers, most likely landing at Margate. They proceeded towards Canterbury where a grand feast was organised in their honour. They then proceeded to London, probably arriving in the city by the second week of May.

England under the rule of the new Yorkist king, Edward IV, experienced relative peace after decades of warfare. It was at this time, after the return of his two brothers, that Edward, who was residing in the interim at Baynard's Castle, is believed to have secretly married Lady Eleanor Talbot. Whether this marriage really took place or was just a ruse for negative propaganda against his wife and children after his death – which resulted in his marriage to Elizabeth Wydeville being declared illegitimate and his children bastardized by his brother, King Richard III – remains a mystery.

The controversy over Edward IV's 'first' marriage to Lady Eleanor would raise its head many times during his reign thanks to his numerous detractors citing this 'second' marriage to Elizabeth Woodville. One such incident would involve George. The first Tudor king, Henry VII, finally put the issue to rest by legitimising the marriage between Edward and Elizabeth, thus restoring their children, especially their firstborn and Henry's queen, Elizabeth of York, to their respectable status.

The exact nature of the relationship between George and Edward after he became the king is not known. While Edward was a benevolent older brother with a slight superior air about him, George may have looked up to his older brother as his sovereign, but may have not idolised him in the way that his younger brother, Richard, had done. George always had a volatile streak, a fickle individual who displayed traces of envy towards Edward time and again during his life.

George and Richard participated in the night of vigil ceremony during the coronation of their brother and were both created Knights of the Bath. On the day of the coronation at Westminster Abbey, on 28 June, George was formally appointed as the Steward of England, and the day after saw him being created Duke of Clarence. A few weeks later George and Richard, newly created Duke of Gloucester, were made Knights of the Garter. They now had lands to govern and George was also appointed Lord Lieutenant of Ireland in 1478. George, Richard and the younger York siblings now began residing at the Palace of Pleasaunce, formerly known as Bella Court, at Greenwich.

The flipside of this newfound fame for George was that he was thrust into the limelight way too early. He had not even completed his education and there was no full-time guardian appointed to help him in that matter. It is quite possible that the duties that George was entrusted with were actually performed by Lord Wenlock, his assistant.

However, through certain Paston letters we see that George built some important connections in his career such as one with the Duke of Norfolk. In the midst of all this, George managed to complete his basic education.

The sudden rise of his eldest brother to King of England and his subsequent prestigious appointments made him quite arrogant and self-centred; an attitude that ultimately led to his downfall and tragic end.

Edward was rumoured to have secretly married or promised marriage to a certain Eleanor Talbot, but kept the news under wraps. Richard Neville, Earl of Warwick, unaware of any such marriage with his wife's niece, carried out Edward's marital negotiations with the sister-in-law of the King of France, Bona of Savoy, in the hope of securing a politically powerful match.

However, on being told by Warwick to conclude the negotiations with Bona of Savoy, Edward dropped a bombshell at the meeting of his royal council at Reading in late September 1464. He announced that he was already married in a secret ceremony to Elizabeth Woodville, a virtually penniless widow with two sons. The news naturally came as a shock to all who were present but no one was more stunned than the Earl of Warwick. He was made to look like a fool, not only in front of some eminent courtiers but also those enormous upstarts, the Woodville clan.

Swallowing his humiliation, Warwick, along with George, the newly appointed Duke of Clarence, formally presented Elizabeth as queen to the nobles and the public at Reading Abbey on Michaelmas Day, on 29 September 1464.

Domenico Mancini, an Italian traveller, records George's reaction to his brother's marriage as: 'Though Edward's brothers, two of whom were then living, were both seriously concerned at the deed – nevertheless, the Duke of Clarence, the one born second after Edward, clearly showed his ill humour, openly denouncing the obscurity of Elizabeth's family, while proclaiming that the king's marriage to a widow (when he should have married a virgin) was contrary to ancestral practice.'

It was clear, through Mancini's account, that there was no love lost between Elizabeth and her family and George. Perhaps he felt threatened by the fact that he would now be pushed down in the line of succession as Edward's heirs would take precedence. However, as George was just fifteen at that time, it may have been the influence of his mother, Cecily Neville, who was also opposed to the match, that defined his dislike towards the new queen and her openly ambitious family.

It seems that George hid his true feelings for the time being as he is said to have participated in her coronation ceremony, eight months after the announcement at Reading. He even held the washbasin as the Earl of Oxford washed the new queen's hands at the coronation banquet. But his enormous and fragile ego took quite a massive hit when Edward's first child, Princess Elizabeth of York, was born in 1465-66.

By 1466 Edward IV sent his messengers to the court in Burgundy seeking a match for his fourteen-year-old brother, George, Duke of Clarence, with Marie of Burgundy, the nine-year-old daughter of Charles, Count of Charolais, who was also the heir to the powerful dukedom of Burgundy. This match would have ensured George's position as second in line to the dukedom of Burgundy. It would also ensure that George would no longer be a contender for the English throne, paving the way for any children that Edward had with Elizabeth.

This idea – although nothing of the sort happened – revealed Edward's insecurity about the fact that George was a serious contender for the throne if anything should happen to him (Edward) now. George was known to be volatile and unpredictable whereas Richard, the youngest brother, was the complete opposite. Moreover, George, his mother's favourite son, clearly had his eyes on the throne, and Edward's marriage to Elizabeth had clearly unnerved him.

Although the Burgundian match for George came to nothing, they showed interest in his sister, Margaret, who later married the Count of Charolais.

By July 1466, when his niece, Elizabeth of York, was five months old, George finally took up his role as an independent working royal and moved to Tutbury Castle in Staffordshire. His relationship with Richard Neville, Earl of Warwick, who also did not approve of Edward IV's marriage to Elizabeth Woodville, grew stronger, despite never having lived with him under the same roof. Both Warwick and George disliked Elizabeth Woodville and her enormous clan and Warwick was eager to oust them from their position of power and negate their influence over the king.

Warwick tried to reignite the Burgundian matter about George, albeit in a different matter. He reached a conjectural settlement with King Louis XI wherein, on the division of Burgundy, George would gain Holland, Zealand and Brabant. This proposition naturally appealed to George, but Edward refused. This fanned the flames of George's resentment towards his brother even further.

Another bone of contention between the two brothers was the fact that Edward rejected the idea of George marrying Warwick's eldest daughter, Isabel. We can only assume that Edward was sceptical about George's growing influence under Warwick's tutelage and did not wish for it to grow further. It is quite likely that this move of Edward was at the suggestion of Elizabeth Woodville.

Warwick was in France, either intentionally staying away from a court that was increasingly becoming pro-Burgundian or at the behest of the king, when the Burgundians, led by Antoine, the Bastard of Burgundy, arrived in England. His brother, George Neville, the Archbishop of York and the king's chancellor, was abruptly stripped of his post with Edward IV personally going to the archbishop's house to collect the royal seal. This move brought the royal rift between Edward and Warwick out into the open. George, however, stayed back in England and played an important role during the festivities at this time.

Richard Neville, the Earl of Warwick arrived in England from France on the very day Philip the Good, the Duke of Burgundy, died, 15 June 1467. There was no one, apart from George, Duke of Clarence, to welcome him back. On his return to court, Warwick tried to press the French alliance once more but to no avail.

Warwick tried to befriend the tempestuous George on their trip to the eastern counties during the plague outbreak in London, presumably using him as a stepping stone to achieve his objectives. Edward had left for Windsor while their youngest brother, Richard, who was Warwick's ward, accompanied Warwick and George. Both shared a common distaste for the current government and thought up strategies to correct the situation. Tactfully, Warwick suggested that George take charge of the government and offered his daughter, Isabel's hand in marriage, a proposition that George accepted wholeheartedly.

Once back in London, Edward IV was furious on learning about the secret marital agreement between George and Isabel Neville and supposedly arrested his brother for siding with Warwick's plans. This move, if true, must have antagonised George and may have played a role in alienating Edward further from his brother. Meanwhile, owing to the close blood relations between George and Isabel, Warwick was trying hard to obtain a papal dispensation, a process that was made additionally difficult due to the disapproval of King Edward IV.

Secretly conniving with his brother, the Archbishop of York, George Neville, to kickstart a rebellion with a 'Robin of Redesdale'[10] as its leader, Warwick and George quietly escaped to Calais. Warwick then arrived in France to a rousing welcome by King Louis XI. George's presence in France is not recorded.

By late 1467 or early 1468, Warwick and George returned to England and Warwick reconciled with Edward and attended a royal council. However, his hatred towards Elizabeth Woodville remained undeterred and this hatred came to the fore when he had the Rivers' estates plundered.

King Edward IV, however, was still wary of the duo and sought to test Warwick's sincerity by giving him the honour of escorting the former's sister, Margaret of York, in the first stage of her wedding journey from the Palace of the Royal Wardrobe to the streets of London and thence to Charles the Bold, the Duke of Burgundy, despite being fully aware of the animosity between Warwick and the Burgundians. Clearly, Edward not only sought to test Warwick but also staged this as a public show of Warwick's approval of the match.

Although George participated in the next leg of the wedding journey, from London to Kent, the final honour was reserved for the queen's brother, Anthony Woodville, Lord Scales, who accompanied Margaret to Burgundy and handed her over to her new husband.

The reconciliation with Edward did have its advantages as by 14 March 1468-69 George received the papal dispensation from Rome to marry Isabel Neville. This was possible due to the intervention of Dr James Goldwell, the king's proctor at the papal curia.

By April 1469 the Earl of Warwick, with King Edward IV's permission, left for Calais to deal with pirates in the English Channel. However, according to Polydore Vergil, he made sure that the Duke of Clarence did not forget his promise of marrying his eldest daughter, Isabel.

After settling down in Calais, Warwick, in a surprising move, sought permission to visit Charles the Bold, the Duke of Burgundy and his new wife, Margaret of York, the king's sister. The king was only too happy to grant his request and Warwick received a warm welcome from the Burgundian duchy at St Omer.

Back in England, the rebels continued their opposition, despite the death of their leader 'Robin of Redesdale' in 1469. This was supposedly masterminded by the Earl of Warwick and the Duke of Clarence who were eager to oust the Woodvilles from their position. Their main objective, apart from overthrowing the queen's family, was to gain control over the government although they did not wish to dethrone Edward IV.

After the Earl of Warwick's return from Burgundy, the preparations of the wedding of George, Duke of Clarence, and Warwick's daughter, Isabel, commenced in earnest and the two were joined in holy matrimony on 11 July 1469. The wedding seemed to have been a low-key affair, as reported by the chronicler Jehan de Wavrin, who accompanied Warwick from Burgundy. The festivities lasted for a mere two days and were attended by a handful of people.

Immediately after his marriage, and emboldened by the Earl of Warwick's support, George launched a manifesto deriding the rule of Elizabeth Woodville as the Queen of England and the growing influence of her huge family. George and the Earl of Warwick then sailed across the Channel from Calais and reached Sandwich. They then rode to Canterbury where they amassed a rebel force before heading for London and on towards Coventry. On {24?} 24 July 1469 both men fought at the Battle of Edgecote in Northamptonshire, a battle fought presumably to dislodge the Woodvilles from their seat of power.

The Earl of Warwick had planned to displace King Edward IV from the throne of England by declaring him illegitimate – a result of Cecily Neville's folly with an archer named Blaybourne. Unlikely as it may have been, the charge of illegitimacy of Edward IV was brought up many times during the course of George's life and Edward's reign.

The culmination of the Battle of Edgecote[11] saw the seemingly unfair execution of Richard Woodville, Earl Rivers, and his son, John Woodville. The aftermath of the battle also saw the queen's mother, Jacquetta Woodville, arrested on charges of witchcraft. A follower of the Earl of Warwick, Thomas Wake tried to denounce her as a witch by producing a lead figurine supposedly depicting the king entwined with a piece of wire claiming that Jacquetta had intended to cause bodily harm to the king through magic spells. Wake also claimed that a parish clerk named John Daunger said that Jacquetta had made images of both the king and her daughter. Clearly the Earl of Warwick and Duke of Clarence had planned to denounce the king's marriage as a false one that was brought about by sorcery.

The audacious plan did not work as King Edward IV managed to free himself from their captivity and Jacquetta Woodville was cleared of all charges. The ball was now in Edward's court, and, as per John Paston II's letter to his mother in October 1469, the Duke of Clarence and Earl of Warwick and their supporters, the Earl of Oxford and Archbishop Neville of York, Warwick's brother, were now trying their best to get into the newly restored King Edward IV's good books. They were successful as the king, too, sought to reconcile with his enemies.

Despite this setback, Warwick and Clarence did not stop plotting against their king. In 1470 George met his royal brother at Baynard's Castle where their mother, Duchess Cecily Neville, resided. Outwardly, the two displayed their brotherly affection to everyone present; however, the tension simmering between the two parties was palpable. Warwick and Clarence had no idea that Edward had captured Sir Robert Welles, the son of Richard, Lord Welles, whose support the former were seeking in their rebellion against the king. Sir Robert Welles had broken down under intense questioning and confessed everything that Warwick and Clarence were plotting. Sir Robert Welles was then beheaded on 27 March 1470 at Doncaster.

Thanks to Sir Robert's confession, Warwick and Clarence were summoned to the royal court to answer to the charges against them. Not assured of a safe passage, they decided to ignore the summons. While the king was at Doncaster, he was informed that Warwick and Clarence were just six miles away at Austerfield. Anticipating a battle, Edward quickly mustered an army only to be disappointed. The two renegades fled westwards towards Manchester hoping to gain the support of Lord Stanley, but to no avail.

King Edward IV then rode out to York where he restored the earldom of Northumberland to the Percy family; it had previously been held by Warwick's brother, John Neville.

Not in an advantageous position anymore, Warwick and Clarence proceeded to the West Country where they prepared to leave England for Calais. It was a risky proposition as Clarence's wife and Warwick's daughter, Isabel Neville, was heavily pregnant yet there was no question of leaving her behind. The travelling party expected a smooth passage and warm welcome as Warwick was the Captain of Calais.

However, fate conspired against them yet again. Learning about their plans, Edward had instructed the Calais garrison to bar their entry. Lord Wenlock, the leader of the army at Calais and Warwick's erstwhile faithful lieutenant, decided to obey the royal orders and fired cannon shots at the rebels.

Caught in a difficult situation and denied the usual comforts of an expectant mother, Isabel Neville delivered Clarence's first child prematurely. The baby, hastily baptised, died soon after and was buried at sea.

Wenlock, in a seemingly uncharacteristic move, advised the rebels to sail to Normandy, which they did. They then proceeded to Honfeur where Warwick presented an extraordinary proposition to King Louis XI. Warwick was proposing to restore the rather timid and evidently mentally unstable King Henry VI to the throne of England. Despite the Duke of Burgundy's constant exhortations to extradite Warwick, the French king decided to give his plan a shot. He sent messengers to Margaret of Anjou, the former Queen of England and Warwick's arch enemy, to meet them at Amboise to discuss Warwick's plan. Margaret, who was in exile and disgrace, was initially hesitant, not trusting Warwick's peace offering, but agreed to come at the French king's request.

Initially, following the king's marriage to Elizabeth Woodville, Warwick had planned to displace King Edward IV from the throne of England with the help of a dubious claim of illegitimacy – by claiming that Edward was the son of Cecily Neville and an archer named Blaybourne. In a surprising move, Duchess Cecily had no qualms about besmirching her name and reputation in order to displace the Woodvilles from their position of power. However, due to the constant defeats, the Yorkist Warwick changed his plans and now hoped to restore King Henry VI to the throne, and to continue his family's influence over the royals through his progeny. This time, though, it wasn't through his eldest daughter, Isabel Neville, and her husband, George, Duke of Clarence. Instead he planned to achieve this through his younger daughter, Anne, and Margaret of Anjou's son, Edward of Westminster, the former Prince of Wales.

A marriage contract between Edward of Westminster and Anne Neville was quickly drawn up and one of the conditions was that the Duke of Clarence was to be recognised as the Duke of York and would be next in line to the throne in the event that the couple died childless.

George must have been angered at this demotion in his status and did not accompany Warwick when he met Margaret of Anjou at Angers. The marriage negotiations concluded by June 1470 and took place on 13 December at Bayeux. Margaret of Anjou, though, refused to allow the consummation of the marriage till Warwick fulfilled his end of the bargain to restore the Lancastrian line to the throne of England. It is quite possible, given the result of the future events, that the marriage between Edward of Westminster and Anne Neville was never consummated.

Disappointed at these latest developments, George, on the advice of a women presumably sent from either the royal court of England or from his mother, Cecily Neville's household, defected to his brother Edward's side.

Preparations were now underway for the Earl of Warwick's entry to London. Accompanied by the Admiral of France, Jasper Tudor, the Earl of Pembroke, and the Earl of Oxford, Warwick set sail for England with George, Duke of Clarence, accompanying them.

Landing unopposed in the West Country on 13 September 1470, a proclamation naming Henry VI as King of England was immediately issued. Soon after, while the rebels were on the move, Lord Stanley and the Earl of Shrewsbury joined them.

King Edward IV, on his way south from York, summoned John Neville, the Earl of Warwick's brother. Although he answered his king's summons, he then turned back, claiming that he had been mistreated by the king when his earldom of Northumberland was taken away. He then defected to the side of his brother. Now genuinely worried about his safety, King Edward IV, along with his brother, Richard, Duke of Gloucester, his brother-in-law, Earl Rivers, Lord William Hastings and a group of loyal Yorkists, fled to the Low Countries, sailing from Bishop's Lynn. In London an eight-months pregnant Queen Elizabeth

Woodville, along with her daughters, sought and was granted sanctuary at Westminster Abbey.

It was either Archbishop George Neville or Richard Neville, Earl of Warwick, himself who set the dishevelled King Henry VI free from his captivity in the Tower of London and installed him on the throne of England for the second time.

A rather disgruntled George was granted the Erber, the former home of Warwick's father, to maintain as his London residence but was denied a chance to play any role, pivotal or not, in the current government. Disappointed at this turn of events, and on the exhortations of his mother and sisters, George reconciled with his now exiled brother who was mustering an army against Warwick.

In exile in the Low Countries, King Edward IV, along with his brother Richard, Duke of Gloucester, embarked on their return journey to England, landing first at Cromer in Norfolk. He then proceeded to York and then Coventry, which forced Warwick to withdraw and seek fortifications. Edward then set up his court at Warwick and arranged a meeting with his brother, the Duke of Clarence, by the end of March.

By early April Edward marched on London where he captured the Tower and also King Henry VI. He spent two days in London – probably meeting his wife and queen Elizabeth Woodville in sanctuary where she had delivered their first son five months previously – and then went on towards Barnet[12] to confront Warwick. Warwick, who presumably had no inkling of Clarence's desertion, was shocked to learn of this development and was greatly distressed.

A short but intensely fought battle followed where nearly everyone, including George, Duke of Clarence, was wounded. However, the biggest loss was the death of Richard Neville, Earl of Warwick. It was now time for King Edward IV and his band of loyal Yorkists to confront one of their deadliest enemies, Margaret of Anjou.

Margaret of Anjou, along with her son, Edward of Westminster, and her new daughter-in-law, Anne Neville, remained in France while the Lancastrian English troops battled it out at Barnet. After Anne's marriage to Edward of Westminster, the Warwick women left for England with the Lancastrian party in a separate barge. It took them two weeks to cross the English Channel in bad weather, landing at Portsmouth. The ship carrying the Countess of Warwick and the Duchess of Clarence reached England first and, as fate would have it, Margaret of Anjou and

Anne Neville, along with their travelling party, reached England on the very day the Earl of Warwick was killed on the battlefield.

In a surprising move, Anne Beauchamp, Countess of Warwick and the Earl of Warwick's widow, abandoned her daughter – who was now totally at the mercy of Margaret of Anjou – and sought refuge at Beaulieu Abbey[13].

Meanwhile, Margaret of Anjou, along with her son, Edward of Westminster, and her daughter-in-law, Anne Neville, and their troops, marched on towards Wales. They were prevented from crossing the River Severn and forced to take a detour to Tewkesbury instead.

The Lancastrians were soon cornered by King Edward IV and his army. An unwilling Margaret of Anjou was forced by her son and the Duke of Somerset to keep fighting for the throne. The result was a complete bloodbath. Edward of Westminster was killed while the Duke of Somerset was captured and executed.

There are many varying accounts with regards to the death of Edward of Westminster. Some say that he was killed on the battlefield whereas others claim that he was captured and executed and that George, Duke of Clarence, was instrumental in this. However, we can dismiss that claim on the basis of a letter written by George himself to his brother, King Edward IV, mentioning that Edward of Westminster was 'slain in plain battle'. His mother, Margaret of Anjou, fled to the protection of sanctuary in a nearby convent where she was discovered three days later.

George and his wife, Isabel, took Edward of Westminster's widow and Isabel's younger sister, Anne, into their custody while the girls' mother remained at Beaulieu Abbey. Isabel and George now stood at a better position to inherit the Warwick fortune with the former's mother and sister being widows. As long as Anne Neville did not remarry, Isabel and George could rightfully keep her and her share of inheritance in their custody, which was what they were eager to do.

Anne Neville, however, gave the couple the slip and married George, Duke of Clarence's younger brother, Richard, Duke of Gloucester in secret in May or June 1472. George was understandably displeased by this turn of events but could do nothing about it.

The Duke and Duchess of Clarence now settled down at Warwick Castle. After losing her baby to a treacherous storm, Isabel was pregnant again and on 14 August 1473 gave birth to a daughter, Margaret, at Farleigh Castle in Hungerford.

Early Life

Born a royal, Margaret in 1473 was the sole heir of the vast fortunes amassed by her parents. King Edward IV's court being one of extreme discipline and formality, Margaret would have been treated with reverence. She would have received an education befitting her stature and made aware of her roles and responsibilities. George, Duke of Clarence maintained a massive household comprising a staff of 188 people and a stable of ninety-three horses. Isabel, too, maintained a staff of some 125 people and forty-three horses. This ensured that Margaret lived comfortably enough.

She had a fixed routine wherein she was required to observe the norms of the holy days amongst other rules of the Clarence household that were strictly adhered to. Apart from her usual lessons, she was also taught to play musical instruments and sew.

Such skills equipped women of noble birth to run households of their own post marriage. And certainly a grand marriage was envisioned for Margaret, given her father's status and influence. Doubtless, there would be no shortage of suitors for her hand.

25 February 1475 saw the birth of Margaret's brother, Edward Plantagenet, at Warwick Castle[14]. It was celebrated in a grand manner and the king himself stood as godfather at his christening. He even granted the earldom of Warwick to the baby, a title that Clarence relinquished in favour of his son.

George did not forget his daughter, however. As he left for a military campaign he granted a large number of manors to his daughter to ensure financial stability in his absence or possible death.

In 1476 Isabel, Duchess of Clarence, was pregnant once again, giving birth to a boy they named Richard after the duke's youngest brother. However, soon after the birth Isabel fell gravely ill, and, in a seemingly foolhardy decision, was taken to Warwick Castle to recuperate. This move did more damage than good as Isabel's condition deteriorated and she passed away on 12 December 1476.

George must have genuinely loved his wife; nothing else can justify his next action, which earned him a place in the Tower and his name on the death warrant signed by his own brother, King Edward IV.

Being a royal widower with immense wealth, George was suddenly thrust into the marriage market for the second time. This time he tried to bring about a marital alliance with Mary of Burgundy, the stepdaughter of his sister, Margaret, and with Margaret, the sister of the King of Scotland. However, it was his brother, King Edward IV, who yet again put a stop to his grand plans.

Thwarted yet again, bitterness against the king crept into Clarence's heart. He accused two of his former servants, Ankarette Twynho and John Thursby, of poisoning his wife, Isabel Neville, and bullied a hastily put together jury to condemn them to death. In April 1477 Clarence had Twynho and Thursby summarily executed. (Twynho was posthumously pardoned the next year by King Edward IV.)

Clarence got away with a reprimand but his mental state was deteriorating. In the same year, one of his retainers, John Stacey, an astronomer from Oxford, was arrested and thrown into the Tower of London. After a round of interrogation and torture, Stacey confessed that he had 'imagined and compassed the death of the king'. Stacey, in turn, incriminated a Thomas Burdett and a Thomas Blake (who happened to be a chaplain at Merton's College in Oxford). The three of them stood trial for treason and were condemned to death. Blake was saved by a last-minute plea by the Bishop of Norwich, but Burdett and Stacey were executed.

Clarence ignored the subtle warning given to him by his brother. John Goddard, an ex-Lancastrian, was chosen by Clarence to burst into the royal court and proclaim the innocence of the two men.

This time King Edward IV had had enough. He summoned Clarence to Windsor, reproached him for his behaviour and had him arrested and incarcerated in the Tower of London. He was put on trial for treason and prosecuted by his royal brother.

Despite their mother's desperate pleas for mercy, George was condemned to death and was privately executed on 18 February 1478, apparently by drowning in a butt of Malmsey wine, the manner he chose to end himself.

Margaret and Edward had lost both their parents in the space of a year, and not only were they orphaned, they were the children of an attainted traitor. Bearing no animosity toward his wayward brother's children, King Edward IV and his queen, Elizabeth Woodville, took them under their wings and made them their wards. Margaret was completely at her royal uncle's mercy as she, unlike her brother, had no lands or fortunes that she could call her own.

King Edward IV kept Margaret comfortably enough; records exist that suggest generous amounts were spent for her clothing and as wages to her retainers. The lands that Clarence held in his own right reverted back to the Crown whereas the lands that he held in the right of his wife were exempted. This made Edward, the new Earl of Warwick, heir to a respectable fortune.

By September 1480 Queen Elizabeth Woodville granted the custody of the Earl of Warwick to Thomas Grey, her son by her first marriage. He was also granted the custody of Margaret. The only reasoning behind this move was that the queen wished to protect Warwick's inheritance from Warwick's uncle, Richard, Duke of Gloucester.

Margaret and Edward remained under the royal wardship, first under King Edward IV and then under King Richard III. While Richard, Duke of Gloucester, was busy putting into motion his plans to mount the throne of England following Edward's death on 9 April 1483, he sent Edward, Earl of Warwick, to the custody of his maternal aunt, Anne Neville, Duchess of Gloucester. Richard's next move of bastardising his dead brother's children (on the basis of an apparently secret marriage between Edward and Lady Eleanor Butler) greatly enhanced Margaret and Edward's social standing. However, the taint of being the child of an attainted traitor barred him from the line of succession, as explained by his royal uncle.

While the two sons of the late King Edward IV, Edward V and Richard of Shrewsbury, Duke of York, were imprisoned in the Tower of London (for their own protection as claimed by their uncle), Margaret and her brother, Edward, were sent to Sheriff Hutton Castle[15]in Yorkshire, which was under the care of Margaret's maternal family, the Nevilles, for 300 years before being handed over to Richard, Duke of Gloucester, under the care of their cousin, John de la Pole. A secure and grand place of residence, Margaret and Edward lived comfortably for the next two years at Sheriff Hutton, enjoying breathtaking views of York Minster from their windows. They were soon joined by the late King Edward IV's daughters, Elizabeth of York, Cecily and Anne.

Tragedy struck the king's family as his only son and heir, Edward, Prince of Wales, died in 1484. The young and frail son of King Richard III was the titular head of the Northern Council formed by his father and his loss came as a big blow to his parents and extended family.

The leadership of the Northern Council was granted nominally to Edward, Earl of Warwick, while King Richard's nephew, the Earl of Lincoln, helmed the affairs of the council. Warwick was also named the heir apparent (some claim that it was John de la Pole, Earl of Lincoln who was named Richard's heir before Warwick) and was accorded preferential treatment at the royal court.

However, disaster loomed just around the corner as King Richard III's army met Henry Tudor's ramshackle ragtag of men at the ill-fated Battle of Bosworth in 1485. Richard was killed and unceremoniously buried in an unmarked grave at Greyfriars in Leicester.

Almost immediately after his victory at Bosworth, the new monarch, King Henry VII, proceeded north, specifically Sheriff Hutton Castle, to gain custody of the erstwhile royals who were housed there. He was especially concerned about Edward, Earl of Warwick, fearing that he might be supported in his claim for the throne of England by the north – his mother being Richard Neville's daughter, Isabel.

Amidst this, he had Henry Percy, Duke of Northumberland, imprisoned as he suspected the latter of stirring up support for the Earl of Warwick. Although hardly any proof exists for this claim, the fact that Northumberland declined to support either Henry Tudor or King Richard III during the Battle of Bosworth makes it believable. Rumours also swirled that the new king, Henry VII, had died of the plague and that Humphrey Stafford, a former member of King Richard III's household, bolstered by speculation that Edward, Earl of Warwick had escaped across the English Channel, had engineered an uprising against the new king.

Fearing an all-out rebellion in favour of Warwick, King Henry VII granted custody of the earl and Margaret to his mother, Margaret Beaufort, now known as My Lady The King's mother. Along with them, he also kept his betrothed, Elizabeth of York, and her sisters in his mother's custody. She began her life at the royal court as the chief lady-in-waiting of her cousin, Queen Elizabeth of York, under the close scrutiny of the king and his mother lest she try and contact any of her kinsmen and stir up a rebellion.

By late 1486 the queen had given birth to her first child, a boy they named Arthur. She walked at the head of the royal and noble ladies during the christening. Later that year, she also watched her cousin being crowned from a special stage that was erected between the pulpit and the high altar of Westminster Abbey.

Considered a threat from the very beginning, Edward, Earl of Warwick, was thrown into the Tower of London almost immediately into the reign of King Henry VII, with the king claiming that it was for his own safety. Initially paying a pension of 500 marks from the

Warwick-Spencer lands to Anne Beauchamp, Countess of Warwick, and Margaret and Edward's maternal grandmother, King Henry VII, in 1490, restored the lands to the countess who immediately made the king her heir, thus disinheriting her grandchildren.

In 1487 a new threat reared its head when an imposter named Lambert Simnel, trained by a priest, claimed to be the Earl of Warwick. The claim was further bolstered by the support of Margaret of Burgundy, the sister of George, Duke of Clarence, and the support and defection of John de la Pole, Earl of Lincoln. The matter was settled through the Battle of Stoke Field[16] and Simnel was quickly subdued, and, instead of being punished, found work in the king's kitchen. However, King Henry VII was intelligent enough to recognise the threat that the young earl posed and despite repeated pleas from his wife and the earl's sister, refused to set him free.

With the intention of pushing her further into obscurity, a need prompted by the rebellion of Lambert Simnel, My Lady the King's Mother got little Margaret married to her kinsman, Sir Richard Pole. The marriage took place sometime between September 1486 and November 1487. A loyal Tudor supporter who was knighted immediately after the Battle of Stoke Field, Sir Richard Pole held several important offices for the king. Although he was far beneath her status – she was an erstwhile royal princess and he was a knight – the marriage was a success, probably because Margaret may have wanted to ward off the suspicion that was attached to her name.

Now known as Lady Margaret Pole, she enjoyed a quiet life after her eventful childhood and adolescence. She stayed by his side at Stourton Castle in Staffordshire as he went about his royal duties in Wales.

Conforming to her new domesticity, Margaret gave birth to five children while fulfilling her duties towards the household of Arthur Tudor, Prince of Wales, who was the first-born son of her cousin and queen, Elizabeth of York, and King Henry VII, at Ludlow Castle in Wales.

Apart from managing Ludlow, Sir Richard Pole was involved in managing many other castles in Wales such as Harlech, Conwy, Caernarfon and Beaumaris. An astute military man, Sir Richard was a part of the royal army as they laid siege to Boulogne in October 1492. Thanks to his military exploits and administrative skills, he was made a Knight of the Garter and was accorded a prominent place at the marriage ceremony of Princess Margaret Tudor with the King of Scotland in 1503.

In the meantime, Margaret lived a quiet life, probably revelling in the anonymity that her marriage to Sir Richard provided. When Arthur, Prince of Wales, married Katherine of Aragon, she developed a close friendship with the Infanta and continued to champion hers, and much later, her daughter Mary's cause throughout their lives. She was by Katherine's side when Arthur died of the sweat merely five months after their marriage.

Sir Richard Pole returned to his other duties in Wales after Arthur's death. Margaret returned to Stourton and alternated between living there and at Bockmer. In 1504, while Margaret was pregnant with her fifth child, Richard was reinstated to his former post as the chamberlain at Chester. However, it is unlikely that he ever got to see his youngest son as he was dead by the end of October.

After the death of Sir Richard in 1505, Margaret lived in penury as she had just a small piece of land. She had no other source of income and no suitor who might marry her and provide comfort and obscurity. She lived in exile at various places, including Syon Abbey, and committed her son, Reginald, to the Church, for which he remained bitter throughout his life. She turned to King Henry VII for help and he grudgingly parted with some funds to help her afford Richard the funeral that he deserved due to his position and kinship with the king's mother, Margaret Beaufort.

It is strange, however, that despite being the king's ward, Margaret's older son, Henry, was never invited to court nor was his education and upkeep funded by his royal guardian. One plausible explanation for this, according to Hazel Pierce, is that as he was the grandson of George, Duke of Clarence, and nephew and heir of Edward, Earl of Warwick, Henry had a greater claim on the throne of England than the usurper, Henry Tudor. He may have likely feared an uprising, as was the case with Edward, in support of Henry Pole.

Katharine of Aragon was facing difficulties of her own. After Arthur's death she was betrothed to Prince Henry, but in November 1503 her mother, Queen Isabella of Castile, died unexpectedly and the political aftermath made Katharine a less viable match for the future King of England. King Henry VII began hunting for more suitable brides for the new heir to the throne, and to add insult to injury, he even stopped Katharine's monthly allowance. In dire straits and shuttled from one derelict house to another, the young widow bore her hardships with admirable resilience. Margaret maintained her friendship with Katharine during these times and it bore fruit later on in their lives.

Margaret's tough life ended when King Henry VIII married Katharine of Aragon on 22 April 1509. Her fortunes took a turn for the better and she was invited back to the court as the new queen's lady-in-waiting. She attended Katharine's coronation, her boarding charges were paid for by the new king and she was welcomed back warmly into the royal fold by the young king. Her oldest son, Henry, was employed as one of the king's attendants and was showered with gifts of fine clothes regularly. King Henry VIII also supported the education of Margaret's third son, Reginald, which helped him move to Magdalen College.

The Earldom of Salisbury was restored to her in 1512 through an Act of Parliament, making her the first woman of that era to hold a peeress in her own right and one of the richest and most influential women in the country. However, the Crown retained her brother Warwick's Spencer lands. It is quite possible that Katharine was behind all this benevolence towards Margaret and her family; she honoured Margaret's friendship during their trying times and also may have wanted to make up for the unfortunate execution of Edward, Earl of Warwick, for which Katharine's parents were responsible. Margaret's kin was also raised to new heights. William Courteney, and later, his son, Henry, were reinstated as earls of Devon, and Charles Somerset, Lord Herbert, was made Earl of Worcester. The illegitimate son of King Edward IV, Arthur Plantagenet, was created Viscount Lisle while Thomas Manners, a cousin of Margaret, was created Earl of Rutland.

Margaret also sought to wipe the taint of treachery from her slain brother's name and approached the king through a carefully drafted letter which sought his kindness and goodness of heart in ridding her brother of his attainder. King Henry VIII complied, and with a few conditions attached, restored her brother's lands to Margaret. She now held estates in seven English counties along with manors in Calais, Isle of Wight, and Wales. She held a total of fifty-six manors in England and Wales by the time she was arrested in 1538, which included her jointure of Ellesborough and Medmenham. Her estate of Le Herber was a grand palace which, during the reign of King Richard III, was known as the King's Palace. Margaret carried out various restoration projects and also rented out the tenements that were a part of Le Herber. Margaret personally commissioned Warblington Castle in Hampshire and it reflects her aesthetics and preferences as well as declaring her rising social standing. She made sure that her coat of arms was emblazoned on each of her residences and estates to reflect her prestigious position as the Countess of Salisbury.

By 1538 Margaret was the fifth richest peeress in England. She supported and endorsed new age learning, especially in the case of Renaissance noblewomen such as Gentian Hervet who translated Erasmus' *de immensa misericordia Dei* (The Great Mercy of God) into English for her.

Her children did immensely well, too, at the royal court. Her eldest son, Henry, was created Baron Montague, which was one of the Neville titles, and her second son, Arthur, was one of King Henry VIII's closest friend and one of the Six Gentlemen of the Privy Chamber. Although he suffered a minor setback when his patron, Edward Stafford, Duke of Buckingham, was executed, he recovered his position soon enough and was restored into the king's inner circle once again. Her third son, Reginald, stayed and received his early education at Sheen Priory and graduated from Magdalen College in Oxford. By 1518 he was made a Dean of Wimbourne Minster at Dorset and then sent to the University of Padua in Italy where he met various notable Renaissance figures such as Pietro Bembo, Gianpietro Carafa (the future Pope Paul IV) and Giovanni Morone amongst others. On his return in 1527 he was made Prebendary of Salisbury and Dean of Exeter. He was also a canon in York, despite not being ordained as a priest, and was trusted and sent to Paris by King Henry to research general opinions with regards to his divorce from Katherine of Aragon.

Margaret displayed her steely side and her business acumen on the untimely death of her son Arthur. In a bid to secure her grandchildren's future (Arthur's children with his wife, Jane Lewkenor), Margaret and her eldest son, Henry, Baron Montague, compelled Arthur's widow to take vows of chastity at Syon Abbey. She was later released from her vows and went on to marry again, though whether she retained her fortune or was forced to give it up is unknown. Her youngest son, Geoffrey, married Constance, the daughter of Edmund Packenham, and inherited the Lordington estate through his marriage.

Margaret's daughter, Ursula, was married to Henry Stafford, the only son and heir of Edward Stafford, Duke of Buckingham. Hers was the most magnificent marriage of all as the Duke of Buckingham was the greatest peer in the kingdom and Henry, as the only heir, stood to inherit it someday. She enjoyed a luxurious life after marriage and there is no record of her having served any of King Henry VIII's six queens.

Margaret's fortunes at the royal court fluctuated. In 1518 she disputed with the king over a land issue. The contested lands in question were handed over to the Duke of Somerset, whose Beaufort ancestors had held them years ago. In 1520 she was appointed governess to Princess Mary but was removed when her sons got involved in the entire Duke of Buckingham episode (see next page). Restored to her position in 1525, her fortunes continued to rise. When Princess Mary was sent to Ludlow, Margaret accompanied her, aware of the responsibilities that the king and the queen trusted to her: good education and lessons in 'virtuous demeanour'. Mary's health was fragile and Margaret was to make sure that the princess got some 'moderate exercise'. Mary was also to receive lessons in dancing, playing the virginals and other musical instruments. Taking care of the princess and her needs was a challenging task. Mary could be quite finicky about her food and suffered from chronic menstrual issues which escalated due to stress while Katharine was going through her divorce with the king, but Margaret rose to the challenge and made a place in the princess' heart for life.

Margaret's position was threatened during the King's Great Matter when her mistress and patron, Queen Katharine of Aragon, was cast aside to enable the king to marry Anne Boleyn. Incidentally, Anne's father, Thomas Boleyn, happened to be Margaret's steward of Bushey in Hertfordshire. In addition to Boleyn, many well-known Tudor luminaries, such as Sir William Compton, Sir Thomas Denys and Sir Thomas Heneage, happened to be stewards in Margaret's service. Many members of her staff were recommended by Cardinal Thomas Wolsey. It is quite notable and praiseworthy that, in an era where infighting between servants was commonplace, Margaret managed to maintain a cordial relationship between herself and her staff.

Fluctuating Fortunes

The King's Great Matter brought about immense political upheavals in England and the Pole family, having a close affinity with the royals, were caught in the middle of it.

The first chink in the Pole armour probably came when Arthur Pole was said to have been dismissed from service in 1519, possibly on the recommendation of Cardinal Wolsey. Wolsey may have feared the rising influence of the Pole family on the king, which would have undermined his own position in the court. However, the facts of this event are unclear as during the Field of Cloth of Gold event in 1520, Arthur is said to have attended as a member of the king's chamber and held the position as the Squire of the King's Body, which allowed him the honour of sleeping near the king in a pallet bed. Meanwhile, Margaret continued to enjoy royal favours and was appointed Princess Mary's governess and ward in 1520.

Two months after a jousting tournament held in York Place in February 1521, the Duke of Buckingham was executed and Henry Pole, Lord Montague, was imprisoned in the Tower along with his father-in-law. Buckingham was accused of treason and conspiring to overthrow the king. He was said to have been speculating about his possible succession to the throne and believed to have been planning to assassinate King Henry VIII. An already paranoid king, Henry wasted no time in sending Buckingham to the block and thus put all those who were friendly with Buckingham in a perilous position.

Arthur Pole was also expelled from the court. It was revealed that he was attempting to convince Leonard Grey to write a letter to someone, most likely Reginald who was in Padua at that time. He was also suspected of concealing a mysterious visitor at Dowgate although it may have just been a messenger or an informer bringing him news about his brother who was imprisoned.

The king began doubting Reginald's loyalty as well while Cardinal Thomas Wolsey tried to convince the French about the Pole family's innocence and dismiss Montague's imprisonment as a minor inconvenience. And despite her impeccable behaviour, Margaret, too, was dismissed from her post. It was abundantly clear that their association and friendship with the Duke of Buckingham threatened their employment at the royal court and also the goodwill that the family had accumulated over the years.

The Pole family were exonerated by the king in due course. However, Margaret did not regain her post as Princess Mary's governess until four years later in 1525. In 1522 the family began receiving Christmas gifts again from Queen Katharine of Aragon and Lord Montague was chosen amongst many others to attend to the king when he met King Charles V at Canterbury in May 1522. Arthur Pole, too, regained his lost goodwill with the king and was able to persuade him to take action against his father-in-law, Sir Roger Lewkenor, and the Earl of Arundel. The following year both Henry and Arthur were sent on the doomed French campaign with Charles Brandon, Duke of Suffolk. Suffolk appointed Henry, Lord Montague, as a captain and knighted Arthur.

Although restored to favour, the Pole family now grew wary of King Henry VIII's unpredictable temper and moods and tread carefully. Margaret would also have to reconcile with the fact that her daughter, Ursula, who was married to the Duke of Buckingham's son and heir, would never inherit the title of Duchess of Buckingham, nor would her son-in-law inherit his father's vast estates. He was finally given a few of his father's manors in 1522 and 1531, namely Shropshire, Cheshire, Staffordshire, Essington, Caus, and Hay in Wales. However, these clearly did produce a suitably lucrative income for Henry Stafford as he kept pleading poverty. Ursula and Stafford's twelve children, previously an asset, were now a burden as the family scrambled for money and to regain even a fragment of their lost honour.

The marriage of Margaret's son, Arthur, to Sir Roger Lewkenor's daughter was an unhappy one. The already sour situation turned worse when Arthur died suddenly sometime around 1528, most likely from sweating sickness. (It was at this time that the virulent disease claimed Sir William Compton's life and almost claimed Cardinal Thomas Wolsey's and Anne Boleyn's lives.) Arthur's death prompted Margaret to write out a new will. Despite taking a vow of chastity, Jane Lewkenor married a Sir William Barentyne and Margaret felt it necessary to safeguard Arthur's inheritance for his children. This need was accelerated when Sir Roger Lewkenor married for the third time and had three daughters by his third wife. Finally, King Henry VIII became the mediator and settled the issue through an Act of Parliament in 1543-4. After dividing all of Arthur's wealth according to the king's stipulations, it was seen that Arthur's children inherited considerably less than Margaret had expected.

As if this wasn't enough, Margaret soon landed in trouble herself. This time it was over the lands that she claimed under the earldom of Salisbury whereas the king argued that they belonged to the Duke of Somerset. This land dispute had been going on for the last eight years and played a part in undermining Margaret's position in the royal court.

Margaret, working as the governess of Princess Mary, gradually saw her friend and queen being usurped by the much younger and vivacious Anne Boleyn. Margaret was soon drawn into the vortex of the matter as King Henry VIII attempted to prove his marriage to Katharine was invalid. As Princess Mary's governess, Margaret hovered around court circles, often moving with her young charge to Ludlow, Thornbury, Tickenhall and Hartlebury. Katharine and Mary corresponded regularly and the queen never failed to remember her old friend in her letters. In 1527 talks of a possible marital alliance between England and France – the potential bridegrooms being King Francis I's second son, the duc d'Orleans and King Francis I himself – commenced and Margaret was ordered to bring Mary to court in April so that she could meet the French ambassadors. King Francis I was an incorrigible lecher and the English courtiers may have breathed a sigh of relief when Princess Mary was contracted to marry his son instead.

Queen Katharine of Aragon, however, continued to fall out of favour with the king as he continued to search for ways to end his marriage. It did not help matters that her nephew, King Charles V, the Holy Roman Emperor, refused to hand over King Francis I to England when the former captured the French King in Pavia in 1525. Moreover, despite her success on the battlefield of Flodden[17] and her brilliant political acumen, Katharine had failed in her most important duty: to bear Henry a living son, and an heir to the English throne.

Katharine refused to accept Henry's claims that their marriage was invalid and retire to a nunnery, and declared that it was God's will that she was King Henry VIII's wife and queen. This position threatened Mary's succession and the queen was separated from her daughter and banished from the court. During this time, Margaret did her best to protect Mary, already of fragile health, from the tensions between her parents. Assuming that the king's fascination for the seductive Anne Boleyn was only a passing fancy, Margaret attempted to maintain normalcy in the princess' household in order to avoid stressing her out. Although Mary's household was reduced, Margaret was retained as her governess and they spent Christmas at the royal court in 1529 and 1530. The king even visited her in Richmond in 1531, which cheered her up considerably.

By 1531 Margaret was running out of ways to shield Mary from the happenings at court. A fifteen-year-old Mary was a sharp and intelligent girl who could no longer be hidden from the truth. King Henry VIII's desertion of Katharine in 1531 coincided with the onset of Mary's puberty and led to a severe emotional crisis with the princess succumbing to hysteria and tantrums before slipping into depression.

The birth of Princess Elizabeth in 1533 raised the question of Mary's position. The king ordered Cromwell to inform Lord Hussey, Mary's chamberlain, to hand over the princess' jewels to Mistress Frances

Elmer. Margaret was finally pushed into a situation where she had to make a choice: obey the king's orders or defend Mary's position. Out of devotion to Katharine of Aragon and Margaret's own relationship with Mary, she took matters in her own hands and prepared an inventory of the princess' jewels herself. She refused to hand it over without seeing an official letter from the king, forcing Lord Hussey to beseech Cromwell for it. Hussey's troubles increased manifold when Cromwell sent another letter demanding Mary's plates. Hussey was forced to inform Cromwell that the jewels were in the custody of Margaret and that she refused to hand them over. The situation worsened when Katharine refused to hand over to Anne Boleyn the christening robes that her mother, Isabella of Castile, had given her. Following Elizabeth's birth, Mary was informed about the reduction in her household and that she was no longer the Princess of Wales. Thankfully for her, familiar faces like Margaret, Lord Hussey and Dr Featherstone remained in her service, much to her relief.

During a visit from a deputation headed by the Earl of Oxford, Mary complicated matters by refusing to accept her illegitimacy and the loss of her royal title. This angered Henry and he decided to dissolve the princess' household completely, placing Mary in Princess Elizabeth's household. Margaret was probably kept away from Mary in order to help her conform to this new situation. Henry blamed Margaret for Mary's obstinacy and refused Eustace Chapuys' request to place the princess back in Margaret's care, saying that the Countess of Salisbury was a 'fool of no experience'.

The erstwhile Princess Mary, now rechristened Lady Mary, took her place in her half-sister's household amidst much trepidation. She feared that she was now amongst people who would not understand and empathise with her. Margaret, worried about her charge, requested that the king let her stay in the employ of Mary, but her request was refused point blank.

The stress of the last few years – Katharine's divorce, protecting Mary, and then, finally losing her custody – took a toll on Margaret's health, as mentioned by her son, Lord Montague, in a letter to Lord Lisle in which he mentions Margaret being extremely weak while she recuperated at her manor in Bisham.

Further troubles lay in store for Margaret as she became embroiled in the infamous Elizabeth Barton case. According to A. Denton Cheney, it was Cromwell who was trying to implicate as many supporters of Queen Katharine of Aragon in the sordid affair, namely the Marchioness of Exeter and Margaret. It has also been suggested that it was the king who attempted to get rid of Katharine's supporters by accusing them of playing a part in the conspiracy. Bishop John Fisher and Sir Thomas More, who had actually met Barton, found themselves in hot water. Margaret's incrimination, however, was through an indirect source, Father Hugh Rich of the Observant Friars, who claimed to have mentioned about Barton's visions to Margaret in a conversation. He also claimed to have repeated the nun's prophecies, which concerned the king's liaison with Anne Boleyn, to the queen, Princess Mary, Lord and Lady Hussey, and the Marchioness of Exeter, thereby putting all of them in grave danger. Barton's influence kept growing and King Henry, fearing that Princess Mary's behaviour was being influenced by the nun's claims, blamed Margaret for contributing to this.

Margaret was put in an even more precarious position when Princess Mary's supporters, buoyed by Barton's predications, were inspired to rebel against the king and fight for Mary's rights. Luckily for Margaret, she hadn't met Barton herself; moreover, Queen Katharine had always refused to meet the nun and must have instructed Margaret to follow suit. Despite this, it is quite likely that she was questioned about the affair.

Margaret must have been exasperated and exhausted with all this stress and decided to maintain a low profile. She remained almost incognito for the next three years, barring one altercation with Thomas Cromwell as she opposed William Barlow's appointment as Prior of Bisham Abbey. Barlow had openly supported Anne Boleyn against Katharine and enjoyed the patronage of both Boleyn and Cromwell. However, her efforts to displace Barlow came to nothing, and she also had to deal with the sudden disappearance of her personal chaplain, John Helyar, in 1534, a move that raised many eyebrows.

In 1535 the king wrote to Reginald Pole, who was studying in Italy, asking his opinion on the Pope's authority and his marriage to Anne Boleyn. Reginald's reply, which arrived in June, was a scathing one. He compared King Henry VIII to a wild animal and accused him of incest. He also called the king a robber and a murderer, describing him as one who is more dangerous than the Turks. He supported and encouraged Charles V to launch an attack on England. Seething with rage, Henry, who had expected a conciliatory reply, feared that the French king, Francis I, would also follow suit. King Henry VIII read out Reginald's letter to Margaret himself, and Margaret, prompted by her oldest son, Montague, denounced Reginald as a traitor. Advised by Montague once again, Margaret wrote to Reginald urging him to serve his king faithfully. Already in a perilous position at court, Montague, too, wrote to Reginald using a stronger tone than their mother.

Exiled from the royal court and residing at the faraway Kimbolton Castle[18] in Huntingdonshire in dire conditions, Katharine of Aragon finally succumbed to what we may assume was a heart attack on 7 January 1536. On one hand, according to Eustace Chapuys, Henry was relieved on hearing the news of Katharine's death. On the other, Margaret must felt an immense pain at losing her friend whose friendship she had enjoyed and cherished for over thirty-five years. That same year, Anne Boleyn fell spectacularly from grace as Thomas Cromwell, an erstwhile supporter of the Boleyn faction, worked against them and pulled off a coup which saw Anne, along with her brother, George, and four more nobles accused of treason and executed. Eleven days after her gruesome death, King Henry VIII married Jane Seymour.

Queen Jane was sympathetic to Katharine of Aragon's cause and brought about a reconciliation between the king and his daughter, Mary. This did come with conditions: Mary had to accept and agree to her father's reasons for breaking away from the Rome and marrying Anne Boleyn. This reconciliation also brought about Margaret's return to court life and former power, much to Princess Mary's happiness. The king also held the hope that Reginald Pole would return to court and accept Henry's supremacy. Margaret's star was rising once again, so much so that Lord Lisle wrote to her urging her to find a place for his daughter in the new queen's household.

The summer of 1536 saw Margaret retire from court life permanently. She had expected an appointment in Mary's household but that was not to be. Mary, probably on the advice of Thomas Cromwell, had drawn up a list of ladies she wanted in her household and the most telling exclusion was Margaret. We can safely assume that Mary, aware of Margaret's fluctuating fortunes at court, wished to keep her away and protect her from any further conspiracies and suspicions. It could also be that Thomas Cromwell, with the support of the king, decided not to appoint Margaret fearing that she shared Reginald's views and would have influenced Mary against her father. Although Margaret kept in touch with Mary, sending her gifts on several occasions, she no longer came to court nor did she attend any important occasions such as Prince Edward's christening. She even stopped sending New Year's gifts to the king. She spent most of her time at Warblington as she managed her vast number of estates and overseeing the rearing and education of her five granddaughters. Her two sons visited her frequently, but the king did not.

The fortunes of Margaret's sons were also precarious. Reginald's stance was well known. Although he initially supported the king during his Great Matter, he grew suspicious of the latter's intents and went against him. He requested permission to leave the court, which was granted happily as he feared, as did the king, that he might speak his mind if he stayed behind. Montague's career was consistently comfortable, barring the seemingly erroneous endorsement of Reginald, while Geoffrey's fortunes oscillated as he was always short of money. Both brothers supported the king and Anne Boleyn on his divorce from Katharine of Aragon, mainly to keep the king's favour on their side. Geoffrey, although charming, was an impulsive person, lacking caution in his actions and unsuitable to hold any official position. He often borrowed money from Thomas Cromwell and accumulated a large debt as he purchased a variety of grains and commodities using the royal commission. It was Montague who held the king's favour towards the family, even though this was merely an illusion. However, even Montague's fragile goodwill could not withstand the storm that the Pole family were about to face.

The Fall of the Pole Family

The disillusioned northerners rose up against the king to protest the dissolution of the monasteries in what we know as the Pilgrimage of Grace. They demanded the expulsion of upstart noblemen such as Thomas Cromwell and also demanded that Mary be relegitimised and restored to the line of succession.

In December 1536 Reginald was made a cardinal, hoping that he could compel Francis I of France and Charles V, the Holy Roman Emperor, to join hands with the rebels against King Henry VIII. However, this plan proved to be a double-edged sword for Reginald as neither the French king nor the emperor wished to antagonize Henry at this point of time. All it did was thrust Reginald and his actions into Henry's suspicious gaze.

After two years of lying low, the Pole family's honour was threatened again when Geoffrey's servant, and an ex-pirate, Hugh Holland, was arrested. Margaret maintained a 'surgeon house' in her estates at Warblington where a doctor named Richard Ayer was employed. Ayer, who had accepted the 'New Learning', suspected Margaret of harbouring priests who influenced and prevented her from embracing the new faith. In the summer of 1538 Ayer readily divulged some incriminating details to Gervase Tyndall, a schoolmaster and a possible spy of Cromwell's who was staying at the hospital, saying that Holland was acting as a messenger between the Pole family and the exiled Reginald.

Margaret's next actions aroused even more suspicion. Believing Tyndall to be of the reformed faith, she ordered Ayer to send him away. Tyndall, though, refused to leave, so she ordered Ayer to send all the other patients away. Cromwell's spy then passed on the information on Hugh Holland that Ayer had given him and Holland was promptly arrested.

In custody, Holland lost no time in implicating his master, Geoffrey Pole, and also on the absconding chaplain, John Helyar. Helyar, who was opposed to the religious changes, left the country in fear of his life without informing Margaret as she would have definitely prevented him from taking such a step. Geoffrey, however, communicated with the fugitive chaplain on a regular basis, as revealed by Holland.

Holland also mentioned that Geoffrey had asked him to deliver a message to Reginald offering to join him when Holland went to Flanders to sell wheat. In reply, Reginald told Holland to carry a message to his mother in which he sought her blessings and another to Geoffrey advising him not to meddle too much in such matters. Nevertheless, Geoffrey kept speaking about going abroad and kissing the Pope's feet.

Geoffrey Pole was promptly arrested on 29 August 1538 and taken to the Tower of London where Holland was already incarcerated. He remained in the Tower for two months until he was formally interrogated. When asked for the names of those with whom he had discussed 'a change of this world', he offered his oldest brother, Lord Montague, hastily adding that Montague no longer shared this belief. The government's interests in Montague grew and Geoffrey, already of fragile mental health and now guilt-stricken, attempted suicide. He is believed to have stabbed himself in the chest with a blunt knife.

Geoffrey recovered quickly and the interrogations resumed. He incriminated Gertrude, Marchioness of Exeter, and, once again, his brother, Montague. This time, he mentioned that Montague had told him that he believed the king's ulcerous leg would be the death of him

Geoffrey also mentioned that Montague told him that he never loved the king and that the king would soon lose his mind.

Montague and the Marquis of Exeter were arrested on 4 November and were soon joined by their young sons and the Marchioness of Exeter. When subjected to rigorous interrogation, Montague managed to retain his composure, unlike his brother, and revealed very little incriminating information, though admitting that he had burned letters.

At Warblington, Margaret heard about Geoffrey's suicide attempt from her comptroller, Oliver Frankelyn, who hoped that Geoffrey would not implicate his mother (though this was not to be). A wary Margaret immediately mentioned that she did not care about Geoffrey any longer and proclaimed her loyalty to the king.

On 12 November William Fitzwilliam, Earl of Southampton, and Thomas Goodrich, Bishop of Ely, descended on Margaret at Warblington to interrogate her. The questioning went on for two days as the fate of her sons hung in the balance. She was questioned about Reginald, whether he had told her that he intended to go abroad as he was disillusioned with England. Margaret refuted all such allegations. She stated that that she was no longer in touch with her errant cardinal son and that she had not wished for him to go abroad. She also denied any knowledge of Hugh Holland meeting Reginald. She did acknowledge, though, that Geoffrey had told her that the king planned to assassinate Reginald and she prayed that the king would change his mind. She must have been relieved when she was told that Reginald was out of danger. When asked whether her sons had planned to join Reginald abroad, she said that she wished she be 'torn to pieces' if she ever heard of such a travesty. She said that she felt sorry at the destruction of the places of worship but was more concerned about her people.

Margaret also mentioned that she never burned the king's letters, only those of little importance, and that she had no knowledge about her sons burning any letters. She did admit that Geoffrey had gone to Guisnes without informing the family, after which Montague had ordered him to return. She denied any involvement in the Pilgrimage of Grace rebellion and continually asserted her loyalty to the king, in front of whom she had earlier denounced Reginald. Lastly, she confirmed that Frankelyn had warned her about Geoffrey 'doing her a displeasure' but that she believed he would not do such a thing.

Finally, the interrogations came to a close and Margaret signed her name at the bottom of each page. The two men then proceeded to seize

Margaret's goods and moved her to Southampton's manor of Cowdray. The countess, it appeared, was not pleased at this development.

Two weeks later, Montague was tried before a jury at Westminster Hall, followed by the trials of the Marquess of Exeter, Geoffrey Pole, Hugh Holland, Edward Neville, George Croftes and John Collins. Lord Montague was accused of supporting his brother Reginald's views on the king and predicting the king's death. Exeter was accused of echoing similar views as that of Montague, and Geoffrey's travesties were already well-known.

Montague and Exeter were tried by twenty-eight noblemen with whom they had worked in better days. The rest were tried before a commission of oyer and terminer. They were all found guilty and sentenced to death by hanging, drawing and quartering. The higher ranked Neville, Exeter and Montague had their punishments commuted to beheading, whereas Croftes, Collins and Holland suffered a gruesome death at Tyburn on 9 December 1538. Immediately after the Tyburn executions, the three erstwhile noblemen were buried at the Chapel of St Peter ad Vincula. Geoffrey was pardoned on 2 January 1539, after which he attempted suicide for the second time.

All the while, Margaret remained at Cowdray as her wealth and treasures were rifled through. On 16 December 1538 Southampton found some money and a will which Margaret had drawn up in September of that year. He forwarded the document to Cromwell and then discovered a second document which was cut in half. Margaret explained that it was her previous will which was made ten years before.

In May 1539, despite ambiguous evidence, Parliament finally attainted her of treason mainly to avoid according her a trial. After the Act of Attainder against Margaret was read, Cromwell produced a tunic which was taken from Margaret's coffers, which, supposedly, was proof of her involvement in the Pilgrimage of Grace. When informed about his mother's attainder, Reginald denounced the king in the strongest of terms, describing his mother as one of the holiest woman in England.

Margaret was put in the Tower, along with her little grandson, Henry Pole, Gertrude, the Marchioness of Exeter, and her son, Edward Courteney. Not much is known about her imprisonment in the Tower, except that she had appealed for some warm clothes and that Queen Katheryn Howard had taken pity on her and provided her with these and blankets.

She would not enjoy the new clothes and blankets for long, though. On 27 May 1541 she was abruptly informed that she was to be executed that very morning, leaving her no time to repose her soul and prepare for death. She was hurriedly escorted to a secluded part of the Tower where she was practically butchered to death by a blundering youth. With his grandmother now dead and buried at Chapel of St Peter ad Vincula, Margaret's grandson, Henry Pole, disappeared from the pages of history.

So, what exactly was Margaret's crime? Was she really a traitor? Did she really conspire with Reginald to overthrow the king? Or was the king suddenly insecure about the fact that Margaret and her family, being the last of the Plantagenets, had a greater claim on the throne of England? We will never know.

Her honour was redeemed in 1886 by Pope Leo XIII when he beatified her as one of the martyrs to suffer death under the regime of King Henry VIII. She shares this honour with Sir Thomas More and Bishop John Fisher.

10

Anne Askew

16th July 1546 Smithfield, London

A crowd – men, women and children – gathered at a cattle market in West Smithfield to witness an execution. The execution of a royal courtier, a noblewoman and writer from Lincolnshire, a tailor from Essex and an ex-friar – the last such one carried out under the terms of the Act of Six Articles – went down as one of the cruellest chapters in the reign of King Henry VIII. The sight of the twenty-five-year-old Anne Askew, a writer, poetess and an ardent Protestant (who went down in history as only the second woman to be subjected to the rack after Margaret Cheyne[1]), being dragged to the stake, her limbs broken at the joints, flailing around, drew collective gasps from the audience, and maybe even a few tears from some secret sympathisers.

John Foxe, in his *Acts and Monuments of these Latter and Perilious Days* commonly known as *Book of Martyrs* describes Anne's interrogations and subsequent torture and execution in heartbreaking details. He mentions that Anne's torturers had a sole purpose: to establish a link between Anne and Queen Catherine Parr, King Henry VIII's sixth wife. However, they were in for a disappointment as Anne steadfastly refused to implicate the queen even on the pain of extreme torture and a prospect of a gruesome death.

Early Life

Anne Askew, in her 'Examinations of Anne Askew', which is akin to an autobiography, says little to nothing about her early life and family. However, John Bale, who first edited and published her 'Examinations' mentioned that she was 'the yonger doughter of Sir Wyllyam Askewe, knight of Lynconshyre'. Going by the fact that she was around twenty-five when two of her examinations occurred, we can say that she was born around 1521 to Sir William Askew (or Ayscough), a knight from Stallinborough in Lincolnshire, and Elizabeth Wrottesley of Reading, Berkshire. Anne's father owned quite a number of properties in Lincolnshire and Nottinghamshire and we can presume that Anne and her family led comfortable lives. Her father was knighted by King Henry VIII at Touraine and was one of the king's attendants, along with two of his sons, at the Field of Cloth of Gold, a diplomatic meeting between King Henry VIII of England and Francois I of France, in 1520. He had a glittering career as the high sheriff of Lincolnshire and was also a member of Parliament.

Anne's mother died soon after her birth and her father subsequently married Elizabeth Hutton Hansard of South Kelsey, a marriage that increased the family's wealth and status considerably. The Askews then moved to South Kelsey which was close to Lincolnshire.

Anne had two sisters: Jane, whose first marriage was to George St Paul, a Protestant and steward in the Duke and Duchess of Suffolk's household, and her second to Richard Disney, a well-known Protestant; and Martha. Anne also had two brothers and two half-brothers: Francis, who was knighted at the siege of Bolougne in 1544 and married his stepmother's granddaughter, Elizabeth Hansard; Edward, who was a member of Archbishop Thomas Cranmer's household and cup bearer to King Henry VIII; Christopher, who was a gentleman of the King's Privy Chamber; and Thomas.

The Askew family was unquestionably of the reformed faith, evidenced by Anne's open conversion and her brother Edward's employment in Archbishop Thomas Cranmer's household, and Anne witnessed the religious and political unrest during her formative years when the Lincolnshire uprising, also known as the Pilgrimage of Grace, took place. Her father, Sir William, who was one of the commissioners of the subsidy, was captured by the rebels and compelled to write a letter to the king asking for a general pardon. King Henry VIII threatened the rebels and intermediaries with dire consequences till the commissioners were released. Thomas Cromwell, too, mentioned Sir William in a letter for failing to convict a heretic and also handing out a light punishment to another priest.

Anne must have received a quality education for her to elucidate her thoughts so clearly later in life, but her marriage to Thomas Kyme became the talking point of her adolescent life. The real identity of Anne's husband, though, remains obscure. He may be Thomas Kyme of Friskney, who later married Alice Tournay, or yet another Thomas Kyme of Friskney, who later married Eleanor Whichcot. The mystery of the identity of her husband is deepened further as Anne never used her married name. She stuck to her maiden name 'Askew' throughout her life.

A devout Protestant, Anne baulked at the thought that her husband was a Catholic. She did not believe in the doctrine of transubstantiation and aired her opinions on this matter openly, which caused quite a bit of controversy in Lincolnshire. Moreover, her marriage to Thomas Kyme had only occurred because of a territorial agreement with her father.

Although Anne bore Kyme two children, he eventually threw her out of his house, probably exasperated with the controversy surrounding her. There are no documents to support this, but it is a well-known fact that Anne was one of those rare women to demand a divorce as an innocent party on scriptural grounds, thus clearly indicating that the marriage was an unhappy one. Anne, in all likeliness, approached the Bishop's Court in Lincoln with her divorce petition first. Failing to convince them, probably due to her subordinate status as a woman, she may have moved on to the Chancery Court in London. In any case, Anne's chances of winning her case at Lincoln were pretty slim, mainly due to her confrontational manner as well as Bishop John Longland's orthodoxy and immense antagonism towards Protestantism.

After her arrival in London, news of her reformist activities found their way into numerous documents in which she is described as a heretic and a martyr. These documents are a mine of information, but they also raise pertinent questions about how they have been interpreted over the years. It may have been in London where Anne laid her hands on William Tyndale's Holy Bible which she may have purchased from the people who managed to smuggle it into the country. In London, she met fellow Protestants, such as the Anabaptist Joan Bocher. She continued to study the Bible and continued her job as a gospeler and preacher.

In 1543 King Henry VIII, the lonely, ailing and irascible monarch of England, married Catherine Parr, the daughter of Maud Parr, a former lady-in-waiting and close friend of his first wife, Katharine of Aragon. Already twice widowed, Catherine was in love with Thomas Seymour, the late Queen Jane Seymour's brother, when Henry began pursuing her for marriage. Left with no other choice but to agree, Catherine reluctantly married the king and became his sixth and final queen. On Henry's adoption of the title of King of Ireland, Catherine, too, became the first Queen of Ireland.

Blessed with a fine education and an astute political acumen, Catherine undertook and published her translation, albeit anonymously, of the Latin work of Bishop John Fisher which was titled *Psalms or Prayers taken out of Holy Scriptures*. Henry also declared her as the regent while he went to France on a campaign in July 1544. She managed the finances, musters and provisions for her husband's French campaign and also maintained contact with the English lieutenant in the north, Lord Shrewsbury, to keep the volatile Scots in check.

Catherine published her second book *Prayers or Meditations* in June 1545 and it was an instant hit. It prompted Princess Elizabeth to translate the work into Italian, Latin and French as a New Year's gift for her father.

By March 1545 Anne was arrested once again on the orders of her husband, Thomas Kyme. He ordered her back to Lincolnshire and demanded that she stay there. However, she escaped and returned to London, where she began preaching again. She was arrested again in early 1546 but was released. Soon, though, she would find that fate was conspiring against her.

By 1546, in order to pursue an alliance with Charles V, Holy Roman Emperor, Stephen Gardiner suggested that it would be prudent to halt the religious reforms that were taking place in England. The traditionalist faction went about arresting minor clergymen in the hope that they would incriminate an influential person. Most of those who were arrested had close links to Thomas Cranmer, Archbishop of Canterbury, who now spent most of his time in Kent rather than the court. It is to be noted that Anne's brother, Edward, was one of Cranmer's servants.

It was suspected that the traditionalist quartet of Thomas Wriothesley, Richard Rich, Edmund Bonner and Thomas Howard were keen to implicate Queen Catherine Parr on the charges of treason and heresy and they tried to achieve this through the queen's ladies: Katherine Willoughby, Anne Calthorpe, Joan Champernowne, Nan Seymour (Lady Hertford) and Anne Parr, the queen's sister. The queen was known to host Bible study sessions in her private apartments and it is suspected that Anne Askew was invited and even attended some of them.

Thomas Wriothesley and Bishop Stephen Gardiner tried to influence the king against her and to get her arrested, but she happened to see the warrant by chance and managed to convince the king of her loyalty to her faith before her enemies got to her. The queen's religious leanings, however, came under suspicion again when, though a Catholic, her reformist views were highlighted in her third publication *Lamentations of a Sinner* which was published after King Henry's death in 1547.

In 1546, according to Wriothesley's records, Anne was arrested and arraigned to stand trial at Guildhall with the former Bishop of Salisbury, Nicholas Shaxton, John Hadlam and Nicholas White. They appeared before the Lord Mayor, Sir Martin Bowes, the Duke of Norfolk, the Bishop of London, the Lord Chief Baron of the Exchequer, the Bishop of Worcester, the Recorder of London, the two chief justices of the King's Bench, and the Bishop of London's archdeacon, chancellor and commissary.

Anne was subjected to intense questioning with regards to her faith and religious leanings. According to Stephen Gardiner, Bishop of Winchester, 'plain-speaking' was the sign of the devil spreading heresy amongst the people, which was what the judges thought that Anne was doing to the population of the country. The questions they asked her were carefully worded so as to extract the names of influential people involved in this heresy. They especially wished to implicate the queen, whom they suspected of being a Protestant.

However, Anne remained tight-lipped, infuriating her interrogators. Edward Bonner was especially angry and ordered her repeatedly to 'utter all thynges that burdened [her] conscience', to which she answered fearlessly that 'God hath geven me the gyfte of knowledge, but not of utterance. And Salomon sayeth, that a woman of fewe words, is a gyfte of God.'[2] Bonner's increasing rage reached its peak when she declared that she wouldn't accept non-scriptural authorities over her own knowledge of the Holy Scriptures. She was questioned about the Eucharist, but did not weaken, often using her gender to its fullest advantage, and also questioned about the Holy Spirit, and being an Anabaptist replied: 'If I had not I was but a reprobate or cast awaye.'[3]

The aldermen of London ordered her to be detained under the Six Articles Act. She was interrogated again by Edward Bonner, the Bishop of London, after which he decreed her to be imprisoned for another twelve days. She was questioned rigorously and intensely but refused to confess or recant. Finally, her cousin, Brittany, arrived and bailed her out after her twelve days of imprisonment.

Anne was arrested once again on 19 June 1546 and imprisoned. This time, she was subjected to questioning and cross-examination by Thomas Wriothesley, John Dudley, Sir William Paget, the king's secretary, and Stephen Gardiner, Bishop of Winchester. Even when she was threatened with execution, she refused to change her stance and name her fellow Protestants. The men then finally decided to torture her

She was taken to the lower room in the White Tower where the rack was awaiting her. This barbaric torture device consisted of a rectangular, wooden frame which was slightly raised from the ground, with a roller on both ends. The prisoner's wrists were fastened with a rope to one roller while his or her ankles were fastened to the other. As the questioning progressed, the handle and ratchet mechanism were used to retract the chains, usually very slowly, which increased the strain on the prisoner's shoulders, hips, knees and elbows. The rollers could also rotate on their own axis with the help of pulleys and levers thus dislocating the prisoner's joints. Too much time on the rack resulted in the snapping of cartilages and bones with loud popping noises.

Anne was shown the rack in an attempt to scare her, but she remained unfazed. She was then asked to remove all her clothing save a shift. She then climbed up onto the rack and her wrists and ankles were fastened. She was asked again if she would name her fellow Protestants. After she refused yet again the handle was turned agonisingly slowly and Anne's joints were stretched. She passed out due to the excruciating pain and was revived, before being strapped to the rack once again. Sir Anthony Knevet, Lieutenant of the Tower, refused to carry on and sought the king's pardon which was granted. Wriothesley and Sir Richard Rich continued to torture her, often taking turns in rotating the handle themselves. Her elbows and knees were dislocated and her shoulders and hips were pulled from their sockets as she cried out in pain. Her cries were so loud and heart-rending that the Lieutenant of the Tower's wife and daughter pleaded with him to release her from her agony, a request that he complied with and ordered her back into her cell.

Even under extreme torture, Anne refused to confess, recant or name her fellow Protestants. Consequently, she was sentenced to die. On 16 July 1546, Anne, along with John Lascelles (the same John Lascelles who contributed to the downfall and execution of Queen Katheryn Howard), Nicholas Belenian and John Adams, was taken to Smithfield to be burnt at the stake. Unable to walk or even stand due to her torture, Anne was carried to her execution site on a chair. Once there, she was dragged out of the chair and taken to the stake which had a small seat attached. She sat astride it as she was chained to the stake and the pyre was lit. It is a testament to her bravery that she did not cry out till the flames reached her chest.

Anne was probably the only non-royal to leave a first-hand account of her ordeals in Tudor England. Her work left England, probably in the hands of Dutch merchants, and was smuggled back to England. The first examination was published at Wesel in the Duchy of Cleves as *The Examinations of Anne Askew* by John Bale.

Anne Askew and John Bale shared the same religious faith and political views, but where Bale interpreted Askew's *Examinations* as a medium to attack the Roman Catholic Church, Askew merely records her confrontations with the male authorities. However, it is interesting to note that Anne exonerates King Henry VIII of any wrongdoing. It is believed that the Privy Council attempted to keep the happenings secret lest the king find out. Moreover, Stephen Gardiner, Bishop of Winchester, understood the political implications of Anne's work and pronounced it as 'pernicious, sedicious and slaunderous', and which was published by 'vile inferior subjects' who questioned the honour of the king by declaring Anne as a martyr. He also claimed that Anne's *Examinations* were 'utterly misreported'.[4] John Foxe's *Acts and Monuments of 1563* names her as a Protestant martyr.

Her *Examinations* offer us a glimpse into the lives of sixteenth-century women and their religion. It does not conform to our usual notions of the lives of women during that era but opposes and questions the prevailing male dominance. It also describes her initiation of divorce from her husband, an extremely brave and progressive move at that time. They also display her refined education and her influence; the fact that she corresponded with eminent fellow Protestants such as John Lascelles stand testimony to that. Finally, Anne Askew's *Examinations* is a testament to her courage under fire and her final sacrifice for her faith and beliefs.

List of People Mentioned in the Book

Agnes Howard: Dowager Duchess of Norfolk and guardian of Katheryn Howard during her childhood.

Alice Tankerville: Petty thief; first woman to escape from the Tower of London; common-law wife of John Wolfe.

Andrew Barton: Scottish seafarer turned pirate.

Anne 'Nan' Seymour: Duchess of Somerset and second wife of Edward Seymour, First Duke of Somerset, the brother of Queen Jane Seymour.

Anne Askew: English writer, poet and preacher; condemned as a heretic and tortured on the rack at the Tower of London before being burnt at the stake at Smithfield.

Anne Boleyn: Daughter of Sir Thomas and Lady Elizabeth Boleyn and sister of Mary Boleyn and George Boleyn. She was the second queen of King Henry VIII.

Anne Hastings: Countess of Huntingdon; possible mistress of King Henry VIII.

Anne Hoo: Wife of Geoffrey Boleyn.

Anne of York: Sister of Queen Elizabeth of York; wife of Sir Thomas Howard, Duke of Norfolk.

Anne Shelton: Anne Boleyn's aunt; Madge Shelton's mother and Anne Boleyn's lady-in-waiting at the Tower of London.

Anthony Woodville, Earl Rivers: English nobleman, courtier, bibliophile and writer; brother of Queen Elizabeth Woodville.

Arthur Pole: Second son of Margaret and Richard Pole; English knight.

Arthur, Prince of Wales: Oldest son and heir apparent of King Henry VII and Queen Elizabeth of York; brother of King Henry VIII, Margaret, Queen of Scotland and Mary Tudor, Queen of France and later, Duchess of Suffolk; first husband of Katharine of Aragon.

Bernard Andre and Giles D'Ewes: King Henry VIII's childhood tutors.

Bishop Ranulf Flambard: A Corrupt Clergyman.

Cardinal Campeggio: Italian Cardinal and politician; last cardinal protector of England; Bishop of Salisbury.

Cardinal Thomas Wolsey: English statesman and Catholic bishop; King Henry VIII's almoner; Archbishop of York.

Catherine Carey: Mary Boleyn's daughter.

Charles Brandon, Duke of Suffolk: English military leader and childhood friend of King Henry VIII; husband of Mary Tudor.

Charles V: Holy Roman Emperor; Katharine of Aragon's nephew.

Charles: Dauphin of France; son of King Louis XI.

Desiderius Erasmus: Dutch humanist.

Dr Edward Bocking: A doctorate in divinity and a university graduate.

Edmund Tudor: Also known as Edmund of Hadham; older son of Owen Tudor and Dowager Queen Catherine of Valois; the First Earl of Richmond; first husband of Lady Margaret Beaufort.

Edmund Walshingham: Lieutenant at the Tower of London during Alice Tankerville's incarceration.

Edward Baynton: Anne Boleyn's Vice-Chamberlain.

Edward Hall: Member of Parliament and lawyer of Gray's Inn.

Edward Thwaites: Local gentleman of Kent.

Edward, Seventeenth Earl of Warwick: Son of George, Duke of Clarence and Isabel Neville, Duchess of Clarence; younger brother of Margaret Pole, Countess of Salisbury.

Elizabeth 'Bessie' Blount: King Henry VIII's mistress and mother of his illegitimate son, Henry FitzRoy, Duke of Richmond.

Elizabeth Barton: A nun from Kent known for her divine prophecies.

Elizabeth Wydeville: Queen of England from her marriage to King Edward IV. Daughter of Jacquetta Wydeville, Duchess of Bedford and Richard Wydeville, Baron Rivers. Mother of Queen Elizabeth of York.

Eustace Chapuys: Imperial ambassador in the court of King Henry VIII.

Ferdinand of Aragon and Isabella of Castile: Monarchs of a unified Spain and parents of Queen Katharine of Aragon.

Francis Dereham: An English courtier and former lover of Queen Katheryn Howard.

Francis Lovell: Ally of King Richard III in the Wars of the Roses; disappeared following the defeat at Battle of Stoke Field in 1487.

Francis Weston: English courtier; Gentleman of the Privy Chamber.

Geoffey de Mandeville: Constable at the Tower of London.

Geoffrey Boleyn; Hatter, merchant and ancestor of Anne Boleyn.

Geoffrey Pole: Youngest son of Margaret and Richard Pole.

George Boleyn: Son of Thomas and Elizabeth Boleyn; brother of Anne and Mary Boleyn; husband of Jane Boleyn, Lady Rochford.

George, Duke of Clarence: The sixth son of Richard Plantagenet, Duke of York and Cecily Neville, and father of Margaret Pole, Countess of Salisbury, and Edward, 17th Earl of Warwick. Although a member of the House of York, he switched to the Lancastrian side before returning to the Yorkist side. He was executed by his brother, King Edward IV, on the charges of treason, by drowning apparently in a butt of Malmsey wine.

Gilbert de Clare: Sixth Earl of Hertford; Seventh Earl of Gloucester; from 1262 to 1295.

Gundulf: Bishop of Rochester.

Henry Bolingbroke or King Henry IV: King of England from 30 September 1399 to 20 March 1413.

Henry FitzRoy: Illegitimate son of King Henry VIII by his mistress, Elizabeth 'Bessie' Blount.

Henry Manox: Katheryn Howard's music teacher.

Henry Percy: Earl of Northumberland; erstwhile paramour of Anne Boleyn.

Henry Pole: Lord Montague; oldest son of Margaret and Richard Pole.

Isabel Neville, Duchess of Clarence: Elder daughter of Richard Neville, Earl of Warwick; wife to George, Duke of Clarence and mother of Margaret Pole, Countess of Salisbury and Edward, Seventeenth Earl of Warwick.

James Butler: An Irish cousin of Anne Boleyn.

Jane Boleyn: Lady Rochford; wife of George Boleyn; executed along with Queen Katheryn Howard.

Jasper Tudor: Also known as Jasper of Hatfield; younger son of Owen Tudor and Dowager Queen Catherine of Valois; instrumental in helping Henry Tudor win the Battle of Bosworth.

Jeffrey Harrison: Close friend of John Bawd.

Joan Vaux, Lady Guildford: Close friend of Queen Elizabeth of York.

John Bawd: Jailor at the Tower of London; lover of Alice Tankerville and instrumental in helping her to escape.

John Beaufort, Duke of Somerset: Father of Lady Margaret Beaufort.

John de la Pole: Son of William de la Pole and Alice Chaucer; husband of Elizabeth of York, King Edward IV's sister.

John Fisher: Bishop of Rochester and a theologian; also the Chancellor of University of Cambridge; martyred along with Sir Thomas More for opposing the Protestant Reformation.

John Lascelles: Mary Lascelles' brother.

John of Gaunt: Son of King Edward III of England and father of King Henry IV of England.

John Skelton: Renowned English poet and King Henry VIII's childhood tutor.

John Skip: Anne Boleyn's almoner.

John Wolfe: Common law husband of Alice Tankerville; thief and, possibly, a pirate.

Katharine of Aragon: Youngest daughter of Ferdinand of Aragon and Isabella of Castile; earlier married to Arthur, Prince of Wales; later, became the first Queen of King Henry VIII.

Katherine de la Pole: Sister of William de la Pole, 1st Duke of Suffolk; abbess of Barking Abbey.

Katherine Swynford: Duchess of Lancaster; third wife of John of Gaunt.

King Edward I: King of England from 20 November 1272 to 7 July 1307.

King Edward II: Also known as Edward of Caernarfon; King of England from 7 July 1307 till he was deposed on 13 or 25 January 1327.

King Edward III: Also known as Edward of Windsor; King of England and Lord of Ireland from 25 January 1327 to 21 June 1377.

King Edward IV: King of England from 4 March 1461 to 3 October 1470 and again from 11 April 1471 to 9 April 1483. Husband of Queen Elizabeth Wydeville and father of Queen Elizabeth of York.

King Francis I: King of France.

King Harold Godwinson: Anglo-Saxon King of England from 5 January to 14 October 1066.

King Henry I: King of England from 5 August 1100 to 1 December 1135.

King Henry III: King of England from 28 October 1216 to 16 November 1272.

King Henry V: Also known as Henry of Monmouth; King of England from 21 March 1413 to 31 August 1422. Victor of Battle of Agincourt.

King Henry VI: King of England from 1 September 1422 to 4 March 1461; again from 3 October 1470 to 11 April 1471; disputed King of France from 1422 to 1453. Only son of King Henry V and Catherine of Valois.

King Henry VII: King of England from 22 August 1485 to 21 April 1509; father of Arthur, Prince of Wales, and King Henry VIII.

King Henry VIII: King of England from 22 April 1509 till his death on 28 January 1547.

King James I of Scotland: King of Scots from 4 April 1406 to 21 February 1437.

King Richard I: King of England from 3 September 1189 to 6 April 1199.

King Richard II: Also known as Richard of Bordeaux; King of England from 22 June 1377 to 29 September 1399.

King William II: Son of William the Conqueror and King of England from 26 September 1087 to 2 August 1100.

Lady Margaret Beaufort: Major figure in the Wars of the Roses; mother of Henry Tudor, the future King Henry VII of England, the first Tudor king.

Lady Margaret Douglas: Daughter of Margaret, Queen of Scots and Archibald Douglas; King Henry VIII's niece.

Lambert Simnel: Pretender to the throne of England; claimed to be Edward, Seventeenth Earl of Warwick; later, employed as a scullion and a falconer.

Lord Edmund and Joyce/Jocasta Howard: Parents of Queen Katheryn Howard.

Lord Herbert Cherbury: King Henry VIII's earliest biographer.

Louis XI of France: King of France from 1461 to 1483; also known as Louis the Prudent.

Louis XII: King of France.

Margaret 'Madge' Shelton: Anne Boleyn's cousin.

Margaret Beauchamp of Bletsoe: Mother of Lady Margaret Beaufort.

Margaret Butler: Daughter and co-heiress of Thomas Butler, 7th Earl of Ormond.

Margaret de Clare: Baroness Badlesmere; Norman-Irish noblewoman, *suo jure* heiress and wife of Bartholomew de Badlesmere, First Baron Badlesmere.

Margaret of Anjou: Queen of England; wife of King Henry VI.

Margaret of Austria: Governor of the Habsburg Netherlands from 1507 to 1515 and again from 1519 to 1530.

Margaret, Queen of Scots: Daughter of King Henry VII and Queen Elizabeth of York; sister of Arthur, Prince of Wales; King Henry VIII, and Mary Tudor, Queen of France.

Maria de Salinas: Baroness Willoughby; closest friend of Katharine of Aragon.

Mark Smeaton: Lute player in the household of Anne Boleyn.

Martin Luther: German priest and theologian.

Mary Boleyn; Daughter of Sir Thomas and Lady Elizabeth Boleyn and sister of Anne Boleyn and George Boleyn. She was the mistress of King Francis I of France and King Henry VIII of England. Married, first to William Carey, and then to William Stafford.

Mary Lascelles, Joan Bulmer, Alice Wilkes, Malyn

Mary Tudor: Briefly the Queen of France by virtue of her marriage to King Louis XII; daughter of King Henry VII and Queen Elizabeth of York; sister of Arthur, Prince of Wales; King Henry VIII, and Margaret, Queen of Scots; wife of Charles Brandon, Duke of Suffolk.

Matthew Parker: Anne Boleyn's chaplain and Protestant reformer.

Nicholas Sanders: English Catholic priest.

Owen Tudor: Welsh courtier and second husband of Queen Catherine of Valois, widow of King Henry V.

Pastons: An eminent noble family; neighbours of the Boleyns at Norfolk; known for their extensive correspondences.

Perkin Warbeck: Another pretender to the throne of England; claimed to be Richard of Shrewsbury, Duke of York; executed, along with Edward, Earl of Warwick, on 23 November 1499.

Prince Edward, Prince of Wales (King Edward V), and Richard of Shrewsbury, Duke of York: The Princes in the Tower; sons of King Edward IV of England and Queen Elizabeth Wydeville.

Prince Edward: Later King Edward VI; son of King Henry VIII and Queen Jane Seymour.

Prince John, later John, King of England: King of England from 27 May 1199 to 19 October 1216.

Princess Elizabeth: Later Queen Elizabeth I; daughter of King Henry VIII and Anne Boleyn.

Princess Mary Tudor: Daughter of King Henry VIII and Katharine of Aragon.

Queen Anne of Cleves: Fourth Queen of King Henry VIII; later known as the King's Beloved Sister.

Queen Catherine of Valois: Queen Consort of England from 1420 to 1422 as wife of King Henry V of England; wife of Owen Tudor whom she married after the death of her first husband; mother of King Henry VI, Edmund and Jasper Tudor.

Queen Catherine Parr: Sixth and final queen of King Henry VIII; later married Thomas Seymour, Queen Jane Seymour's brother.

Queen Claude: Wife of King Francis I of France.

Queen Elizabeth of York: Wife of King Henry VII and mother to Arthur, Prince of Wales and King Henry VIII.

Queen Isabella: Queen of England as the wife of King Edward II and regent of England from 1327 till 1330; described as the She-Wolf of France.

Queen Jane Seymour: Third Queen of King Henry VIII and mother of his only legitimate son, Prince Edward, later King Edward VI.

Queen Katheryn Howard: Fifth Queen of King Henry VIII; executed on the charges of adultery and treason.

Queen Matilda: Claimant of the English Throne; Holy Roman Empress, and Queen of the Romans from 7 January 1114 to 23 May 1125.

Reginald Pole: English cardinal of the Roman Catholic Church; last Roman Catholic Archbishop of Canterbury.

Richard Masters: A renowned rector.

Richard Neville, Earl of Warwick: Also known as Warwick the Kingmaker; English nobleman, administrator and military commander; became the Earl of Warwick through his marriage to Anne Beauchamp, Countess of Warwick; originally a Yorkist, he later switched to the Lancastrian side.

Richard Rich: Beneficiary of the Dissolution of the Monasteries; played a role in the executions of Sir Thomas More and Bishop John Fisher and also in the torture and execution of Anne Askew.

Richard, Duke of Gloucester, later, King Richard III: King of England and Lord of Ireland from 26 June 1483 to 22 August 1485. He was married to Anne Neville, younger daughter of Richard Neville, Earl of Warwick, and sister of Isabel Neville, Duchess of Clarence. Suspected to have killed his nephews in the Tower of London, he was defeated and killed in the Battle of Bosworth by the armies of Henry Tudor, the future King Henry VII.

Robert Aske: Leader of the Pilgrimage of Grace rebellion.

Robert Fitzwalter: One of the leaders of the baronial opposition against King John, and one of the twenty-five sureties of the Magna Carta.

Roger Mortimer: Third Baron Mortimer of Wigmore; 1st Earl of March.

Roger of Howden: 12th century English chronicler.

Simon de Montfort: Sixth Earl of Leicester; from 1239 to 4 August 1265.

Simon Sudbury: Bishop of London from 1361 to 1375; Archbishop of Canterbury from 1375 till his death in 1381; and Lord Chancellor of England in the last year of his life.

Sir Henry Norris: English courtier; Groom of the Stool in the court of King Henry VIII.

Sir Richard Page: English courtier; Gentleman of the Privy Chamber.

Sir Richard Pole: Husband of Margaret Pole, Countess of Salisbury.

Sir Thomas More: English lawyer, judge, social philosopher, author, statesman, philosopher and an eminent humanist; author of 'Utopia'; Lord Chancellor from October 1529 to May 1532; martyred due to his opposition to the Protestant Reformation.

Sir Thomas Wriothesley: King Henry VIII's Secretary of State and Lord Chancellor.

Sir William Kingston: Constable of the Tower.

Stephen Gardiner: Bishop of Winchester.

Stephen of Blois: King of England from 22 December 1135 to 25 October 1154.

Thomas Abel: Katharine of Aragon's chaplain.

Thomas and Elizabeth Boleyn: Parents of Anne, Mary and George Boleyn.

Thomas Audeley: Lord Chancellor of England from 1533 to 1544.

Thomas Cobb: Gentleman at the parish parish of Aldington, Kent.

Thomas Cranmer: Archbishop of Canterbury and leader of the Protestant Reformation in England.

Thomas Cromwell: English lawyer and statesman; served as chief minister to King Henry VIII from 1534 to 1540. Leading figure of the English Reformation.

Thomas Culpeper: English courtier and close friend of King Henry VIII; lover of Queen Katheryn Howard.

Thomas Howard: Duke of Norfolk and Katheryn's uncle.

Thomas Sutton: Sherriff of Norwich.

Thomas Wyatt: Neighbours of the Boleyns at Kent; poet and admirer of Anne Boleyn.

Tilney, Katherine Tylney: Katheryn Howard's housemate at the Dowager Duchess' household.

Ursula Pole: Only daughter of Margaret and Richard Pole.

Wat Tyler: Leader of the 1381 Peasants' Revolt in England. Killed by officers loyal to King Richard II at Smithfield, London.

William Askew and Elizabeth Wrottesley: Anne Askew's parents.

William Brereton: English courtier; Groom of the Privy Chamber.

William Carey: Mary Boleyn's first husband.

William de la Pole: First Duke of Suffolk and a favourite of King Henry VI of England.

William Denys: Alice Tankerville's jailor at the Tower of London.

William Fiennes: Lord Saye and Sele.

William Fitzwilliam: Treasurer of the Household.

William Knight: King Henry VIII's secretary.

William Longchamp: Lord Chancellor during the reign of King Richard I; also Constable of the Tower.

William of Poitiers: William the Conqueror's biographer.

William Stafford: Mary Boleyn's second husband.

William the Conqueror: King of England from 25 December 1066 to 9 September 1087.

William Tyndale: English scholar; leading figure of the Protestant Reformation in England.

William Warham: Archbishop of Canterbury.

Endnotes

1. The History of the Tower of London

1. *Tower: An Epic History* by Nigel Jones. Jones mentions that William was the illegitimate son of Duke Robert 'the Devil of Normandy' through his relationship with Herleva, a tanner's daughter.
2. *Ibid.* William the Conqueror was crowned King of England despite protests by Londoners against a foreign-born king, by Stigand, the Archbishop of Canterbury, at the newly constructed Westminster Abbey on Christmas Day 1066.
3. *Wikipedia* entry on the Tower of London.
4. *Tower: An Epic History* by Nigel Jones. Poitiers, too, mentions the brutality of the Londoners.
5. *Ibid.* Gundulf was born in 1024 near Caen. Demonstrating a knack towards architecture, Gundulf earned a rather unflattering moniker 'The Wailing Monk' for being overly emotional and prone to outbursts of weeping.
6. *Ibid.* Ranulf Flambard was loyal to King William II, William the Conqueror's son, who viewed the English as hostile and potentially rebellious serfs.
7. *Ibid.* William the Conqueror's son, Rufus, succeeded him as King William II. He was a tyrant who quarreled violently with the Church and was suspected to be a homosexual. An enthusiastic builder, his lasting legacy was the Westminster Hall and he also supervised the completion of Gundulf's work at the Tower.
8. *jpost.com/Jerusalem-report/the-tower-of-london-and-the-jews-556561*
9. *Tower: An Epic History* by Nigel Jones. Geoffrey de Mandeville was described by his biographer, the Victorian historian J.H. Round as 'the most perfect and typical presentment of the feudal and anarchic spirit that stamps the reign of Stephen.'

10. *Ibid.* Stephen of Blois was the first monarch to reside in the Tower of London.
11. *Ibid.*
12. *Ibid.*
13. *Ibid.* An arrogant and vain, William Longchamp was the Bishop of Ely and King Richard I's chancellor, justiciar and the Constable of the Tower.
14. *Ibid.*
15. *Ibid.* King Henry III's justiciar, Hubert de Burgh, Constable of the Tower, was an able administrator and kept the dissenting barons at bay. However, in 1232 he was suddenly dismissed and charged with embezzlement, maladministration and other such trumped-up offences and was arrested. He was imprisoned in the Tower and eventually lived in disgrace till his death in 1243.
16. *Ibid.*
17. *Ibid.* Cardinal Ottobuono was the Italian papal legate living in England. The king used him to pronounce penalties and even excommunication on the clergymen who supported the rebellious barons.
18. *Ibid.* Gilbert de Clare became the head of the rebels after the death of Simon Montfort.
19. *Wikipedia.* Queen Isabella, the wife of King Edward II, was also known as the 'She-Wolf of France'.
20. *Tower: An Epic History* by Nigel Jones.
21. *Wikipedia.*
22. *Wikipedia.*
23. *Tower: An Epic History* by Nigel Jones. Walter (or Wat) Tyler may have been a soldier from the wars in France or a common highway robber.
24. *Wikipedia.* Simon Sudbury, the son of Nigel Theobald, was born in Sudbury in Suffolk in around 1316. He studied at the University of Paris and then became the Bishop of London from 1361 to 1375 after which he was appointed the Archbishop of Canterbury from 1375 until his violent death on Tower Hill in 1381.
25. *Tower: An Epic History* by Nigel Jones. Henry Bolingbroke overthrew King Richard II and crowned himself King Henry IV. He had the erstwhile king thrown into the Tower. After the coup by Richard II's supporters, realising the risk of keeping Richard II alive, he had him secretly removed in chains and taken to Leeds Castle

in Kent and then to Pontefract Castle wherein he died a mysterious death.

26. *Tower: An Epic History* by Nigel Jones. The deposed King Henry VI was held captive at Wakefield Tower with a dog and sparrow for company.
27. *Ibid.*
28. *Ibid.* King Henry VII was the last monarch to treat the Tower as a residence. His personal bodyguards – the Yeomen of the Guard – were direct ancestors of the Yeomen warders of the Tower today.
29. *Wikipedia.* King Henry VII's contribution to the Tower's military architecture had been the construction of mounts to support his heavy artillery.

3. Henry VIII: A Brief History

1. *quotes.yourdictionary.com/author/king-henry-viii/61887*
2. *Uncrowned Queen: The Life of Margaret Beaufort* by Nicola Tallis
3. *exclassics.com/skelton/skel069.htm*

5. Alice Tankerville

1. *thevintagenews.com/2018/04/21/little-ease/?chrome=/* and *rct.co.uk/collection/2102216/little-ease-torture-cell-beneath-the-white-tower*
2. *roughdiplomacy.com/whos-afraid-of-alice-wolfe-a-true-tale-from-the-tower-of-london* and *Tales from the Tower of London* by Daniel Diehl and Mark P Donnelly
3. *roughdiplomacy.com/whos-afraid-of-alice-wolfe-a-true-tale-from-the-tower-of-london*
4. *Wikipedia* entry on Hanseatic League.

6. Anne Boleyn

1. *Anne Boleyn* by Amy Licence.
2. *The Boleyn Women* by Elizabeth Norton.

3. *Wikipedia.* The Battle of Wakefield took place in Sandal Magna near Wakefield in Northern England on 30 December 1460 and was one of the major battles of the Wars of the Roses.
4. *Anne Boleyn* by Amy Licence.
5. *Anne Boleyn: Henry VIII's Obsession* by Elizabeth Norton
6. *Pretty Dukkys: The Love Letters of Henry VIII to Anne Boleyn*
7. *Anne Boleyn* by Amy Licence.
8. *Anne Boleyn: Henry VIII's Obsession* by Elizabeth Norton.
9. *Ibid.*
10. *The Life and Death of Anne Boleyn* by Eric Ives.
11. *The Life of Cardinal Wolsey* by George Cavendish.
12. *englishhistory.net/tudor/monarchs/Catherine-of-aragon*
13. *Anne Boleyn* by Amy Licence.
14. *Ibid.*
15. *Anne Boleyn's Letter from the Tower: A New Assessment by* Sandra Vasoli.
16. *Anne Boleyn* by Amy Licence.
17. *Ibid.*
18. *Ibid.*
19. *smithsonianmag.com/smart-news/why-henry-viii-orchestrated-every-detail-anne-boleyn-execution-180976135/*

7. Elizabeth Barton

1. *kentonline.co.uk/ashford/news/ancient-chapel-is-one-of-kents-best-kept-secrets-238691/*
2. *Wikipedia* page of Aldington.
3. *The Hidden Lives of Tudor Women: A Social History* by Elizabeth Norton.
4. *Ibid.*
5. *theanneboleynfiles.com/easter-in-tudor-times/*
6. *The Hidden Lives of Tudor Women: A Social History* by Elizabeth Norton.
7. *Ibid.*

8. Katheryn Howard

1. *tudortimes.co.uk/people/howard-family*
2. *Ibid.*

3. *royalhistorygeeks.com/new-research-reveals-the-true-age-of-catherine-howard-says-gareth-russell/*
4. *Katherine Howard: A New History* by Conor Byrne.
5. *Ibid.*
6. *Katherine Howard* by Josephine Wilkinson.
7. *Ibid.*
8. *Anne of Cleves: Henry VIII's Unwanted Wife* by Elizabeth Norton.
9. *Young and Damned and Fair* by Gareth Russell.
10. *Katherine Howard* by Josephine Wilkinson.
11. (Details of the progress) *Katherine Howard* by Josephine Wilkinson; *Young and Damned and Fair* by Gareth Russell.
12. *Katherine Howard* by Josephine Wilkinson.

9. Margaret Pole

1. *Wikipedia*. Sir Thomas Hungerford was the first person to be recorded in the Rolls of the Parliament of England as holding the office of the Speaker of the House of Commons.
2. *Castles of Ireland: Some Fortress Histories and Legends* by C.L. Adams.
3. Richard Plantagenet, third Duke of York was the son of Richard, Earl of Cambridge and Anne Mortimer, both descendants of King Edward III.
4. Also a descendant of King Edward III, Cecily Neville was the youngest of twenty-two children of Ralph Neville, first Earl of Westmorland. She was born to his second wife, Joan Beaufort.
5. (Readeption of Henry VI) *The Wars of the Roses* by Alison Weir.
6. Fotheringhay Castle was founded by Simon de Senlis whose wife, Maud, inherited the land from her mother, Judith of Lens, wife of Waltheof, Earl of Northumbria. The land was granted to Judith by William the Conqueror.
7. Founded in the early 1120s by Geoffrey de Clinton who was the treasurer and Lord Chamberlain to King Henry I, Kenilworth Castle played an important role during the Wars of the Roses acting as a base for Lancastrian operations.
8. Ludlow Castle was probably built by Walter de Lacy in around 1075 during the Norman Conquest of England.

9. Mickelgate Bar was the most important of York's four main medieval gateways and the focus for grand events. The name comes from 'Mickelith' meaning 'great street'.
10. Robin of Redesdale or Robin Mend-All was the leader of a rebellion against King Edward IV of England. Although his real identity is unknown, he is believed to have been either Sir John Conyers, steward of Middleham or his brother, Sir William Conyers of Marske, or both. They were both retainers of Richard Neville, Earl of Warwick.
11. Also known as the Battle of Banbury or the Battle of Danes Moor, the Battle of Edgecote took place on 24 July 1469 between the Royal Army led by the Earls of Pembroke and Devon and a rebel army led by the supporters of the Earl of Warwick.
12. The Battle of Barnet, along with the Battle of Tewkesbury, was a decisive battle of the Wars of the Roses. Fought between the House of York led by King Edward IV and the House of Lancaster led by Richard Neville, Earl of Warwick on 14 April 1471 near Barnet, a small town near Hertfordshire, this battle ended with the death of Richard Neville thereby leading to a Yorkist victory.
13. Beaulieu Abbey, founded in 1203-1204 by King John, was a Cistercian Abbey in Hampshire.
14. Originally a wooden motte-and-bailey castle built by William the Conqueror in 1068, Warwick Castle is a medieval castle located in the county town of Warwickshire.
15. Sheriff Hutton is a ruined quadrangular castle in Northern Yorkshire.
16. The Battle of Stoke can be considered as the last battle of the Wars of the Roses. Fought between King Henry VII and the armies supporting the pretender, Lambert Simnel, the battle saw the death of many leading Yorkists.
17. The Battle of Flodden Field was fought on 9 September 1513 between the Kingdom of England and the Kingdom of Scotland which resulted in the death of King James IV of Scotland and an English victory.
18. Kimbolton Castle was built in the late twelfth century by Geoffrey FitzPeter, first Earl of Essex. Located in Huntingdonshire, Kimbolton Castle was the final home of Queen Katharine of Aragon.

10. Anne Askew

1. Margaret Cheyne (Bulmer) was a woman accused of high treason and burnt at the stake in the aftermath of the Pilgrimage of Grace rebellion. She was rumoured to be an illegitimate child of Edward Stafford, third Duke of Buckingham.
2. *The Examinations of Anne Askew* by Anne Askew.
3. *Ibid.*
4. *Ibid.*

Bibliography and Sources

Websites

The Tragic Tale of Elizabeth Barton (www.kentonline.co.uk/ashford/news/ancient-chapel-is-one-of-kents-best-kept-secrets-238691/)
Crime and Punishment during Tudor Times (https://www.bbc.co.uk/bitesize/topics/z8w3n9q/articles/z26w4xs)
www.tudortimes.co.uk
www.tudorsdynasty.com
www.thefreelancehistorywriter.com
https://meanderingthroughtime.weebly.com/history-blog/category/joan-vaux

Books

Ackroyd, Peter: The Tudors
Ashdown-Hill, John: The Third Plantagenet: George, Duke of Clarence, Richard III's Brother
Askew, Anne: The Examinations of Anne Askew
Borman, Tracy: Henry VIII and the Men who made him
Bruce, Marie Louise: The Making of Henry VIII
Byrne, Conor: Katherine Howard: A New History
Cavendish, George: The Life of Cardinal Wolsey
Darsie, Heather R: Anna, Duchess of Cleves: The King's Beloved Sister
Davies, John Paul: A Hidden History of the Tower of London
Diehl, Daniel and Donnelly, Mark P: Tales from the Tower of London
Emmerson, Owen and Ridgway, Claire: The Boleyns of Hever Castle
Higginbotham, Susan: Margaret Pole: The Countess in the Tower
Ives, Eric: The Life and Death of Anne Boleyn
Jones, Nigel H: Tower: An Epic History of the Tower of London
Licence, Amy: Anne Boleyn

Loades, David: The Boleyns

Mackay, Lauren: Inside the Tudor Court

McCall, Janet: Queenship, Power and Politics: A Comparison between the roles of Catherine of Aragon and Anne Boleyn at the Tudor Court

Norton, Elizabeth: The Boleyn Women

Norton, Elizabeth: Anne Boleyn: Henry VIII's Obsession

Norton, Elizabeth: Anne of Cleves: Henry VIII's Discarded Bride

Norton, Elizabeth: The Hidden Lives of Tudor Women: A Social History

Norton, Elizabeth: Jane Seymour: Henry VIII's True Love

Norton, Elizabeth: Catherine Parr: Wife, Widow, Mother, Survivor. The Story of the Last Queen of Henry VIII

Pierce, Hazel: Margaret Pole: Countess of Salisbury

Plowden, Alison: Tudor Women: Queens and Commoners

Pollard, A.F.: Henry VIII

Ridgway, Claire: The Anne Boleyn Collection

Ridgway, Claire: On This Day in Tudor History

Russell, Gareth: Young and Damned and Fair: The Life and Tragedy of Catherine Howard at the Court of Henry VIII

Smith, Lacey Baldwin: A Tudor Tragedy: The Life and Times of Catherine Howard

Strickland, Agnes: Lives of the Queens of England

Tallis, Nicola: Uncrowned Queen: The Life of Margaret Beaufort

Thurley, Simon: Houses of Power: The Places that shaped the Tudor World

Tremlett, Giles: Catherine of Aragon: Henry's Spanish Queen

Vasoli, Sandra: Anne Boleyn's Letter from the Tower: A New Assessment

Weir, Alison: Elizabeth of York: A Tudor Queen and Her World

Weir, Alison: Henry VIII: The King and his Court

Weir, Alison: Mary Boleyn: The Mistress of Kings

Wilkinson, Josephine: Katherine Howard: The Tragic Story of Henry VIII's Fifth Queen

Author's Note

This book was not just a project for me. It is a journey. A journey that I embarked on two years ago when I picked up my first Tudor book. After that, there was no looking back. I could not get enough! I began traversing a medieval world through modern gadgets namely my Kindle and iPad. Initially confused between all the Edwards, Marys, Margarets et al, I began making notes along with a list of people mentioned in each book. This was the first time I actually did something of this sort but it did help me get a hang of the events and the people involved. The Tudors gave me my idea for my blog, something that I wanted to do for the longest time but was stuck in a limbo for the want of a good topic.

This book is a culmination of all those notes. When I began working on this book, the first thing I had to do is bring in some order to all the notes and highlights on the two gadgets. Being in India, I faced a major constraint of non-availability or difficult to procure hard copies which would have made my life easier. It took me around two months to collate them all together and I was finally confident of starting the whole writing process.

However, writing for a publisher for the first time, I approached the entire project like a headless chicken and very soon, I was stuck. I tried a different strategy and I ended up spending weeks just writing one chapter.

In the meanwhile, Covid reared up its ugly head and struck our family. However, I must say that the pandemic and the subsequent lockdown did give me a chance to explore this part of history.

I finally decided to draw up a time table with all my chapters assigned on different days. This ploy worked wonders and I finally got a grip. It was then time to power on!

For a bibliophile like me, writing this book gave me a golden opportunity to read various books on my subjects for each chapter. As someone staying outside UK, books were my major source of information. Through these books, I managed to put myself in each of their shoes.... imagine myself in their situation and delve into their psyche. Ever since I began my writing journey as a 21-year-old, writing about people has always been my strong point.

Deciphering King Henry VIII was an interesting journey. How did a golden king who held so much of promise turn into a power hungry, egoistic maniac? Injury aside, according to me, it may have been the fact that he was unprepared. Firstly, he wasn't meant to be a king. Had Arthur not died unexpectedly, Henry would have been on his way to a quiet Church life. Probably, the Reformation wouldn't have happened. Or it may have happened in a much more controlled manner.

In any case, I feel, he was thrust into a position that he was unprepared for. Moreover, he was surrounded by a household full of eminent names, influential people and officers who were adept at handling political matters with elan. His father, King Henry VII, had no such problems; he did not have a Sir Thomas More or a Thomas Cromwell in his court. Cardinal Wolsey was just a mere officer in King Henry VII's court.

Whereas, in King Henry VIII's case, the new king preferred enjoying and whiling his time away and thrust nearly all the responsibilities on the shoulders of his officers. Already capable of handling state matters, they thus grew in power and influence.

It was Katharine of Aragon, Henry's first wife, who showed the young boy turned king a mirror. She made him aware of his duties and responsibilities. Not only that, she was astute enough to share them.

I believe that the seeds of insecurity, albeit inconspicuous, were sown at that time. King Henry VIII was aware that he had in his court, people more capable than him in ruling the realm.

The need to assert his authority manifested itself in his decisions that he took henceforth. I, initially, felt sympathetic towards him but it was difficult to continue empathising with him at the latest stage of his life as he grew in megalomania and attention seeking behaviour.

I guess it is quite obvious that I enjoyed researching for Anne Boleyn the most. It started with finding out more about Anne's early life which was when I thought to include a short background on the early Boleyns. I found out that Geoffrey Boleyn led quite an adventurous life. And the lives of the other Boleyns weren't that simple either. Also, they mingled with some of the eminent families at that time namely, the Pastons and the Wyatts, the latter boasting of eminent poets in their clan. Anne, herself, had an eventful childhood in the glittering courts of Burgundy and France that it was quite natural that she began feeling the staidness of the English court. She tried, in her own small way, to bring in the opulence and glamour of the two European courts that she had been a part of but it was to go horribly wrong for her in the end. It proved to be her undoing as was evident by the charges that were levelled against her which led her to her prison in the Tower and subsequent execution. So, where did Anne go wrong? What was her crime? I believe that her only crime was to be born in the wrong era. I highly doubt she fully supported the English Reformation that was initiated due to King Henry VIII not being able to secure a divorce from his first queen, Katharine of Aragon. Her frank and amiable nature was misconstrued as flirtatious. Moreover, the Tudor era was a male-dominated one and did not look upon kindly to a woman, let alone a queen, put forth her views and opinions in an open manner. The quality of Anne's that attracted King Henry VIII in the beginning, began to wane post their marriage. The charges against her were definitely false as I have no doubt that, however flirtatious she may have been, she would have never, knowingly, taken such a huge risk. A commoner raised to such dizzying heights would have never risked her life in such a foolish manner. And Anne was no fool. Although, I have always rooted for Katharine of Aragon due to the entire injustice with regards to her annulment, I couldn't help but sympathise for Anne while I wrote out her chapter.

I chanced upon Alice Tankerville's story when I first read Tales from the Tower of London. It made for an interesting read and I included it here as it offers a fresh change from the usual political intrigues. Here we have a woman who not only dared to help rob the king's gold, but also break out of the Tower of London. There is absolutely no political agenda attached to Alice's story yet her optimism in planning her escape was so infectious that I actually began to visualise the entire scene in front of my eyes while writing about her.

Elizabeth Barton's life was, again, a little tough to research on as mere fragments of her life are described in the books dedicated to the Tudor reign, King Henry VIII or Anne Boleyn. However, Elizabeth Norton's book and an article on the ruins of an ancient church in Kent helped me get through a chapter that I considered giving up at one point of time.

It is a common misconception that Katheryn Howard was a naïve airhead. The TV series on the Tudors did not do much justice to her either. I believe that she was forced into situations that she did not agree to (her affairs with Manox and Dereham, and her marriage to King Henry VIII) and was subsequently exploited. While Katheryn thought of her 'marriage' to Dereham as a mere sham, a playacting between two friends, Dereham certainly took it seriously. He must have known that Katheryn did not understand the implications of it all yet he conveniently kept it all a secret from her and continued to exploit her as she mentioned later in her life when she was questioned against the charges of adultery and treason. Moreover, she was blackmailed at every step of her life causing her to take decisions that benefitted others rather than herself.

Margaret Pole's life has always fascinated me. The last remaining relic of the Plantagenet dynasty, her life was marred with tragedy from her very birth to her death. A favourite cousin of Queen Elizabeth of York, and an aunt to King Henry VIII, she witnessed the metamorphosis of the chubby toddler that she must have adored: from an easy-going and exuberant youth to an irascible and obese king who did not think twice before eliminating those who opposed him and his policies. The surprising part was that Margaret and her family never did so. I believe that the only thing that may have played on King Henry VIII's mind was the superior claim of Margaret and Lord Montague on the throne of England.

Anne Askew's *Examinations* is a fascinating read. It provides a vivid picture of life in Tudor England through the eyes of a woman, which is a rare thing. She challenges male authority in every step of her life beginning from her divorce from her fiercely Catholic husband, Thomas Kyme, to her altercations with the king's men as they tried to subdue her and her voice in the most gruesome and appalling manner.

As mentioned in the beginning, this book, for me, was a journey. A journey through Renaissance England….through the lives of these incredible women who decided to face the challenges thrown to them and paid the ultimate price. I have lived their lives this one year, cheered at their achievements and mourned when they fell from grace.The accounts of their lives clearly show us that women, especially those in power, had to tread on very carefully and watch their word. One misstep and one careless word resulted in dire consequences. Ultimately, despite the power and the riches that the royal women held, their lives and fates were not very different from those of the common women.

I have included a list of noteworthy people mentioned in the book to aid the first time readers of the Tudor dynasty.

I have also included a list of books that I have read to research for this book.

I hope you all enjoy reading this as much as I enjoyed writing it.

Happy Reading!

Acknowledgements

Writing, whether a book or a blog, is not just a one person job. There are many people involved who are instrumental in bringing this project to fruition. My dream in life was to see my name printed on the cover of a book that I have penned. And these are those who were with me in every step of my writing journey.

Eleri Pipien, who reached out to me on Twitter with a proposal to write a book on the Tudors. I had just revamped my blog and had never expected this offer so soon. Being not so Twitter savvy, I almost missed the bus but she was gracious enough to carry it forward.

Claire Hopkins and Lucy May, for helping me out with all my doubts and queries. I would also like to thank Laura Hirst and Alan Murphy for helping me throughout the editing and publishing journey. I hope I wasn't insufferable as I tend to get with all my questions!

To all the Tudor authors and bloggers, thank you for fanning the flames of my Tudor interest with all the interesting books and articles.

The numerous Tudor podcasts that I listened to were instrumental in helping me draw up a timeline for the events. Thank you for putting in so much time and effort for creating such wonderful content.

I owe a huge debt of gratitude to my grandfather, Naresh Chandra Banerjee, for igniting the love of books and history right from my childhood as he regaled me with stories from his experiences in the past.

My family: my grandmother, Rekha Banerjee, parents, Ashok and Mousumi Banerjee, for being there for me; my mother-in-law, Kasturi Roy, for setting deadlines that I did not know I needed and making sure that I adhered to them. Thank you for being my constant source of encouragement and inspiration; my father-in-law, Arjun Roy, for keeping me motivated throughout the journey of writing this book.

My husband, Abir, for tolerating me as I spouted (and still do) historical and Tudor facts all the time! And also for the constant encouragement and motivation to keep me going; I needed some harsh words at times to get back on track and I now know how much it helped me.

To my alma mater, St Joseph's Convent High School, and all my teachers. I am what I am today because of all your teachings and values that you all have instilled in me in the twelve years that I spent there.

To the two of my closest friends, Sneha and Falak, who have been in my life since we were three ten-year-old pigtailed misfits in our school. Thank you for sticking on with me till date and tolerating all my idiosyncrasies with a smile. You girls are angels!

To another of my school buddy, Anuja, who is based in London and never fails to send me photos of any Tudor-related place that she visits. The breathtaking Hampton Court photos are all her handiwork!

During the first lockdown, I responded to a Zoom meeting post by Rebecca Larson of Tudors Dynasty podcast. Through her, I got to meet some outstanding people who shared the same love for the dynasty as me. The book recommendations that we discussed during these meetings were of immense help while researching for this book. So, thank you Heather, Jennifer, Karla, Julia, Susan and, last but not the least, Rebecca, for making my lockdown so much more interesting.

To Susan Abernathy. Thank you for pointing me at the right direction when I first began blogging about the Tudors. I owe you a lot.

To all my friends back home in Gurgaon, thank you for being a bunch of amazing people. I hope you understand the reason for my caginess this past one year.

To all my readers, some of you who have followed my blog, Instagram and Facebook page, thank you for all the support despite me being such an irregular poster.

And finally, a note of thanks to the person for whom I wrote this book: my little daughter, Aryana. This book is for you. I hope I am leaving you something for which you would be proud of your mother just as I am proud of being your mother!

THE END